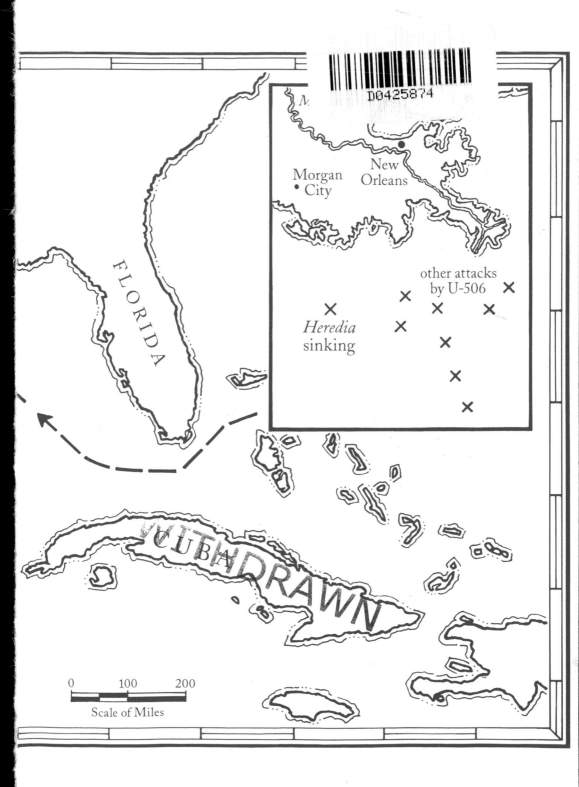

FLORIDA

M.

New
Orleans

Morgan
City

other attacks
by U-506

×

× ×   ×

× × ×

Heredia
sinking   ×

×

×

CUBA

0   100   200

Scale of Miles

SO CLOSE
TO HOME

ALSO BY MICHAEL J. TOUGIAS

Overboard!: A True Blue-water Odyssey of Disaster and Survival

Fatal Forecast: An Incredible True Tale of Disaster and Survival at Sea

Ten Hours Until Dawn: The True Story of Heroism and Tragedy Aboard the Can Do

The Finest Hours: The True Story of the U.S. Coast Guard's Most Daring Sea Rescue (coauthor Casey Sherman)

Until I Have No Country: A Novel of King Philip's War

River Days: Exploring the Connecticut River from Source to Sea

King Philip's War: The History and Legacy of America's Forgotten Conflict (coauthor Eric Schultz)

Quabbin: A History and Explorers Guide

The Blizzard of '78

There's a Porcupine in My Outhouse: Misadventures of a Mountain Man Wannabe

AMC's Best Day Hikes Near Boston (coauthor John Burke)

Inns and Adventures: A History and Explorers Guide to VT, NH and the Berkshires (coauthor Alison O'Leary)

Derek's Gift: A True Story of Love, Courage and Lessons Learned (coauthor Buck Harris)

The Cringe Chronicles: Mortifying Misadventures with My Dad (coauthor Kristin Tougias)

Rescue of the Bounty: Disaster and Survival in Superstorm Sandy (coauthor Douglas Campbell)

A Storm Too Soon: A True Story of Disaster, Survival, and Incredible Rescue

SO CLOSE
TO HOME

A TRUE STORY OF AN AMERICAN FAMILY'S
FIGHT FOR SURVIVAL DURING WORLD WAR II

MICHAEL J. TOUGIAS
AND ALISON O'LEARY

PEGASUS BOOKS
NEW YORK LONDON

SO CLOSE TO HOME

Pegasus Books Ltd.
80 Broad Street, 5th Floor
New York, NY 10004

Copyright © 2016 by Michael J. Tougias

First Pegasus Books cloth edition May 2016

Interior design by Maria Fernandez

All rights reserved. No part of this book may be reproduced in whole or in part without written permission from the publisher, except by reviewers who may quote brief excerpts in connection with a review in a newspaper, magazine, or electronic publication; nor may any part of this book be reproduced, stored in a retrieval system, or transmitted in any form or by any means electronic, mechanical, photocopying, recording, or other, without written permission from the publisher.

Library of Congress Cataloging-in-Publication Data is available.

ISBN: 978-1-68177-130-4

10 9 8 7 6 5 4 3 2 1

Printed in the United States of America
Distributed by W. W. Norton & Company

To the Downs Family:
Ray, Ina, Lucille, Terry, and Sonny

Contents

Prologue

In January 1942, a handful of German submarines, called U-boats (short for *Unterseeboot*), cruised toward the American shores, ready to change the dynamics of the war that had been under way in Europe for over two years. They were instructed to take the war to North America, and that more U-boats would be following them to ramp up the attacks. The orders, written by Vice Admiral Karl Dönitz and approved by the Führer, gave the U-boat commanders considerable freedom to choose targets of opportunity rather than spend time locating a specific ship or even class of ship. Dönitz had a "tonnage" plan: sink Allied ships faster than they could be replaced, and sink them quick, before the American military implemented effective countermeasures on its home waters. Each U-boat would keep track of the approximate tonnage of the ships sunk so that Dönitz and Hitler could measure the success of the plan. Called *Unternehmen Paukenschlag*, or Operation Drumbeat, the mission would bring devastation to the doorstep of the U.S. now that America had entered World War II following the Japanese bombing of Pearl Harbor.

At first, the U-boat crews were subdued when their commanders explained the operation and informed them how little navigational intelligence they had about U.S. waters. The crews could not have guessed just how easy it would be to glide into American waters and achieve success beyond their wildest imagination.

The United States was ill prepared to defend itself against the U-boats, even though the British—who had cracked the German encryption code called Enigma—gave ample warning that subs were headed straight to America. Instead of marshaling its defensive resources, the U.S. Navy had most of its limited resources employed in the Pacific and had done little to prepare for the U-boat onslaught. Many coastal cities ignored blackout requests, while navigational buoys and lighthouses still shone brightly, all of which helped the enemy enter shipping lanes and establish positions for spotting ships. American freighters and tankers traveled alone in coastal waters rather than in convoys with protection, and the ships usually remained lighted while frequently using their radios, which the Germans monitored. U-boat commanders could not believe their good fortune as they surfaced at night and saw the clear silhouette of a ship steaming by. Often, there were multiple targets to choose from, and commanders had to decide which one to home in on first. The success of the U-boats was so great just off the coast of the U.S. that the Nazi leaders referred to the next six months as the "Second Happy Time," similar to successes the Germans had had against British shipping in the opening months of the war.

One U-boat captain adopted the strategy of waiting for prey near a navigational buoy and picking off ships as they passed by, rather than burning his valuable fuel searching for vessels. In New York, the *Jacob Jones* (DD130), the first destroyer assigned to anti-submarine patrol along the East Coast, was sent out to locate and bomb a particularly successful U-boat, only to become more fodder for the enemy. On the *Jacob Jones'* second day of patrol, a U-boat torpedoed the destroyer, killing 138 sailors. Farther down the coast, in North Carolina, so much oil spilled from torpedoed tankers that several beaches had to be closed. In some instances, people on shore could actually see the tankers erupt into flames before the ocean swallowed the ships and their crews.

Approximately 170 ships were sunk off the eastern coast of North America and in the Caribbean in a period of just four months. Finally, in April 1942, the U.S. improved its aircraft surveillance of German subs while simultaneously experimenting with the convoy system. This change, however, was only employed along the East Coast, and Admiral Dönitz simply diverted some of his subs to Central America and the Gulf of Mexico where the happy hunting could continue.

Two U-boats, U-506 and U-507, were the first to head toward the Gulf. Commanding U-506 was Erich Würdemann, a young and daring opponent who had shown considerable skill. Würdemann's hunt would take him deep into the Gulf, just off the coast of New Orleans and toward a freighter, SS *Heredia*, which carried the Downs family of San Antonio, Texas. This is the story of that family, U-boat 506, and what happened when their paths intersected on a May night in 1942.

SO CLOSE
TO HOME

PART I

CHAPTER ONE

A TIRED OLD
WORKHORSE

*"Some experts think that if Hitler had had fifty more U-boats in
1939, he probably would have won the war."*
—Wolfgang Frank, *The Sea Wolves*

E ight-year-old Raymond "Sonny" Downs, Jr. was disappointed by
the drab grey freighter called *Heredia* looming above him at a port
in Costa Rica. Sonny had steamed from the United States to South
America eleven months earlier, and that ship had been a cruise liner with
all the comforts of a five-star hotel. Now, on May 12, 1942, his return trip
to the States would be aboard the *Heredia*, an old ship that was primarily
transporting produce rather than pampered passengers. The big difference,
however, between his earlier voyage and the one he was about to embark
on was the risk. The United States had entered World War II five months
earlier, and Germany had sent her U-boats toward the Americas for what
they considered easy "hunting."

Sonny was aware that war had broken out, but at this moment he was more intrigued with the giant cargo nets of bananas that were being loaded onto the *Heredia*. He and his eleven-year-old sister Betty Lucille, who preferred the name Lucille over Betty, ran up the gangplank to the ship's deck for a better view of the stevedores working below. Lucille, brown-eyed with a dimpled chin and a full head taller than Sonny, didn't know there were this many bananas in all of Costa Rica and Colombia, where they had been living these last few months. Other workers were loading heavy sacks onto the ship, and Sonny, never shy, asked a senior crew member of the *Heredia* what was in them. "Coffee, young man. All bound for the U.S."

"We thought so," said Lucille, "thought we could smell coffee."

"Well, you're too young for coffee, but would you two like a Coke?"

"You bet!" exclaimed Sonny.

"Okay, follow me to the galley."

Lucille shouted down the gangplank to their parents, telling them they were going to the galley, and the two youngsters skipped away, Sonny barefoot. *Maybe this trip is going to be a good one*, thought Sonny. *It doesn't matter how old the ship is if the crew is nice.*

Sonny was correct: it wasn't every day that children were onboard the freighter, and the crew was more than accommodating. In fact, only ten of the sixty-two people aboard the ship were passengers; six were members of the Navy assigned to man the guns mounted on top of the bridge; and the rest were crew. And yes, the 4,700-ton *Heredia* had steamed many a mile since she was built thirty-four years earlier in 1908. Powered by an oil-burning engine that turned a massive propeller, the steel ship was 378 feet long and had a large funnel that belched black smoke from the spent fuel. Although the vessel was originally a passenger ship named the *General Pershing*, it had been converted to a freighter by the United Fruit and Steamship Company and renamed *Heredia*. Most of its former elegance had been worn away by time and rust, and now it was a tired old workhorse. But as Sonny and Lucille Downs bounded after the crewman toward the galley, they couldn't wait to get under way and explore every inch of the freighter before they expected to reach New Orleans in seven days.

The children's father, Raymond Downs, Sr., who worked as a steam engine [railroad] mechanic, also looked forward to the voyage and returning to the States. When the Japanese bombed Pearl Harbor five months earlier on December 7, 1941, Ray had made up his mind that it was time for him and his family to leave South America and return home. Although he was thirty-six years old, he was hoping to join the Marines and serve his country. Ray was certainly in good enough shape to fight; at six feet and two hundred pounds, he had strong upper-body strength and unending stamina. Couple that with his quick and ambidextrous fists, and Ray was a formidable opponent should anyone underestimate him in a challenge. He'd had his share of fights, yet he told Sonny more than once, "Don't go looking for a fight; but if there is one, get the first lick in."

Ray lived life in a straightforward, no-nonsense manner and taught his children that if they worked hard, good things would come. That mindset had served Ray well, and his job with United Fruit in Colombia had paid handsomely; but now he was anxious to get home and be a part of his country's response to Japan's sneak attack. Like many young men at the time, patriotism was running high in Ray's veins, and he wanted to have his family secure in their hometown of San Antonio, Texas before he enlisted.

Sonny had some of his dad's characteristics, showing athletic promise even at eight years of age, and sharing the trait of a competitive and deter-mined nature. But while Ray, with his close-set eyes, had an intense, even threatening, look about him, Sonny usually wore a wide, welcoming smile and would strike up a conversation with anyone nearby. The boy had tre-mendous respect for his father, but recognized that his dad was set in his ways and usually unyielding. Sonny knew better than to try to argue with him. When Ray announced the family was going to leave South America, Sonny wasn't happy about the decision, but he didn't question his father. Instead, he told his mother, Ina, that he wanted to stay right where they were because he was having fun and had made new friends. Ina, however, was in complete agreement with her husband, although for a different reason.

Ina Downs was a beautiful woman who was every bit as strong-willed and opinionated as her husband. While she understood Ray's desire to return home with a war under way, the thirty-three-year-old mother's primary concern was her children's well-being. Besides Sonny and Lucille, she and Ray had a third child, fourteen-year-old Terry, who was living back in America with his grandparents. Terry had made the trip with the family to South America, but only stayed a couple of months before he was sent back to Texas to continue his schooling. Ina missed the boy terribly. She also felt out of place and out of sorts in South America, and didn't quite fit in with either the locals or the other Americans who worked for United Fruit. Even before the war broke out, she had broached the subject of returning home, especially after she observed a couple of raucous parties hosted by other expatriates. It bothered her that while she was trying to raise Sonny and Lucille with strong Christian values, there was excessive drinking and carousing going on all around them.

Now, as Ina looked up at the towering grey hull of the ship that would take her home, she said a silent prayer that her family would be safe. Although reliable news about the German U-boat threat had been hard to come by, she knew of a couple of attacks in the Caribbean and off the east coast of Florida. She was unaware of any attacks in the Gulf of Mexico, through which the family would be traveling, and like most people she assumed the Gulf was out of U-boat range.

Ina reflected on the last eleven months the family had spent in Colombia and Costa Rica, and despite her desire to leave, she did not regret the experiment of living abroad or her husband's decision to take the job. His position at the United Fruit Company had allowed them to save a considerable sum of money, which was sorely needed. That money, along with their furniture, personal belongings, and their car—all their earthly possessions—were being loaded onto the *Heredia*. Prior to Ray's job in South America, they'd been financially strapped; but now they were returning home in good shape, and might even be able to put a down payment on a house of their own. *When we came down*, Ina thought, *we barely had two nickels to rub together, so the grand adventure was worth it.*

Ina let her mind drift back to the beginning of the journey. . . .

CHAPTER TWO

INA AND THE SOUTH AMERICAN VENTURE

"Ain't that something. I have to pinch myself every once in a while to realize this is me."

—Ina Downs

There was so much to do to prepare for the year in South America: digging up birth records, sewing traveling outfits for the growing boys and Lucille, saying good-bye to friends at church.

No one in Ina's immediate family had had a passport made before, but she had confidence that she'd clear all of the hurdles, from gathering the children's birth certificates to getting affidavits from relatives swearing to her and Ray's own birth dates. Getting photos made of herself and the children, and Ray separately, meant pressing clean clothes and going downtown to a studio where the photographer stood under the hood of a large black camera. She only hoped to get the children home and changed into their play clothes before anything happened to the Sunday outfits they wore for the picture. Ray also needed a physical exam for the company, which Ina knew wouldn't be an issue for her healthy, strapping husband.

The passport photos caught the family in an adventurous mood, the children smiling brightly behind their young mother, the boys with their hair slicked to one side. Their resemblance to their father was unmistakable, but Ray's photo showed him unsmiling, even grave. Perhaps his brow was knit with the weight of the decision to move his family to another country. Sitting for a photo was something they'd only done once or twice before, so the children knew it was an important occasion. The State Department had banned travel to Europe due to the ongoing war, so the passports would be processed quickly, but they set the family back a hefty twenty dollars.

For Ina, a hardworking Texas girl with a high school education, the activity of organizing her family's papers and possessions was a welcome distraction from thinking about being away from home for more than a year. While her church groups celebrated the big move with special gatherings to say good-bye over tea and cookies—and promises of prayers throughout the adventure—she found herself awake at night hoping she'd covered all of the necessary bases. In letters, she tried to reassure her parents about the decision to move to Colombia; and in the process, she was reassuring herself as well. She'd never been far from her home state before, not even across the great Mississippi River.

Ray and Ina put great faith in United Fruit as their ticket to the future: they'd own a home on a nice lot and a newer car someday. They knew Ray had the ability and the skills to succeed as a railroad mechanic: he just needed the opportunity to prove himself. At night, the couple talked quietly about the position, always mentioning his future boss, Mr. Brennan, as a good man who was smart enough to recognize Ray's work ethic and potential. He'd do right by them.

For Ina, arriving at her new South American home would be like winning the lottery. They'd been told United Fruit would provide them a home that featured a dining room, kitchen with electric range and refrigerator, two bedrooms, a bathroom, and a laundry room. And the company would try and find them an even larger home over the coming months so there was plenty of room for the children. Ina laughed when she first heard that news: *if only they could see how we live now!*

Indeed, the family home in San Antonio was a bit cramped and always humming with activity. Lucille had the second bedroom, and the boys shared a large storage room as their bedroom. But there was always space for Ina to spread out her sewing—she made most of the kids' clothes as well as sewing for her employer, a costume shop. And they made room when family visited, whether Ina's sisters or her brother, who all lived in Texas. In those post-Depression years, the Downses didn't have a lot, but then nobody in their corner of San Antonio did.

It wouldn't be easy for the children to leave the home they'd known all their lives, Ina knew, and she worried over it. On Denver Street, they roamed freely with other children after school. Terry, then thirteen, had a job sweeping up in the store down the block, as well as selling copies of *Liberty* magazine to neighbors for a nickel apiece. Lucille tagged along with him when he delivered one of Ina's fresh-baked pies to a customer. And the boys in the neighborhood knew that Lucille, a tall girl for ten years old, could keep up with them in running races and stickball games. Denver Street would be hard to duplicate in far-off Colombia.

The family packed up in early June and left San Antonio with only the things they needed. It was nearly a day's drive to Ina's parents' home in Gainesville, Texas, where the kids tearfully left the family dog, Boy. While Ina's parents were saddened to see the family leaving for such an extended period of time, they knew Ina and Ray had to follow the money and the opportunity south. They stood on the porch and waved the young family good-bye, holding back their emotions as best they could. The house was small and quiet after the tumult of the children's voices and busy-ness.

—∞—

Before Ina's dream home in South America materialized, the family had a rough trip to the port in New Orleans. "Everything seemed to go wrong," Ina wrote to her parents. First, the sky opened up and it rained in sheets, dampening everyone's spirits. In Huntsville, Texas, they stopped for gas, and the Bendix spring on the car's starter broke—so Ray had to get out in the rain and crank the car to start it. They stayed the night with friends, and in the morning discovered a flat tire. There was another blowout on the short drive from Houston to Beaumont. Then there was a racket in the gearbox that began near the state line, making the car almost impossible to drive.

Limping into Louisiana, the streets were quiet in the small town of Vinton, but the Downses found an understanding Chevrolet mechanic who allowed the bedraggled family to bring their car in at dinnertime—5 P.M. The tired and dirty children, haggard parents, and worn-out car had been treated roughly by the road, so the mechanic agreed to set things right. He got to work right away with Ray watching over his shoulder, while Ina fed the children from a picnic basket in the office. When he was finished, it was midnight, and the younger two were asleep in the chairs. While Ina packed the sleepy little ones back into the car, Ray settled up: they'd need extra tires, because flats were a regular part of travel, and the family had a schedule to keep. But the $12.45 in repairs and new tires were more than Ray could pay out of pocket, so he asked the mechanic if the man would take his watch for a portion of it. It was agreed, and he slid it off his wrist while Ina looked away. But she set her jaw and got back in the car before they drove off into the night. Everything would work out fine once they got to Colombia.

By morning, the family was worn out from travel but awakened to green, lush surroundings that were unlike most of what they knew in Texas. The wide, brown Mississippi came next, and the kids stuck their heads out the windows to get a glimpse as they crossed it on the giant Huey P. Long Bridge. A sense of excitement was growing in Ina and Ray as they realized the adventure they'd talked about and planned for was really beginning. New Orleans wasn't much farther down the road.

Once in the city, they were deluged with information and their excitement mounted further: Ray returned from the United Fruit offices with information about their trip; they were leaving immediately for Cristóbal, Panama on the SS *Santa Marta*. The trip would take six days, then there would be a layover of five days until the next ship took them to Barranquilla, where they'd meet a plane for the final leg to Santa Marta, Colombia.

United Fruit Co.'s Great White Fleet was a passenger line that operated between the Gulf states and South America, transporting both employees and paying passengers. The ship the Downses sailed on initially was a luxury liner of sorts—a huge departure from their everyday lives in Texas—that made them feel cared for and pampered by Ray's new employer. Indeed, they were living like movie stars, albeit briefly.

"They put us in Suite B, the Bridal Suite," Ina wrote to her father. "Ain't that something. I have to pinch myself every once in a while to realize this is me."

The family was among eighty-nine passengers, many going to Havana or Panama to work for the government, and some just on a cruise. Fortunately, there were a few other children aboard, and Sonny found another boy about his age with whom he could roam the decks.

Terry and Ray watched with interest as a pilot boat led the big ship through the ever-changing estuaries at the mouth of the Mississippi. Once they reached the open water of the Gulf of Mexico, the Mississippi's muddy flow disappeared a little at a time until the water beneath them was aqua green. The pilot then left the wheelhouse, descended a rope ladder on the side of the ship to his own boat, and waved to the passengers as the big liner slowly slipped by, leaving land behind.

Ina and Ray stood by the rail, mesmerized by the crystal-clear water. Soon they spotted movement in the ocean near the bow of the boat and called the children over to see: dolphins racing alongside the boat, arching up out of the water and seeming to swim on top of one another. There were so many new things to experience that they all forgot any worries about moving far from home.

Some of the wealthier passengers on board were there simply to take a cruise. With travel to Europe forbidden due to the war, United Fruit carried a significant number of people to the casinos of Havana and the wonder of the Panama Canal. Folks aboard ship dressed nicely and gentlemen removed their jackets in the heat to play shuffleboard on deck. It was a real vacation: the sort the Downses never imagined they'd take. Ina and Ray strolled on deck, chatting with others at meals and watching the children play as the ocean stretched as far as the eye could see.

Unfortunately, the family's enjoyment of the riches of the cruise ship did not last long. Once the ship was deep in the Gulf, it pitched and rolled continuously, and the effects of the vaccinations everyone had received in

New Orleans were being felt. Ina spent two days lying down, while other members of the family stayed close by. The tropical heat was also oppressive, making their stay in Cristóbal, Panama subdued.

In Colombia, United Fruit and similar companies had developed whole towns of expatriates and local workers, supplying nearly everything the families needed to stay productive for the company. Started some fifty years earlier as a railroad company, the founders discovered the potential in exporting bananas to the U.S., and these banana barons quickly became the largest employers in several countries of Central America, influencing governments and even running the postal service in one. With hundreds of miles of railroad used to transport employees and produce, men with skills like Raymond's mechanical knowledge were key to keeping things running smoothly for United Fruit. There were also dozens of ships either owned by or leased to the company that regularly moved employees and products alike.

Growing bananas requires tropical heat, and it was difficult for the Downses to adjust to the oppressive humidity, although it didn't keep the kids from playing with new friends or exploring their surroundings in the tidy company town deep in a lush jungle. They felt like royalty, with a sparkling new home, servants, and a well-paying job for Ray. The children stared in wonder the first time a man came by to leave a giant bunch of bananas on a hook outside the kitchen, as he did weekly for every household in the village.

The novelty of having hired help quickly dissipated for Ina, as did her energy, sapped by the heat and lack of purpose. "I don't have to do a thing all day—just dress and go to eat," she wrote to her parents. "A maid does the cleaning and we eat at the clubhouse and I have a laundress who washes and irons for me. A person just doesn't have the energy to do anything, though—white people, I mean. Some days all I do is sleep."

While Raymond had work to attend to, Ina's isolation was compounded by the strangeness of the people around her and her apparent inability to connect across cultural barriers. Missing news from home, Ina was particularly homesick after spraining two bones in her foot. The family didn't have a radio, no newspapers were available, and letters were few and far between. In reality, it was difficult to make the transition from a busy San

Antonio household of sewing women's party dresses and baking pies, to reading and simply directing the maids' work and shopping. She found fault with the United Fruit community's lack of religious observance and other lifestyle choices that didn't suit her vision of a family-friendly environment.

During one holiday break, Ray took part in a company softball game and was quickly recognized as a strong athlete, but the revelry went a little too far. While the whole family cheered as Ray slammed a home run with two men on base, winning the game for his team, the holiday cheer didn't end there. After the game, the other employees had a cocktail party, dinner, and dancing until the wee hours. Ina didn't need an excuse not to dance, as her foot was in a splint, but the atmosphere rubbed her and Ray the wrong way. They were hardworking Christians with a family, and they felt the other employees spent too much time imbibing.

Ina poured out her frustration in a letter to her parents: "The people here are mostly English. They are rather hard to understand and I find some are snobs. They are all very, very friendly in a distant sort of way. They give you the feeling you are on the outside looking in and you are classed according to your husband's job: rather like a caste system and you know we come from a democratic state and those things are rather hard to take. If things don't change we are not staying any longer than our contract calls for—what would we gain? Oh, if you throw drinking parties etc. you can be popular enough and we don't do that so there you are. Don't worry about us, we will make the grade. Raymond is doing fine in his work and seems to like it."

While Ina and Ray felt like fish out of water among the expatriate employees of the company, the children adjusted quickly. Terry and Sonny figured out that the clubhouse was a source of lime rickeys that were free for the asking (or so they thought) until Ray got the bill and caught them there one day, sipping the sweet tonic, acting like a couple of rich kids. He shooed the boys home and admonished them against bellying up to the bar for "free" drinks again.

Other parents did communicate enough to inform Ina that school in the United Fruit colony wouldn't be rigorous enough for Terry. Most families were sending their teens back to the States for high school. Ina and Ray decided to do the same, even though Terry was having a great time playing golf with some hand-me-down clubs, swimming and running with a crowd of other youngsters. Ina alerted her parents that he'd be sent back to Gainesville and live with them while he went to school. The fourteen-year-old was packed up and back in Texas within a month, traveling by plane, train, and freighter alone through several countries and concluding the trip with a train ride from the port in New Orleans back to Texas.

Meanwhile Ina made efforts to fit in, planning to learn Spanish by trading lessons with a local woman, and joining a group of women sewing woolen dresses for the British War Relief effort. She and Ray often visited a neighbor to listen to radio broadcasts of President Roosevelt's fireside chats and other news of the day. World events were discussed among expatriates in South America, particularly the British who had been largely isolated by the escalating German U-boat attacks that made travel and trade by ship a perilous endeavor. Just three months before Pearl Harbor, President Roosevelt had been preparing the country for the inevitable by discussing a series of what he called unprovoked attacks on American ships by German U-boats. Although America hadn't entered the war and a large portion of the population still hoped to avoid another armed conflict, the U.S. was actively supplying countries like Great Britain not only with raw materials to support its manufacturing but with ships to replenish its fleet. While the U.S. was officially neutral, these actions infuriated the Germans, who often had American ships in their sights but usually restrained the urge to fire upon them.

Roosevelt was compelled to discuss the situation in his September 11, 1941 fireside chat that was broadcast on the radio.

We are not becoming hysterical or losing our sense of proportion. Therefore, what I am thinking and saying tonight does not relate to any isolated episode," the President said. *"Instead, we Americans are taking a long-range point of view in regard to certain funda-mentals—a point of view in regard to a series of events on land and on sea which must be considered as a whole—as a part of a world pattern. It would be unworthy of a great nation to exaggerate an isolated incident, or to become inflamed by some one act of violence. But it would be inexcusable folly to minimize such incidents in the face of evidence which makes it clear that the incident is not isolated, but is part of a general plan. The important truth is that these acts of international lawlessness are a manifestation of a design—a design that has been made clear to the American people for a long time. It is the Nazi design to abolish the freedom of the seas, and to acquire absolute control and domination of these seas for themselves. For with control of the seas in their own hands, the way can obviously become clear for their next step—domination of the United States—domination of the Western Hemisphere by force of arms.*

Momentum toward war was gaining speed. Folk singer Woody Guthrie underscored the country's reluctant advance toward war with his popular song "The Sinking of the *Reuben James*," which memorialized the first sinking of a U.S. ship, a convoy escort that went down in October 1941 with 115 men near Iceland when a U-boat torpedoed it.

The war was far from Santa Marta but never far from the minds of the people there. The local company manager invited Raymond and Ina to a fancy dinner party where funds would be raised to help the people in Great Britain during their time of need. Ina enjoyed the evening immensely, especially the opportunity to dress up. "Everything was very correct and nice," Ina wrote, explaining to her parents that the proceeds from games of rummy and horse racing were going to support the Red Cross in the U.K.

Then things began to change for the couple in unforeseen ways. Sigatoka, a fungal disease that kills the leaves of banana plants, was rampaging through the plantations. United Fruit attempted to get the Colombian government to pay for some of the costs of spraying the plants to keep them alive, but the government refused. This was followed by a hurricane that damaged the crop. The war also hurt the banana market; only American ships could then take produce out of the ports to markets in the U.S. All of these issues meant that fewer workers were needed in the plantations. Workers were laid off, or transferred to Costa Rica, and Ina anticipated a major shakeup in Ray's railroad department as a result.

Having a teen far away also occupied Ina's mind. In a letter to Terry, she chided him for not working hard enough in school. After a sweet sentimental line or two about how much he was missed, she dug in with her real message: "I was not so proud of your grades. You have football on your mind instead of making very good grades," Ina wrote. "Football is fun but just remember you are going to school to equip yourself for a lifetime of work of some kind so make the most of your studies."

Ina was very concerned about getting money to her parents for Terry's care. She was impatient with the system of cashing out of company stock to send support money home. She learned that the stock took a month to sell, then taxes were discounted from the proceeds. It was another reason to be discontent with life in Colombia.

That problem was solved when the company's troubles with shipping, hurricanes, and plant blights prompted them to send Ray to Costa Rica. "It's a much nicer country," Ina wrote, anticipating better conditions and a different class of people. Getting mail and other communications from home faster would be an added bonus in moving to Costa Rica.

Resettling on the west coast of Costa Rica awakened Ina's interest in travel, as she was entranced by their train's route along a mountainside. The ground was covered in almost every species of fern known, the world around them lush and green. As the train skirted the mountainside, she pointed out to Lucille and Sonny a valley far below them where a mountain river hurried to the sea over huge boulders and rocks with many beautiful waterfalls along its path.

The family's sense of wonder was piqued, and soon after arriving at their new home they awakened at 3 A.M. to drive to the top of the Igazu volcano by sunrise. "I never dreamed I'd be able to gaze upon such a thing," Ina whispered to Raymond.

The December 7 attack by the Japanese on Pearl Harbor shattered Ina's newfound sense of wellbeing, and both she and Ray continually tried to learn more about the U.S. involvement in the War. In the winter months of 1942, Ina's letters home only allude to the worldwide turmoil and the U.S. entry into the war, perhaps out of concern of being censored. Some arrived in Gainesville bearing stamps that show they had been opened by inspectors before reaching Terry and her parents. She longed for a radio, to know more about the country's progress into war, so she and Ray could make a clear decision about their future. United Fruit's boats were being commissioned by the government and put into service, eliminating much of the work available in Costa Rica. The U.S. government also tightened access to the Panama Canal, giving warships priority, so the fruit trade was further limited. The uncertainty ate at the couple, and Ray's desire to join the Marines grew by the day.

"We aren't satisfied with this life to bring up babies in it," wrote Ina to her parents. "There is so much drinking going on and other things and Lucille is growing by leaps and bounds. It is not a healthy environment for a growing child. Ray is anxious to be doing something for the government, just now feels he should offer his services in some way."

Shortly after this letter, Ina and Ray made their final decision: they would leave South America and return to Texas. United Fruit secured passage for the family on the *Heredia*. A week before boarding, Ray had to sign a waiver releasing the company from all liability should their ship be attacked by a U-boat. Ray and Ina readily agreed, never imagining what was to come.

CHAPTER THREE

ADMIRAL DÖNITZ AND HIS GREY WOLVES

"The only thing to really frighten me was the U-boat war."
—Winston Churchill

S onny gazed up at the small deck on top of the *Heredia*'s wheelhouse and wondered at the machine guns mounted there, one on the starboard side and the other on the port side. His parents had told him they were for defense against German submarines; but being ever curious, he later found the captain and questioned him about the weapons. "Well, young Downs, the ones mounted at the top of the ship are machine guns and the ones mounted on the bow and stern are a bit more powerful. Those are 23-caliber, 3-inch cannons." Sonny wanted to fire one, but knowing that was out of the question, he thanked the captain and ran off to tell Lucille what he had learned.

Captain Erwin Colburn, originally from Somerville, Massachusetts, was personable and approachable. Red-haired and fair-skinned, the captain usually had a pipe in his mouth and always dressed in a crisp white uniform and captain's hat. Sonny liked the man; whenever their paths crossed on the ship, the captain had a kind word and the boy usually had a question. The crew was comprised of Americans and a few Filipino sailors, who invariably wore their dark blue pea coats around the clock, even when Sonny was quite comfortable in his bare feet and shorts. Taking a cue from their captain, the crew was friendly and took the time to answer Sonny and Lucille's many questions. The one group of men who Sonny and Lucille didn't know very well was the six Navy armed guards, who rotated shifts manning the guns or scanning the horizon with binoculars. Sonny spent a considerable amount of time watching the men in uniform, hoping to see them at least fire the machine gun in a practice round. He knew his dad wanted to fight the Germans and Japanese too, but the eight-year-old quickly came to the conclusion that the Navy men had the most boring job on earth. All they did was stare out to sea, occasionally switching positions with one another to break the monotony.

After *Heredia* made a brief stop in Puerto Barrios, Guatemala, the Downs family settled into a routine as the ship plowed northwestward at a steady 12 knots. After breakfast each morning were emergency drills: an alarm would sound and everyone was required to grab their cork-and-canvas life jackets, put them on and tie them tight, and then assemble at their assigned lifeboats. Because the Downses were passengers rather than crew, they were told that in the event of a real emergency, the crew would instruct them when to enter the lifeboats and the sailors would handle lowering the boats from deck level to the water. Everyone was reminded by the captain and the officers not to drop anything overboard, lest they leave a clue for the Germans that a ship had recently passed. And all were instructed to immediately report any objects in the water they might spot—it just might be a sub in the distance or even a periscope nearby. The captain also explained that the ship would mostly travel in a zigzag pattern to make it more difficult for U-boats to track them down. And while the captain could listen to incoming radio messages and alerts, he would not transmit, he said, because it might allow the enemy to zero in on their position. Lights on the ship, however, were not completely shut down at night.

Once the drills were over, the family had the rest of the morning and early afternoon free. Ray and Ina usually read, while Lucille and Sonny went exploring. Ina's joy of heading home was not complete, because of an uneasy feeling about the U-boat menace. During the day, she was able to put the threat out of her mind; but each evening she'd look out at the ocean, half expecting a grey steel monster to rise up from the shadow of the swells. She knew her fear was probably misplaced. Like most people, she believed the Gulf was simply too far from Europe for a U-boat to travel to and the odds of a U-boat locating the *Heredia* seemed near impossible. Ina had heard rumors of an attack in the Florida Straits, but that might have been a hit-and-run occurrence with the U-boat quickly moving out of the region, because no other incidents had been reported. The east coast of the U.S., especially off Cape Hatteras, was a different matter, but that was a long distance from the Gulf. Ina also tried to allay her fears by reminding herself that the *Heredia* was carrying bananas rather than oil or gasoline, which was the real prize U-boats were after. Still, she'd feel a lot better when they were safely in New Orleans.

Lack of information about U-boats wasn't due solely to Ina's being far from home. Upon the start of the war, the U.S. government created an Office of Censorship, and the full scale of the U-boat attacks and successes was downplayed. Censorship couldn't keep the lid on certain attacks—sometimes hundreds of civilians witnessed attacks from shorefront communities—but hard news was kept to a minimum. So while Ina, and others like her, worried about the possibility of an attack, she had no idea that all merchant shipping was turning into a turkey shoot for the U-boats.

Sonny and Lucille had no idea that their mother was worried; they were having too much fun. The children had complete run of the ship except for the ammunition room. The crew was always offering them snacks or a beverage, and it wasn't long before Sonny decided this voyage was every bit as good as the earlier trip to South America. He wished his brother Terry could have been with him and Lucille, as Terry would have organized games and contests, the competition that Sonny loved.

The *Heredia* wasn't the only vessel to have recently entered the Gulf of Mexico. U-boat 507, commanded by Korvettenkapitän Harro Schacht sneaked into the Gulf via the Florida Straits on May 1, and U-506, commanded by Kapitänleutnant Erich Würdemann, followed on May 3. Their mission was simple: sink as many U.S. ships as possible. The commanders were to proceed toward the mouth of the Mississippi, where they might be able to send enough ships to the bottom to block river traffic. Schacht and Würdemann, however, were also given plenty of leeway on where to operate, depending on the defenses they encountered and the opportunities they might come across. They were instructed to use their torpedoes wisely, focusing on oil tankers and large freighters.

The mastermind behind their movements was 4,500 miles away at his headquarters in Lorient, France, now occupied by the Nazis. Admiral Karl Dönitz, age fifty, was a tall, thin, tight-lipped serious man, who worked tirelessly to extract maximum efficiency from his U-boats. A sub commander in the First World War, Dönitz was promoted to full Admiral during Operation Drumbeat, rose through the ranks to become the commander of all U-boats, and would later, in 1943, become Grand Admiral in charge of the entire *Kriegsmarine* (German Navy). Dönitz called his U-boats and crew his "Grey Wolves." The U-boats were painted grey and the men often dressed in grey leather, and both were always on the prowl. Sometimes a sub hunted alone, but frequently they worked together like a pack of wolves to find the enemy and make the kill.

Headquarters for Dönitz and his staff was at the Chateau de Ter in Lorient, which included a newly constructed 10,000-square-foot bunker to shelter his command post. (He stayed here until the late spring of 1942, when his superior, Großadmiral Erich Raeder, ordered him to move to Paris, afraid that if the British launched a commando raid it might include capture of his Vice Admiral. Karl Dönitz was that important. Both Raeder and Winston Churchill knew it.) Lorient was just one of several U-boat bases among the French Atlantic ports in the Bay of Biscay. This location made perfect sense; by leaving from France instead of from the German ports, his grey wolves could save fuel and travel time while adding an additional ten days of patrol in the Atlantic. To keep the U-boats safe from British airplanes while in port, Dönitz ordered an elaborate system of impregnable U-boat pens to be constructed. Looking like caves, the tops and sides of the pens were comprised of several feet of reinforced concrete, complete with three-foot-thick steel doors. Here the U-boats could be resupplied and overhauled, as many of the pens had drydock facilities with slips for lifting a U-boat out of the water quickly. The Allies were well aware of the location of these pens, and dropped tons of bombs on them, leading Churchill to think the bombing was having an impact. In actuality, however, it wasn't until the last year of the war that any significant damage was done.

Hitler was almost as surprised as the Americans when the Japanese attacked Pearl Harbor. Dönitz, however, felt relieved—he already considered the U.S. his enemy because American ships had long ferried supplies to Great Britain, helping to keep this foe from succumbing. Hitler, trying to avoid war with the U.S. prior to Pearl Harbor, limited Dönitz's actions against American ships. December 7 changed all that. Hitler immediately convened three days of meetings and deliberation regarding the implications of the Japanese surprise attack, and on December 11 the Führer addressed the Reichstag to declare that Germany and Italy had joined the Japanese in waging war on the United States. Dönitz could finally fight the Americans the way he had wanted to since the start of the war.

The initial attacks along the Eastern seaboard by Operation Drumbeat were so successful that the only complaint Dönitz had (later writing in his memoirs) was that he wished for more than "the six to eight boats available to take advantage of this pre-eminently favorable situation." He was, however, able to keep constant pressure on the U.S. by sending fresh U-boats to the Americas when depleted subs needed to return to Lorient and the Bay of Biscay to resupply after weeks in U.S. waters. The tactic was simple, yet highly successful: from January to mid-April, German torpedoes sank 1.2 million tons of shipping with only one U-boat sunk. And some of the easiest hunting was within five miles of the U.S. coast. Despite the U.S. government's efforts to downplay the carnage, people who lived along the coast could guess what was happening: all manner of maritime shipping debris was washing ashore, including oil, broken lifeboats, life vests, and even body parts.

The American public clamored for a solution, but they didn't want the answer to cause significant inconvenience. When pressure was put on commercial areas to abide by the blackout rules, chambers of commerce cried that it would be bad for business. Shore lights often stayed on at night, even though it was well known that U-boats could use those lights to their advantage whenever a ship passed between a sub and the illuminated shore.

Finally, toward the end of April, improved U.S. defensive measures began to make things more difficult for the U-boats picking off ships along the East Coast. Dönitz wasn't about to pull his subs out of the region just because of better defenses. He wrote that when a U.S. patrol boat found the location of a U-boat, "they give wide berth rather than going over to attack." Yet, the Admiral could foresee the day coming when the U.S. would put up stiffer resistance. The time was right for Dönitz to further stretch the American defenses, and he did so by sending a few U-boats to the Caribbean and Gulf of Mexico, knowing that much of the oil needed for the American war effort was traveling in the holds of tankers leaving the Gulf. The Admiral concluded that the extra travel time would pay dividends in the disruption of oil delivery: without adequate fuel, both the U.S. and Great Britain's ability to wage war would suffer. He also thought it likely that the first U-boats to enter the Gulf would find easy pickings with minimal threats.

U-507 and U-506 were the perfect vessels to send into the Gulf because they were of the larger, long-range class called Type IXC, both built in 1939 in Hamburg. They were 249 feet in length, with a beam of 22 feet, and usually carried 22 torpedoes which could be loaded in one of six different tubes (four at the bow and two at the stern). Mounted on deck were a 4.1-inch gun and a 37-mm anti-aircraft gun. A second anti-aircraft gun was in the conning tower. The IXC could dive to a maximum depth of 755 feet, protected by an outer steel hull and an inner pressure hull. Two nine-cylinder diesel engines powered the U-boat when traveling on the surface. These same engines recharged the enormous batteries for the electrical systems that powered not only the lights and radio, but also electric motors that allowed the U-boat to stay submerged for brief periods. While submerged, the vessel could only travel 63 nautical miles at 4 knots before it had to surface to both recharge the batteries (by running the diesel engines) and replace built-up CO_2 gases with fresh air. Crews typically averaged fifty-two men.

The range of subs was an incredible 13,400 nautical miles when the vessel cruised on the surface at 10 knots. Maximum surface speed was 18.3 knots, while maximum submerged speed was 7.3 knots. Additionally, the deployment of the recently completed refueling Type XIV subs, which sailors called *Milchkühe* (milk cows), allowed the U-boats to stay operational at sea for double the length of time. The massive 1,700-ton milk cows crossed the Atlantic in March 1942 and rendezvoused with U-boats at a secret, designated spot in the ocean. A long hose carried the diesel fuel from the big resupply sub to the attack sub, as both moved slowly ahead on the ocean's surface about 150 feet apart. Besides carrying the all-important fuel and lubricating oil, the resupply U-boat brought fresh bread (from an onboard bakery), medications, and mail from Germany, all of which could be rowed across in a dingy or pulled over by raft. Occasionally the milk cow brought additional torpedoes. The big sub also removed sick or wounded crewmen. There were no torpedo tubes on the milk cows, and they were not designed to attack ships—their only weapons were defensive anti-aircraft guns.

Several U-boats could be serviced by a single resupply sub, and they became instrumental in the success of the operations against the U.S. Even without the aid of the milk cows, U-boats spent more operational time off our coast than the U.S. Navy estimated. This led American military brass to overestimate the number of German subs operating off our shores and hypothesize that enemy agents were offering assistance to extend patrol time. In the War Diary of the U.S. Eastern Sea Frontier (the military organization created to defend against U-boats from Maine to Jacksonville, Florida), there was speculation in April 1942 that the U-boats were being refueled by German sympathizers: "There has been a belief that enemy agents or sympathizers have been assisting U-boats in their campaign. Such assistance could have many forms—fueling the submarines from isolated places along the coast, radioing information about ship departures, meeting them at sea in small boats filled with oil and provisions. Submarines were quite possibly making rendezvous with tankers flying neutral flags and operating out of Colombia, Venezuela, or Mexico."

Americans who lived along the coast were certain that Nazi spies were in their midst. Wild rumors circulated about German scouts (or even U-boat men themselves) coming ashore, blending in perfectly with American citizens, gaining information about shipping, and then relaying that back to their comrades on the subs. How else to account for so many American ships going up in flames?

The men who served for Dönitz—sometimes calling themselves "The Dönitz Volunteer Corps"—had tremendous respect for, and loyalty to, their leader, whom they nicknamed "The Lion." Although the Admiral rarely showed emotion, appearing stiff and correct, the submariners knew he was a master strategist who cared about his men, making a point to meet returning crews in person. He made an effort to learn personal facts about his commanders and sometimes even their crewmen, and upon meeting his officers he would inquire of their family and their well-being.

In the first few months of 1942, most U-boats were returning to Lorient unscathed and victorious after surprise hits on Allied vessels. During Operation Drumbeat, the U-boats were sinking ships faster than the U.S. could build them. Oil shortages quickly became a problem for Roosevelt and his war advisers, with gasoline rationing initiated for civilians so there would be enough fuel for the war effort in the Pacific, Europe, and Africa. Dönitz's plan was working.

Despite the U-boat success, Dönitz and Hitler did not always see eye to eye. Hitler's World War I experience had been on land, and he tended to view the ground forces, along with the Luftwaffe, as the key to success. He once said, "On land I am a hero, at sea I am a coward," when referring to his lack of experience and understanding of naval matters.

In the constant struggle for the most effective use of Germany's resources and manufacturing efforts, the Admiral was not always successful. Dönitz, who believed his U-boats would be the leaders in winning the war, was always pushing for more to be built, and for those in operation to be sent on missions to America, which he thought had a "soft underbelly" along its coast. His frustration grew whenever Hitler diverted U-boats to areas such as the Mediterranean or the Arctic, which Dönitz did not believe had the same strategic value as the North Atlantic and coastal waters off the U.S.

Hitler had an "intuition" that the Allies would try to invade through a landing in Norway, and ordered several U-boats to remain in the North Sea for defensive purposes. Dönitz considered U-boats most effective when they were used offensively, and thought they could help Germany more than even the Luftwaffe planes that tried to destroy the United Kingdom's war machinery. Sinking enemy oil tankers, he thought, was perhaps the best possible use of a U-boat. In a conversation with one of his U-boat aces, Commander Reinhard Hardegen, he once poured out his frustration, saying, "Can anyone tell me what good tanks and trucks and airplanes are if the enemy doesn't have fuel for them?" Dönitz made his case for more subs to be sent to America in an April letter to Berlin, writing that since the U-boats had been sent to America, "total sinkings per month increased very considerably, and also the total tonnage sunk per ship and day at sea. Operations off the American coast have not cost us a single boat."

When this summary of success was ignored, he tried again in May, writing: "To sum up, U-boat Command is of the opinion that keeping U-boats in the polar sea will not pay dividends. As far as possible enemy landings are concerned, the U-boat can best make its contribution by sinking shipping while the invasion is still in process of preparation, rather than by attempting to oppose the actual onslaught off our own shores." His argument fell on deaf ears, and the number of U-boats operating off America and the Caribbean at any one time was never more than a dozen.

Part of the success of the Grey Wolves can be traced back to the intense training all U-boat men and commanders underwent. The U-boat training had Dönitz's fingerprints on it, and it was drilled into officers that the entire crew had to operate at the level of perfection. One person's mistake could have deadly consequences for all. Dönitz wrote that "every man's well-being was in the hands of all and where every single man was indispensable." He knew it was up to the U-boat commander to instill the importance of comradeship and teamwork in the face of the exceptional hardship they experienced. Dönitz's leadership and his gift for choosing top-notch people to serve as commanders worked: morale on U-boats was exceptionally high, despite the awful working conditions that came with being sealed in an iron tube under the sea. In fact, the fighting spirit of his men was so strong that they willingly gave up what little comfort they had on the vessels to increase their patrol time off America. "In their eagerness to operate in American waters, the crews sought every means to help themselves," wrote the Admiral in his memoirs. "They filled some of the drinking and washing-water tanks with fuel. Of their own free will, they sacrificed many of the amenities of their living quarters in order to make room for the larger quantities of stores, spare parts, and other expendable articles which an increase in the radius of action demanded."

The submariners felt they were in an elite corps, working for a man, Dönitz, who inspired confidence and the belief that they were leading the way to Germany's ultimate success. Those on U-boats sent to America were the best of the best, on a new mission that might decide the outcome of the war. They were traveling thousands of miles from home deep into enemy territory, and in some cases into shallow bays a stone's throw from shore. And the two U-boats directed to the mouth of the Mississippi were going further than all others with no advance intelligence from earlier subs.

Dönitz had not only experienced firsthand the deprivations of life on a U-boat during his WWI service, he also had narrowly escaped death. While getting ready to attack a convoy off Sicily in 1918, a mechanical failure caused his vessel to drop nose-first like a rock, to a dangerous depth of 300 feet. Dönitz ordered the tanks blown for buoyancy, and just when it seemed the vessel would break apart, it paused and then shot to the surface. It broke water right in the middle of the convoy, where it was fired upon. Unable to dive again, the crew abandoned the U-boat. Seven died in the escape, but Dönitz and the rest were captured and imprisoned in Britain. It was there that Dönitz dreamed of revenge, but also concluded that several U-boats, a "wolf pack," would have far better success when attacking a well-armed convoy. And if he got the chance, he envisioned selecting U-boat commanders who could handle intense training and then implement it without fear, whose motto would be ATTACK!!

Commanders Harro Schacht and Erich Würdemann fit that profile.

CHAPTER FOUR

HARRO SCHACHT AND U-507

"The Gulf Sea Frontier had the melancholy distinction of having the most sinkings in May of any area in any month during this war."
—Historian Samuel Eliot Morison

Commander Harro Schacht, age thirty-four, and his crew on U-507 were on high alert as they passed between Cuba and Florida on April 30. They had just crossed the entire Atlantic Ocean in a twenty-six-day period and would soon be sailing the first U-boat to ever penetrate the Gulf of Mexico. Spirits were high, and the men looked forward to engaging the enemy. They knew that by being the first of the German subs to enter virgin waters, they would have plenty of opportunities to sink American ships. All the U-boats competed with Schacht to sink the most ships or "tonnage" on a single patrol. The crew of U-507 liked their chances of being recognized as one of the best, with Schacht (pronounced "Shot") as their ace. He had trained under Erich Topp, one of Germany's most successful U-boat commanders, and Schacht was a sixteen-year veteran of the German Navy.

―∞―

Off the northwestern shores of Cuba, the lookout on U-507 spotted a tanker, but it was quite small. Schacht had a decision to make. The American tanker, named *Federal*, was alone with no protection, but Schacht was far from the mouth of the Mississippi where he had been ordered to sink as many ships as possible. He weighed his options. He hated to waste a torpedo on a small ship so distant from his designated area of engagement, yet he also didn't want to squander an opportunity. Like a coach who wants to gauge his team's readiness with a relatively easy scrimmage, Schacht was curious to see how his crew would respond in action after the uneventful ocean crossing.

The commander decided to take action. He ordered his crew to bring the submerged sub close to the tanker. When they were approximately 400 yards away, directly in the wake of the tanker, the U-boat surfaced, water cascading off its grey hull. As soon as the conning tower broke the surface, crewmen sprang through the hatch to the deck gun. Schacht was going to try to sink the *Federal* without firing a single torpedo!

The men opened fire with the 4-inch cannon. In Schacht's U-boat log, also known as his War Diary (*Kriegstagebuchen* or KTB), he wrote, "After the first shot the bridge was hit after which the steamer turned toward land, however after the second hit (third shot) stopped and set out boats." Four sailors were killed almost instantly and the rest managed to climb in a lifeboat before the tanker sank a short time later.

Schacht stayed on the surface to make sure the *Federal* sank. He did this despite writing, "My presence is also known, as the sinking took place within sight of the coast." Moving westward, another ship came into view, but this time he had to quickly submerge, noting in the log "Crash dive for flying boat type Consolidated range 3,000 meters." He continued west, entering the Gulf of Mexico, where he prowled around the area of the Dry Tortugas, writing, "The Tortugas navigational lights burn as though it were peacetime."

It wasn't until three days later that he launched a torpedo (sometimes called an "eel" by the U-boat crew). The torpedo passed aft of its target, and Schacht was sure the eel was faulty, noting that it could not have passed beneath the ship because "the depth setting of two meters makes passing under impossible." The commander thought the torpedo moved too slow and vowed that at the next firing he would increase the enemy's speed setting in his calculations while also moving closer to his target before launching the eel. This would not be the last time a torpedo malfunctioned on Schacht.

The torpedoes inside Schacht's U-boat, called G7e's, were complex weapons with warheads, propulsion and guidance systems, a depth device, and a pistol (either magnetic or contact or a combination of both) that detonated the warhead. They were electrically powered by lead-acid batteries, and the term "eel" was an apt one, because they were long and slender, a full 21.5 feet long and 21 inches in diameter. They had a range of 5,470 yards and could travel at 30 knots, but commanders preferred to be much closer to their prey to ensure a hit. It was perfect for daytime attacks because, since it was electric, it did not leave a trail of bubbles. These German torpedoes, like their American counterparts, had their share of technical problems, and nothing infuriated a sub commander more than working for hours to get into prime firing position, only to have the torpedo go haywire. Some of the issues included torpedoes that hit the target and did not explode, premature detonations, and torpedoes running deeper than the setting and passing right underneath the target.

On May 4, Schacht found his next target eighty miles to the west of the Tortugas, the small merchant freighter *Norlindo*. The unarmed ship and her crew of twenty-eight were steaming from Mobile, Alabama to Havana, Cuba: another sitting duck for U-507.

Schacht ordered the firing of one torpedo from a forward tube, which found its target. The ship heeled to starboard and within minutes was swallowed by the sea. Schacht recorded in his log that the ship "goes down right away at the stern, and in three minutes stands vertical," before sinking. Twenty-three of the crew managed to jump overboard and climb into rafts.

Schacht had his vessel approach the life rafts. Those survivors onboard likely feared that the U-boat's machine guns might mow them down. Instead, Schacht stood on the bridge in a pair of shorts and, looking fit and tanned, said in perfect English, "Hope you get ashore okay." Then he asked the name of the ship and its tonnage since it did not have time to put out an SOS. The sailors refused to answer. Schacht surprised them once again, this time handing them forty packs of cigarettes, water, crackers, lime juice, matches, and even a cake decorated with French writing. Then the U-boat commander bade them farewell and ended the strange meeting by saying, "Sorry we can't help you further."

U-507 had sunk two ships, but neither was the prize Schacht was looking for. The next night, however, the hunting improved. The 5,100-ton tanker *Munger T. Ball* was twice the size of the earlier two ships sunk; and unlike those, this one was fully loaded with gasoline. The tanker, traveling from Port Arthur, Texas to Norfolk, Virginia, with a crew of forty-one, was unarmed and unescorted, and did not try to evade detection by zigzagging. Schacht could hardly believe how easy the shooting would be. He maneuvered to within 500 yards, ordered a forward torpedo to be fired, and then watched the ship explode in flames, sending aloft what the commander called "a rising mushroom cloud of smoke." Flaming gasoline spread completely around the ship, preventing most of the sailors from jumping overboard, resulting in thirty-seven crewmen going down with the ship.

Just a few miles away, a second tanker, the *Joseph M. Cudahy*, saw the smoke from the torpedoed *Ball*, and the captain radioed that a ship had been hit, and added that he was only nine miles away at "position 65 nautical miles northwest of Tortugas." Schacht, of course, was monitoring the radio. In his U-boat log, he wrote "the vessel that made the report must be within visual range. Therefore searched the horizon especially attentively." A half-hour later, he added, "Tanker sighted. This was the one that reported us. Maneuvered ahead. The tanker has obviously moved off from sinking location and steers a zigzag course. The night very dark, therefore surface attack." When U-507 was 600 meters away, Schacht fired his first torpedo but missed. "Apparently the steamer has seen me and stopped at the last minute." Feeling safe on the surface despite the fact that he'd been spotted, the commander moved to within 400 meters, fired again, and this time "Hit center. Steamer exploded and immediately burst into bright flames from forward to aft." The *Cudahy* joined the *Munger T. Ball* at the bottom of the ocean.

Schacht slowly pulled away and headed toward New Orleans and the Mississippi River mouth.

Erich Würdemann and his U-506 crew provided Schacht with competition as to who would sink the most Allied ships. Würdemann had left Lorient on April 6 and was now at the doorstep of the Gulf. Like Schacht, Würdemann could not resist an easy target, and while approaching the Gulf on the afternoon of May 3 he spotted a small, unarmed ship just sixty miles south-southwest of Miami. Due to his proximity to shore, the commander elected to dive, maneuver into firing position, and then order the release of a single torpedo from tube 5. The men inside the sub all stood stock-still, holding their breath, waiting for the soundman wearing the hydrophone headset to confirm whether or not the shot was true. Seconds ticked away, then on the twenty-ninth second the U-boat crew felt a slight jolt and the soundman heard the concussion loud and clear over his headset: the torpedo had traveled 440 meters, striking its target portside amidships. Würdemann had to see his first score for himself, and ordered the sub to the surface. Up it came like a killer whale breaching near its prey. Looking through binoculars, he saw a seven-foot hole in the hull, and crewmen running to the one lifeboat that had not been blown to bits. The sailors launched the lifeboat, just clearing the ship a minute or two before she went on her side.

Würdemann had bagged his first ship on his first shot, later writing a simple summary in his War Diary: "Steamer sinks slowly over the forestem. Nothing heard on the 600 meter wave [radio]."

The ship was named *Sama*, a small Nicaraguan freighter carrying bananas, and its fourteen-man crew was fortunate indeed. Not only did they escape the sinking freighter in the nick of time, they only had to spend six hours in the lifeboat before being rescued by a British ship. The only injury among the sailors was a scratch on the captain's head. They may have been lucky but the Navy interrogator who debriefed these survivors did not believe their story. In the Survivor Statement Report, the crew felt certain they'd been attacked by a U-boat. "All survivors," said the report, "were of the opinion that the explosion resulted from a torpedo, although no submarine or torpedo track was ever seen." This led the interviewing officer to write, "In my opinion there is a strong possibility that the vessel struck a mine." The Navy investigator simply couldn't wrap his head around the fact that a U-boat would be so brazen as to strike in broad daylight, and to select a small freighter loaded with bananas as a target. So while the Navy personnel responsible for defending the Gulf worried about mines, U-506 and U-507 focused on finding their next sitting duck.

After Würdemann watched the *Sama* go down, he quickly guided his sub away from the carnage, continuing on into the Gulf of Mexico. The *Sama* was his first kill, but it was only a warmup.

Erich Würdemann was a relatively inexperienced U-boat commander, having graduated from submarine school just a few months earlier in September 1941. Born in Hamburg—the same city his U-boat was built in—the twenty-eight-year-old Kapitänleutnant was a quick learner. He had graduated from the German Naval Academy in 1933 and served on destroyers before switching to U-boats.

Photographs of Erich Würdemann always show him with an intense look: thick black eyebrows shadowing penetrating eyes, and a furrowed brow as if he's staring right through the camera. He was a good-looking young man with black hair, slicked straight back. The photos taken of him during the war give a sense that he was a confident man who knew how to seize success. Strangely enough, his searing stare, thick dark hair, and serious demeanor are almost a mirror image of the photos taken of Ray Downs, Sonny's dad. Both young men had a no-nonsense aura of both competence and controlled power.

Ray was on his way to serve his country, while Erich Würdemann was already risking his life for his homeland. And on this patrol, the twenty-eight-year-old U-boat commander was so focused on destroying the enemy that he was on track to earn himself the Iron Cross, First Class.

⸻

Now, after sinking the *Sama*, Würdemann was intent on proceeding straight to the waters off New Orleans, where he expected to find bigger game. He tried to keep U-506 on the surface, where the vessel could travel the fastest while also recharging its batteries; but when passing through the Florida Straits, the U-boat was running against the eastward current. Consequently the sub was moving slower than its maximum speed of 18 knots and was in a vulnerable position, close to land-based aircraft. Würdemann likely stationed four lookouts with binoculars on U-506's conning-tower bridge, each scanning an assigned ninety degrees of ocean and sky, searching for both ships and aircraft.

They saw plenty. Twice a lookout spotted a plane, and he shouted for a crash dive. The lookouts on the bridge leaped through the open hatch and slid down the ladder, landing seven feet below inside the sub while the watch officer closed the hatch. The engineering personnel shut off the diesels and turned on the electric motors, while Würdemann ordered the vents open to let the air out of the ballast tanks. A crew member adjusted the U-boat's hydroplanes, and to quicken the sub's descent all available crew dashed to the bow of the vessel and crammed themselves in tight. This added weight assisted the sub as it dropped nose-first away from its exposed position on the surface. The crash dive was a race against time to submerge the U-boat before pilots in the aircraft could see it, or, if the pilots had spotted it, to get as deep as possible and change its position before the depth charges started dropping from the plane. If just one crew member on the sub was slow to his task, it might mean the end for all of them.

In the second crash dive, the U-boat must have been located by the American aircraft, because Würdemann later wrote, "2 aircraft bombs at depth of 60 meters. No damage." So while defenses in the Gulf were sorely lacking—and the commander recorded how Americans on shore acted "as in peacetime with bright light glow seen over the city of

Miami"—Würdemann knew that he and his crew could never let their guard down when on the surface.

Should U.S. aircraft surprise the U-boat crew by coming out of cloud cover or the glare of the sun, Dönitz had instructed his commanders to fight it out if there was not sufficient time to dive. "Do not dive," said Dönitz in an April 27 radiogram; "instead shoot (using deck anti-aircraft cannon), increase speed, turn away hard." He went on to say if firing at the plane failed to deter it, the U-boat commander should dive deep while the aircraft is turning for the next approach. Most bombs and depth charges had to land surprisingly close to the double-hulled U-boat (within twenty feet) to cause significant damage.

For most of his voyage into the Gulf, Würdemann simply played it safe, spending daylight hours underwater while using the cover of darkness to proceed on the surface. At night, the low silhouette of U-506 made it virtually impossible for spotters on a ship or a plane to see with the naked eye. (Rudimentary radar for aircraft and sonar for ships was in existence, but the new technology had not yet been installed on Gulf-based planes or vessels.) Würdemann knew that in the dark of night he could easily find ships that either kept their lights on or were silhouetted by illumination from shore. Once the prey was located, the commander could maneuver unobserved and get surprisingly close to the enemy.

Würdemann continued on a direct course for the mouth of the Mississippi, but a radiogram from headquarters on May 6 forced him to alter course slightly. Commander Schacht on U-507 needed his assistance regarding a seriously injured radioman.

The injury aboard U-507 happened shortly after Schacht's successful sinking of both the *Ball* and *Cudahy* tankers in a single day. That night, Schacht surfaced to rearm, a process whereby torpedoes stored on the deck are carefully moved through the open torpedo-loading hatches and into the firing tubes. During the transfer, the winch broke and a torpedo slid down the gliding rails, where it surprised a radioman assisting with the job, crashing into his arm, splintering bones and causing excruciating pain. The crew carried the groaning man below, but soon realized the sub's supply of morphine and other painkillers wasn't on board. There wasn't so much as an aspirin available, and fellow crew members helplessly watched as the radioman writhed in agony. Schacht sent off a radiogram to Kerneval, France, which was Dönitz's headquarters outside Lorient. The message described "a multiple open arm fracture . . . no pain-relieving means on board. Requesting instructions." A few hours later, headquarters conveyed medical advice, along with the suggestion that "if no morphine onboard, give cognac." Schacht responded that this had been done, adding, "The patient lies in a bunk in the officers' mess and is attended to by a constant vigil."

Headquarters (*Befehlshaber der Unterseeboote*, "BdU," Command of U-boats) then issued instructions for Schacht on U-507 and Würdemann on U-506 to meet "for delivery of relieving drugs, on May 6 at 1500 be in grid square DL 31 upper right. In case of late arrival, Würdemann report by short signal." The grid reference was a clever way of replacing latitude and longitude with a zone designation whereby the entire ocean was divided into squares designated by two letters, and within each of these were smaller squares designated by two to four numbers. This provided brevity in radio communications and also a measure of secrecy.

The rendezvous for Würdemann and Schacht was easier said than done. Coast Guard and Navy planes were patrolling the area after the torpedoing of the *Ball* and *Cudahy* tankers, making it difficult for either sub to stay on the surface for extended periods. The two U-boats missed each other at the first rendezvous point, and then again at two others.

Schacht decided that the injured man was resting fairly comfortably, having given him sleeping pills, dressing his wounds, splinting his arm, and letting him sleep in an officer's bunk. After a day and a half of wasted time trying to meet U-506, Schacht ordered the boat on a westward course and arrived in waters near the mouth of the Mississippi, where he promptly spotted the *Alcoa Puritan*, which was loaded with bauxite, the raw material for aluminum. Schacht's first torpedo missed the vessel, and a lookout on the ship saw it zip by the stern just fifteen feet away. The captain immediately swung the vessel so its stern would be facing the direction the torpedo came from, thus making the smallest area of the hull the target rather than lying abeam to the U-boat. Then the ship sped away at full speed. Schacht gave chase and, not wanting to waste another torpedo, started shelling the *Alcoa Puritan*. Schacht's radioman heard the ship's frantic message for help: "SSS, *Alcoa Puritan*. U-boat on the surface, position 2840N 8822W. U-boat still shoots, torpedo did not hit." (The SOS was a general distress call, while the SSS meant submarine attack.)

Several shells hit the ship, disabling its steering gear, and sailors quickly lowered their lifeboat and rafts and climbed aboard, furiously paddling away from the stricken ship, knowing what would happen next. Schacht then sent a torpedo into the abandoned ship, sinking it stern-first in a few minutes. Next, the commander maneuvered alongside the lifeboat and rafts and hollered his trademark, "Sorry we can't help you. Hope you get ashore."

In his War Diary, Schacht recorded that he "brought the steamer to a halt with artillery" and "Coup de grace from Tube 1. Steamer sinks. It was the newly constructed *Alcoa Puritan*."

One can only imagine what the drifting *Alcoa Puritan* crewmen felt when they heard Schacht shout his jaunty apology and encouragement, but it's very likely that seven of the men thought they had the worst luck of anyone on the planet. Those seven sailors had already endured a submarine attack while aboard a different vessel in March off the eastern coast of the U.S. They spent eleven awful days in a lifeboat before being rescued! This time, however, they were picked up the same day by a Coast Guard vessel.

A few hours later, in the early morning hours of May 7, Schacht followed up the *Alcoa Puritan* attack with another, sinking the *Ontario*, a vessel eerily similar to the *Heredia*. Owned by United Fruit and loaded with bananas, the freighter had left from Honduras and had almost reached the United States. The ship had been notified of the sinking of the *Alcoa Puritan*, and was racing on a zigzag course to the nearest port. Schacht and his crew aboard U-507 came fully to the surface, recording ". . . at first shot, which hit the forward mast, [it] stopped. The crew went to the boats." Once the crew was safely off, Schacht peppered the ship with shells until he was out of ammunition. The ship was burning but did not sink, so the commander readied a torpedo. Before he could fire, however, he crash-dived at the approach of an oncoming aircraft. "Maneuvered for a coup de grace submerged. Steamer suddenly starts to burn brightly, takes a list and settles deeper. Departed since a total loss can be assumed."

A day later, on May 8, Schacht did it again, torpedoing the *Torny*, a Norwegian freighter carrying nitrate. "Must retract periscope," wrote Schacht in his log, "due to wreckage flying about. After surfacing, an explosive piece of our own torpedo lay on the over-deck." Most of the *Torny's* crew managed to escape the sinking ship in a lifeboat and a motorboat. But the ship's propeller was still turning and began to suck the motorboat toward it. The fifteen men in the motorboat jumped overboard, saving themselves, as the ship suddenly plunged toward the depths. A few days later, the New Orleans *Times-Picayune* quoted a surviving sailor who said that just prior to the attack, the crew thought they had reached safe waters. "Just the night before, I said to the captain, 'Well, I guess we're safe now here in the Gulf.'"

Later that evening, Schacht had another close call with an aircraft that forced him to crash-dive again. When he came up to periscope depth, "a distant detonation heard. Possibly a torpedo hit from Würdemann. Aircraft still circling." A half hour later, Schacht fully surfaced and wrote in his log, "while surfacing four quick in succession detonations as from bombs heard. Distance about 15 nautical miles. Perhaps Würdemann had torpedoed a steamer and had just been bombed." (Würdemann did not fire on a ship that day, and the detonations might very well have been from a trigger-happy pilot dropping depth charges at a shadow.)

Schacht's aggressive hunting did cause a couple of close calls with an attacking U.S. Navy PBY Catalina flying from its base at Pensacola, Florida. The Catalina, a "flying boat," could land on the ocean; and although this patrol bomber was slow, it was perfect for long-range searches over the ocean. A bombardier could sit in the nose of the plane and have a perfect vantage point from which to fire its big gun from the turret. Additionally, there were machine guns in the waist position, and bombs on the wings. When the PBY spotted U-507 on the surface, it opened fire with everything it had; but both times, Schacht evaded the attacking plane and continued his hunt for more ships.

The next vessel Schacht found was a wee bit smaller than a ship, but the commander proved his resourcefulness. Through the periscope on May 9, a crew member of U-507 spotted an empty floating lifeboat, and Schacht thought it was worth investigating. "Checked to see if floating lifeboat had medical supplies." No medical materials were found, but the effort proved to be worthwhile because "a number of charts were fished out."

On May 10, U-507 had almost reached its goal: "The previous deep blue clear water is dark green and slightly milky. This color promises good cover from being seen from above. The distance to the Mississippi and the coast is the same at eighty nautical miles."

Seven ships were sunk in eight days by Schacht and U-507. Würdemann on the U-506 would have a lot of catching up to do. For Dönitz and Hitler, Schacht's success was a series of incredible victories, but for the Allies an absolute disaster. It is not known if the news of this carnage reached Captain Colburn on the *Heredia*, but if it did, he elected not to worry the Downs family with it.

CHAPTER FIVE

THE GREY WOLVES
AND THE MISSISSIPPI

"We just entered the Gulf of Mexico, and we're about half way home."

—Ray Downs

Sonny and Lucille were in the galley eating ham-and-cheese sandwiches made up especially for them. A senior crew member sat at their table chatting with the two children when Sonny blurted out that he would probably become bored on the voyage.

"Why's that?" asked the sailor.

Lucille answered before Sonny could. "Because we've seen the entire ship, even where the captain does the steering."

"Well, have you seen the engine room?"

"No! Can we?" shouted Sonny.

"First get permission from your parents. And if they say yes, meet me back here in two minutes."

The children raced through passageways, down a mahogany staircase that was one of the few ornate features from the ship's earlier days as a passenger ship, and then onward to their parents' cabin. The tiny room had a bunk bed, a table and chair, and a closet. A door led into a bathroom that they shared with their children, who had an identical cabin on the other side of the bathroom.

Finding their mother reading on the lower bunk, they told her about their opportunity to see the engine room of the ship. Ina thought for a minute, and said, "If you stay right next to the officer who is taking you there, you may go." The kids raced away, shouting "Thanks, Mom!"

Ina smiled and shook her head: Sonny and Lucille were so happy, so healthy. She couldn't wait to get home. *We finally have money, there will be no more scraping by, day to day, the way it was before. This time our children will get what they need*, she thought.

Once in the engine room, both children covered their ears from the deafening roar of the giant pistons hammering up and down. The room smelled of oil and grease, and Sonny thought the sight of the enormous moving parts was the most fascinating thing he'd ever seen, as if he had entered an enormous cave where giants might live. When Lucille tapped him on the shoulder and shouted it was time to leave, Sonny took one last look around so that he could tell his brother Terry exactly what he'd seen.

Sonny reluctantly climbed the steps up from the engine room and into the fresh air. Once on the deck, he raced off to find his father to explain how the ship was able to power through the seas. He located his dad lounging on a deck chair, enjoying the warm May sunshine. After Sonny described his adventure in the engine room, his dad said, "Well, I've got news for you. We just entered the Gulf of Mexico, and we're about half way home. Won't be long before you get to see your brother and Boy."

Sonny had missed the dog as much as he did his brother. "Can't wait!" said Sonny. "And Dad, do you think we can sleep on the deck again tonight?"

The prior day and night had been warm, and the family found their cabin stuffy, so the whole family had taken blankets and pillows and laid them out on reclining chairs topside. Sonny loved looking at the stars, which were so clear that they appeared closer than he'd ever seen. A gentle breeze kept him cool, and the periodic passing of the Navy Armed Guard on watch made him feel safe.

"I don't see why not," answered Ray. "It's another warm day."

"All right!" shouted Sonny. He skipped away, heading down to the galley for a soda. His mind raced ahead to another night under the stars where he secretly pretended he was a pirate sailing to distant adventure.

⁂

The crewmen on U-506 and U-507 could only dream of escaping the heat and humidity inside their iron tubes. Their only relief was at night, when it was safe to surface and open the hatch. Those lucky enough to have conning-tower duty took deep breaths of the salt air, then breathed a sigh of relief whenever a breeze cooled their perspiring bodies. It must have been close to heaven to be on the conning tower, considering the sheer hell-hole the inside of a U-boat became after weeks at sea. The sub's batteries and electric motors generated heat, and the ventilation system never could keep up with the carbon dioxide buildup. Couple that with the warm waters of the Gulf of Mexico, and the temperature in the U-boat rose well above 110 degrees. Even without the high temperatures or carbon dioxide, the air was foul. Consider that fifty men had to share a confined space with no bathing facility and only one toilet available (the second head was used for storage). The unwashed bodies alone could make a person gag, but the men also had to contend with the constant smell of diesel and a humidity level so high, it kept the men's dirty clothes and bedding perpetually clammy. The fresh food had long since been consumed, leaving the men little choice but to either eat canned items or force down moldy bread. Dysentery and seasickness often occurred, making the stink even worse.

A sailor's specialty and level of training did not earn greater privilege or better conditions in the U-boat service. Even Erich Würdemann grew a long beard and had no more privacy than the lowest-ranking sailor except for a thin curtain separating his bunk from the twenty-four-hour operation of the vessel.

⁂

So why would young men volunteer (and most crewmen were volunteers, not conscripts) for a branch of the military whose living conditions were deplorable and the survival rate low? Some of it had to do with the prestige that came with being a U-boatman. German propaganda glorified the feats that the U-boats performed in glowing newspaper articles, and special magazines were dedicated to submariners' exploits. There were even postcard photographs (similar to American baseball cards) of U-boat aces and a 1941 German movie *U-boat Westward*, which was wildly popular. Consequently, returning U-boat crews were treated like heroes.

Another factor that might push a young man toward joining the U-boat branch of the Kriegsmarine was that the primary alternative, the infantry, was no more appealing, particularly after the Wehrmacht invaded Russia in June 1941. Hitler sent millions of scantily prepared troops to the distant Russian battlefields for more than a year of unrelenting toil, unbearable cold, and terrible bloodshed. At least on a U-boat, a crew member felt important, had a shared sense of camaraderie, and an informality that would never have been tolerated in the infantry, or for that matter in the Luftwaffe or ship duty in the Navy. On U-506 and U-507, the crew could dress in whatever they wanted, and in the Gulf that often meant a pair of pants or shorts and maybe a T-shirt. Life was so cramped in the U-boat that lowly crew members couldn't help but see and exchange a word or two with their commanders, Würdemann and Schacht.

Five crewmen who had almost daily contact with the commanders were the First Watch Officer/Second in Command (Oberleutnant Fritz Schneewind on U-506), the engineer, the radio and hydrophone operator, and the navigator. The stations of these last three were located near the heart of the boat.

During a submerged attack, the U-boat commander spent considerable time with the combat helmsman in the enclosed conning tower that rose amidships above the flat outside deck. Here, the commander had access to the attack periscope that could be raised or lowered by hydraulic power. A ladder led from this tiny tower up to the exposed bridge, where a railing encircled the 20-mm anti-aircraft gun. There was no radar aboard, so locating an enemy ship was done either through the periscope, the Zeiss binoculars on the bridge, or the sound of its propellers heard via the hydrophone. A voice tube on the bridge allowed communication with the radioman and the control room. In rough weather, men on the bridge wore a steel safety belt tethered to the vessel, which just might save their lives should a wave sweep over the vessel.

The *Zentrale* or control room was just below the conning tower, and it was loaded with an array of gauges, valves, and meters, and a gyro compass. The electrical gear to control the rudder and hydroplane was housed here, as was the chart closet and the lower-level periscope used for reconnaissance.

All crewmen on U-507 and U-506 were totally focused on their tasks and felt the weight of the responsibility. They knew it was an honor to be the first two U-boats sent into the Gulf, and they wanted to make Admiral Dönitz proud of his decision to entrust them with such a crucial mission.

Near midnight on May 10, Schacht and U-507 turned toward the mouth of the Mississippi. The night was as still as can be: hazy, cloudless, no wind. In the commander's War Diary, a reader can feel his excitement: "Want to be there [mouth of river] in the morning [May 11], to operate the entire day off the entrance." He made good on his plan, prowling just off the mouth of the Mississippi. "Mississippi lights as in peacetime," Schacht noted in his log. "Frequent mist off the Mississippi. Dirty water gives good cover at periscope depth but bad listening conditions [hydrophone could only pick up the sound of propellers with difficulty]. Boat is difficult to handle because of unaccountable drifts. Patrol by 2 PC-boats. Air patrol along main shipping." Adding to the risk, U-507 was in shallow water, sometimes with as little as twenty feet between the keel of the sub and the ocean's bottom.

Schacht moved in and out of the river delta, noting that even several miles away from the Mississippi the water was dirty. The commander spent most of the daytime hours submerged deep enough so that he could not be spotted by plane, and then toward dusk he'd come up to periscope level, have a look around and if all was safe, bring the vessel completely to the surface and use his diesel engines to both hunt his quarry and recharge his batteries.

On May 12 at 2 A.M., Schacht "again entered the yellow Mississippi water," surprised that the lighthouse burns "as in peacetime." Just before dawn, he steered for the south passage into the river, dodging a patrol boat that was so small, it was hard to see its silhouette. As the sun came up, U-507 submerged but continued a slow prowl at the mouth of the river, gradually moving to the west side of the delta. A short time later, he sighted a slow-moving minesweeper, and Schacht couldn't resist taking a shot with one of his precious torpedoes. The aim was off, and the torpedo passed by the minesweeper, exploding into the jetty at the southwest entrance to the river. Incredibly, boat traffic continued coming and going through the river channel at the Southwest Pass.

Schacht had the pleasure of seeing potential targets seemingly everywhere, but the mighty Mississippi proved a formidable foe in itself. "The entire day am overrun by steamers and tankers from the west, south, and east, in and out," wrote the commander in his log. "Despite all efforts, I cannot get into shooting position." He cited the current, shallow areas, and ships frequently turning as the reasons for his frustration. His irritation increased when he finally maneuvered into a favorable firing position, only to have a patrol boat head his way. Steering the U-boat was incredibly difficult because he was in the grip of the Mississippi's current, and Schacht was in a deadly game of cat and mouse with patrol boats and reconnaissance aircraft both hunting for him. "I have to run the periscope up and down," he recorded, knowing that to keep the periscope up for too long increased his risk of being spotted.

Later that evening, Schacht finally found what he was looking for. A large ship, which lay unmoving just outside the river mouth, caught the commander's full attention. It was a 10,000-ton turbine tanker (carrying gasoline) named *Virginia*, with forty-one crew members on board, and the ship floated unarmed and unescorted, apparently waiting for dawn to move up the river. Schacht had the sitting duck he'd been looking for. He wasted no time maneuvering his vessel into firing position, and launched a torpedo that sliced through the steel hull on the port side. Members of the crew ran to their emergency stations in a state of disbelief that they'd been hit by a U-boat: apparently the captain had decided to keep the information he was receiving about the presence of German subs to himself.

Schacht, watching through the periscope, was also in a state of disbelief. The ship did not explode, and barely shuddered, lying motionless on the surface. In his log, Schacht wrote "because then nothing more happens, shot from tube 4." This time he got his intended result, a direct hit to the engine room that caused the *Virginia* to burst into flames. Schacht noted that the tanker flew apart and burned in two sections, with the sea ablaze in a widening circle.

Surviving crew members later told the *Times-Picayune* that there had been no time to launch lifeboats. Flaming oil spread around the stricken ship, and the men ran to the windward side of the vessel and hurled themselves into the water. Seamen who were not burned to death on the ship or in the ocean tried to swim away from the inferno. Survivor Michael Kuzma showed real bravery when, despite burns to his face and arms, and wearing no life jacket, he supported two injured shipmates and swam them to a buoy, where they hung on for two hours before rescue.

Another seaman, Herbert Dann, said he owed his life to God. "I was in my bunk when the first torpedo hit," he said. "I jumped out and ran on deck. I saw no fire right then, so I went back to get a life preserver and papers and pants and shirt. I ran back on the deck and went to the starboard rail. I was there when the second torpedo hit. Flames burst out over the whole section. I had to drop the preserver. I ran down behind the port housing to protect myself from the flames. I knew I was a goner until I called on the Lord. The smoke and flames parted and a way was cleared to the port side of the ship. Found a preserver there. Put it on, kicked off my shoes, and went over the side and started swimming." A Coast Guard cutter eventually picked him up.

Twenty-seven of his crewmates were not as lucky, and died horrible deaths by burning or drowning or a combination of the two.

Schacht tempted fate by watching the *Virginia* burn, even though he could also see two patrol boats through his periscope. He lay in a precarious position in shallow water "still only eight meters under the keel." It wasn't the patrol boats that finally prompted him to slip away, but the need to move farther out in the ocean where he could fully surface and recharge his batteries in the dark.

CHAPTER SIX

MOVING EVER CLOSER

"After two and one-half years of war experience our [U-boat] crews were at the peak of efficiency, while the American [defenses] and air forces would lack experience."
— Gunter Hessler, senior staff officer to Dönitz

S chacht had the prime pickings by virtue of being the first in the Gulf and the first outside New Orleans at the mouth of the Mississippi. Erich Würdemann, following behind, was likely growing frustrated. After sinking the *Sama*, he had a series of issues that slowed his progress toward the Mississippi. First was a mechanical problem where a broken oil cooler affected the performance of his starboard diesel engine. Next was a series of harassing U.S. aircraft and a patrol boat. One aircraft on May 6 was particularly persistent. The plane made visual contact with Würdemann's sub when it was on the surface, trying to make better time toward New Orleans. The young commander ordered the usual crash dive, waited almost an hour submerged, and then slowly surfaced—only to find that the plane was still in sight, circling the spot where he had initially dived. The pilot must have spotted the sub surfacing, because Würdemann reported that the "aircraft again turns toward the boat," prompting the commander to dive once more. These cat-and-mouse games were helping to educate the young commander, and he balanced the need to sink ships with the welfare of his crew.

Two days later, he had another close call, this time from a Navy patrol boat. "Vessel in sight in the haze," wrote the commander. "Distinguished as a U-boat hunter type PC-450. Crash dive." The soundman then listened to the drone of the boat's propellers and knew it was circling the diving site. Würdemann guessed that the boat lacked sonar because there was no explosion from a depth charge, and no "pinging" noise coming through the soundman's headset that would indicate sonar. Still, the commander didn't take any needless risk or try to sink the vessel but instead slowly eased away from the area, keeping any talk to a whisper and the electric motors as quiet as possible. That turned out to be a smart decision, because later he did hear depth charges "at some distance."

Würdemann was being prudent but he certainly wasn't alarmed. While the U.S. was getting better at locating subs, the Navy and Air Force had a long way to go before becoming skilled at sinking them. From the start of Operation Drumbeat in January through the end of April, the U.S. had sunk the grand total of one U-boat (U-85), whereas the U-boats off the coast of the U.S. and in the Caribbean had sunk 173 ships! Almost every U-boat commander who operated off the coast of the U.S. mentioned, in his War Diary, his astonishment over the lack of convoys and blackouts, and how relatively easy it was to locate ships to sink. Commander Peter Cremer on U-333 observed that the kills he made were "almost textbook style. None of us imagined it to be so easy. . . ."

In perhaps the understatement of the year, President Roosevelt wrote to Fleet Admiral Ernest King about the slow implementation of convoys, saying "Frankly, I think it has taken unconscionable time to get things going."

King might have been slow in implementing the convoy system, but some historians point out just how difficult it was to fight a war in both the Pacific and the Atlantic with limited resources. They remind us that in the years leading up to WWII, King had repeatedly made the case for more ships and aircraft, but the requests fell on deaf ears. A further strain on resources occurred in 1940 when the U.S. gave the British fifty older destroyers in exchange for land rights on British possessions in the Caribbean for the establishment of naval and air bases. Pro-King historians say the Admiral made tough, well-informed decisions as to where to designate the limited resources, and that implementing convoys along the east coast was virtually impossible without the proper escort vessels. But with the loss of so many ships so close to home, one can't help but wonder if more could have been done with the few resources available.

———

Erich Würdemann—knowing he had a golden opportunity with so many ships steaming unescorted—undoubtedly wanted to start sinking a ship a day to catch up with Schacht. But his frustration must have only grown, because while he was dodging aircraft and patrol boats, he learned via radiogram that Schacht had just sank the *Torny*.

The young commander's luck finally changed when, on May 10, he glided undetected into the prime hunting ground of the shipping lanes off the mouth of the Mississippi, and there would be enough tankers and freighters for both commanders to take their pick.

Würdemann got his chance when he spotted a mid-sized oil tanker, the *Aurora*, and he started stalking. The commander fired two torpedoes toward the *Aurora*'s starboard side, and then he waited and after a minute he must have assumed both missed. But then, a full three minutes after he had fired, an explosion. He explained the delay, saying "Range was substantially underestimated, first after 188 seconds (2,800 meters) a hit center."

The tanker, which was carrying water for ballast rather than fuel, listed slightly toward the gaping hole in its hull, but did not sink. Instead, the *Aurora*'s captain, thinking fast, quickly shifted the water ballast, righted the vessel, and gave it full power and started zigzagging away.

Würdemann wasn't going to let his prize escape, so he sent a second and third torpedo into the ship. Incredibly, the vessel still remained afloat, although her crew had taken to the lifeboats. U-506 surfaced next to the wounded ship and the gunner raked the *Aurora* with the large deck gun, then Würdemann ordered the sub below before enemy planes could pinpoint his location. The commander reported that he had sunk the ship, but the old tanker remained afloat and was later towed to port in Louisiana.

The May 12 edition of New Orleans's daily newspaper, the *Times-Picayune*, did not mention the carnage that U-506 and U-507 had brought to the Gulf, because information of submarine attacks had to first be cleared by the government. However, the paper did feature several other war-related stories, most notably the land battles between the Germans and the Russians. HITLER ARMIES PLUNGE TOWARD RED OIL SUPPLY was the day's front-page headline, and the subsequent article went on to say "a battle of major proportions was under way on the narrow peninsula [Crimea] which points the way toward the oil riches Hitler so urgently needs." Other articles on the front page focused on the Pacific Theatre, such as the headline that read: SHIPLOADS OF JAPS MAY HAVE DIED IN CORAL SEA.

But perceptive readers who read a small article at the bottom of the front page, and more articles buried further back in the paper, should have felt an ominous chill that the war was moving their way. One article, headlined PUBLIC BARRED ON FLORIDA BEACH AS GOODS WASH ASHORE, recapped how shiploads of goods from torpedoed vessels were scattered over twenty miles of beach. Another article, headlined EIGHT REACH SHORE, 42 ARE MISSING, described how survivors from a U.S. freighter sunk near Bermuda had spent two days adrift in a lifeboat.

A third story attempted to show that the U.S. was fighting back, but the retaliatory measures must have looked anemic to any reader who digested the entire article. THREE VESSELS TORPEDOED OFF ATLANTIC COAST (NAVY GETS IN SHOTS AT ONE OF THE RAIDERS) was the headline for this article on page 7. It explained how surviving crewmen said that after two subs torpedoed their ship just a half mile from shore, a Navy vessel fired on the U-boats. But H. K. Johnsen, the captain of the stricken ship, was quoted in the article as saying he "doubted that the submarines were damaged." The captain went on to say that the ship initially stayed afloat and he and some surviving crew in a lifeboat tried to return to the ship, but the fumes kept them from boarding. The lifeboat had just turned away from the ship when it burst into flames. "I wish I hadn't seen it," Johnsen said. "Why, the flames shot up five hundred feet into the air." The article went on to explain that the torpedoing had occurred in broad daylight and the explosion had brought hundreds of nearby residents to the beach.

Although Gulf Coast authorities and residents should have initiated strict blackouts, they did not, initially thinking that U-boats simply did not have the fuel capacity to travel from Europe, through the Straits of Florida, and continue westward all the way to the Mississippi. And now, even after authorities knew that the U-boats had arrived, they were slow to demand defensive efforts such as blackouts.

Schacht and Würdemann welcomed that kind of thinking. Their "Happy Times" of easy hunting would continue.

⁂

After torpedoing the *Aurora*, Würdemann and U-506 lurked just off the mouth of the Mississippi for the next day and a half, staying mostly submerged during the daytime but hunting on the surface at night. Once, when trying to rendezvous with Schacht, he surfaced at dawn, and a lazy lookout almost caused a catastrophe. The lookout, wrote Würdemann moments after the attack, recognized an approaching aircraft too late because the plane "came out of the sun." When the men on the sub's bridge knew they had been seen, they shouted for a crash dive and dove down the hatch, probably followed by gallons of incoming water before the hatch could be sealed. The sub had made it thirty meters deep when the depth charges exploded. The U-boat "was literally lifted," said Würdemann in his War Diary. The crew was shaken, and equipment slightly damaged, but the only lasting failure was to tube 5, rendering that tube and its torpedo useless.

It's uncertain whether this incident caused Würdemann to become more cautious, or if he was simply closely following what he had learned in his training. But, whatever the reason, he was more alert than ever in the coming days, even at night. He not only assumed that aircraft could come out of the clouds or the sun at any time with little notice, he also considered what lookouts on ships could see even at night. One of his War Diary entries comments on how marine phosphorescence (micro-organisms that glow in the dark) could betray a sub's position. Explaining how he approached a potential target, he said, "I can only run on an attack course at low speed due to heavy marine phosphorescence." He worried that the shining wake from his surfaced sub would give it away, causing him to either lose the element of surprise or, if the ship were armed, to alert the ship's gunners where to aim their cannons.

Two days after his close call with the aircraft, Würdemann was back in business, finding easy pickings: "multiple freighters and tankers with east or west courses in sight." (Incredibly, the ships traveled without even a single escort vessel, even though the Navy now knew traveling with escorts was the only effective way to prevent ships from being sunk.) Over the next few days, the young commander sank almost a tanker a day. On May 13, he sank the *Gulfpenn* while Schacht, just five miles away, torpedoed its sister ship the *Gulfprince* but was unable to sink it.

May 13 was also the day most newspapers were allowed to acknowledge that the Germans had arrived in the Gulf. On page 3 of the New Orleans *Times-Picayune*, an article proclaimed AXIS SUBMARINES INVADE GULF AND INFEST THE ATLANTIC. The story described how U-boats, which were described as "raiders," have "violated waters impregnable in the last World War." The newspaper had some catching up to do with verifying the number of ships sunk and the number of subs in the Gulf, but they broke the silence regarding the terrible toll the Germans were inflicting. "Reports of at least two ships sunk in the Gulf of Mexico showed that this body of water has been dared by the Axis under-sea raiders." The lack of detailed information and the delay of reporting what little information they did have was not the fault of the newspapers, but rather part of the Navy's strategy to use the cover of "national security" to cloud the Navy's own incompetence in fighting the U-boats. As far back as the opening month of Operation Drumbeat, the Navy had been spinning news or creating outright fabrications to calm the public. A Navy press release on January 23 falsely claimed that they had sunk a U-boat off the coast of the U.S. The press release then boasted that "Some of the recent visitors to our territorial waters will never enjoy the return portion of their voyage."

Schacht was more than just a little irritated over his inability to send the *Gulfprince* to the bottom of the sea. He fired three torpedoes at the ship, and only one struck a glancing blow. The *Gulfprince* crew later said that they had spotted U-507's periscope just before the first torpedo was fired, and their defensive maneuvers were what saved them. And to make matters worse from Schacht's perspective, he couldn't bring the ship down using his deck guns: "steamer runs away. Can do nothing about it. It is not possible to get him on the surface because I am out of artillery ammunition and additionally the entire area is alarmed." He had used all of his 10.5-cm ammunition, and only had smaller 3.7-cm, which he decided would be ineffective at the range he was at.

The next day was no better for U-507, only this time the commander doubted the accuracy of the torpedo settings. He had spotted the tanker *Eastern Sun*, and his first torpedo "went exactly under the center of the tanker without a hit. Running track is easily recognized in marine phosphorescence." Then the tanker opened fire on Schacht with its stern cannon, and U-507 had to crash-dive. Schacht waited thirty minutes, surfaced, and relocated the tanker. He was one pissed-off U-boat captain, and he fired again. "Miss. Surface runner." There were no more eels in his bow tube, but he didn't give up, and maneuvered to fire from the stern tube, which he did. "Miss. A circle runner, easily distinguished in the marine phosphorescence."

Schacht was furious, writing "I have no further trust in the last torpedo remaining on board. I must let the tanker go, as frustrating as it is." He then gave himself a chance to cool down: "Dived to give the crew some peace after the events of the night." He used this time to do a thorough review of the settings for his last torpedo, found it in order, and then hoped for the best. The wily veteran probably didn't want the young upstart Würdemann to eclipse him in kills at the river mouth, and Schacht chose to stay in the area. Like an angry tiger that narrowly missed running down its prey, the senior commander continued to hunt, intent on sinking one last ship before he had to leave the Gulf for good. He found his quarry two days later, with the merchant ship *Amapala*.

The *Amapala* had recently left New Orleans with mixed cargo and a complement of fifty-seven sailors, when at 4:30 P.M. the ship's lookouts spotted U-507 closing in on the surface. (The *Amapala* had been traveling at over 10 knots, and the only way Schacht could hope to overtake it was to run on the surface.) Captain Christiansen of Brooklyn, New York, immediately put out an SSS signal (signifying it was under submarine attack) while he ordered the engines full steam ahead at 16 knots. The distress signal was heard by the radioman on U-507, and he in turn warned his commander that Allied airplanes would respond and soon be on the scene with their bombs. Yet Schacht kept his submarine on the surface and raced after his prize, even using the electric motors to supplement the diesel. The chase was on, with the *Amapala*'s captain sending out updates to the Coast Guard giving his position and repeating that "a U-boat is pursuing us."

Knifing ahead at its maximum surface speed of 18 knots, U-507 closed the distance on the *Amapala*. When Schacht felt he was near enough, he had his gunner open fire with the smaller deck gun.

Captain Christiansen's pleas were getting desperate, at one point saying "Airplane, hurry up, I'm being shot at."

Schacht had his gunners move the light machine gun to the forward bridge and recorded that he "headed directly for the steamer," adding, "He [the *Amapala*] has received numerous hits on the bridge." One of the sailors, Jose Rodrigues of Santiago, Cuba, was wounded by the gunfire (and later died), yet still the freighter did not stop.

Schacht was staying on the surface much too long, knowing that aircraft would be closing in on him. But he gambled that in the "gloomy, rainy weather there is the hope that the launched U.S.A. aircraft will not find us." He was pushing his luck, almost the opposite of the way Würdemann used caution.

The sub continued to blast away with its machine gun.

Finally, with the ship's bridge full of bullet holes, Captain Christiansen had had enough, and he stopped the engines so he and his men could scramble into lifeboats.

Schacht wrote in his War Diary how he ceased firing to allow the ship's crew to leave, and then he "maneuvered his boat abeam for a coup de grace."

He ordered his last torpedo to be fired. Another circle runner! The *Amapala* would apparently stay afloat and live to sail again.

But Schacht, undaunted by the prospect of aircraft arriving any minute, approached one of the lifeboats. After he demanded and received information about the ship, the U-boat commander said he needed to use the lifeboat so his men could row it over and open the hull valves on the still-floating ship so it would finally sink. The men in the lifeboat did as they were told and threw a line to the U-boat crew, which they secured to the sub. As the little boat was being pulled to U-507, it slammed repeatedly into the side of the submarine, threatening to sink the lifeboat. Not knowing what Schacht would do, the lifeboat men made a bold decision and cut the line. (Schacht's version of this part of the story was different from the sailors', as the commander simply recorded that he abandoned the attempt to bring the lifeboats directly to the U-boat.) Whether Schacht let the sailors go or they cut the line, the commander surprised *Amapala's* crew by throwing them cigarette packs.

Schacht continued to tempt fate, this time by positioning the U-boat closer to the *Amapala*. He then ordered two of his men to swim to the ship and sink it by opening the seacocks.

The two submariners stripped down to their shorts, dove into the water, and climbed aboard the *Amapala*, going below to scuttle the ship. Minutes later, a U.S. bomber arrived on the scene, and U-507 had to crash-dive, leaving the two comrades on the ship!

The airplane dropped depth charges, shaking the sub but causing no serious damage. The stranded Germans on the *Amapala*—who had found dry clothing and put it on—came running out on the deck to see what was happening. Somehow the pilots of the aircraft knew the enemy had boarded the ship, and they strafed the deck with machine gun fire. The outlook for those two Germans looked bleak. It appeared that their U-boat had fled, leaving them aboard an enemy vessel with no safe exit. Still, they followed their orders, opened the seacocks, and abandoned ship in a life raft. Imagine their surprise when Schacht and U-507 surfaced and hauled them inside!

Schacht recorded in detail how he brought his "commandos" back inside the sub and they presented him with "the papers of the steamer, among them the zigzag plan. It was the 4,148 GRT steamer *Amapala* of the Standard Fruit and Steamship Company, proceeding under the Honduras Flag." Schacht went on to say that the ship's captain was still within shouting distance of the sub, and that Captain Christensen hollered that he did not know Germany was at war with Honduras or why his ship was sunk. Schacht countered that the captain had ordered U.S. aircraft to bomb him. In the War Diary, Schacht says the captain answered that "he had orders to do it. I then said that I had orders to sink his ship." And on that exchange Schacht finally decided he had pushed his luck far enough, and made course for the Florida Straits because "A further stay at this location seemed unwise to me."

Würdemann wasn't as reckless as Schacht (nor was he as colorful or detailed a writer in his War Diary), but he was smart enough to stay in the vicinity of the Mississippi, knowing that without Schacht around he'd have prime pickings. He took full advantage of this and sank or severely damaged three tankers from May 14 to 17. The *David McKelvy* took two textbook shots from 600 meters (Dönitz's preferred range), which Würdemann said hit in the bow and center: "burning oil pours on the sea," wrote the commander. The fuel ignited, creating an inferno that killed seventeen but the ship itself didn't sink. Its charred hull drifted for several days before coming to rest on the Louisiana shore, a monument to the U-boat's deadly presence.

Next was the *William C. Mctarnhan*, a medium-sized tanker, with forty-five crew members of whom eighteen were trapped below in the aft section of the vessel when the German eel hit and exploded. Four days later, the *Times-Picayune* tried to put a positive spin on part of the story with a sub-headline in the article that read GUN CREW READY. The story went on to say that there was a four-man gun crew (Naval Guard) ready on the bridge, but they had "no time for counter-offensive measures because the Axis U-boat was not spotted until after the ship was hit and sinking." In many newspapers of the period, including the *Times-Picayune*, articles about U-boat attacks started with a headline about the attack by saying NO WARNING GIVEN, as if the U-boat code of conduct should have first been to tell the ship they were about to be torpedoed!

The next target was the *Gulfoil*, which culminated in an attack that was particularly deadly with several sailors perishing either by being blown up when the torpedoes hit, burned by flaming oil, or drowning. The *Times-Picayune* reported that as soon as the first torpedo hit, Captain Henry Rowe began gathering important papers and ignored the pleas of his crew to get in a life raft. "I asked him if he was all right," said a crewman, "and he [the captain] said no, but kept getting the papers." The crew member described how while he was in a life raft he saw the "skipper, still standing on the bridge, go under as the ship plunged downward." Then, incredibly, a few minutes later the crewmen saw the captain bob to the surface and they pulled him into the raft. Later, Captain Rowe mused, "I still have no idea how I got back to the surface." Twenty-one of his crewmen were not as fortunate.

Since entering the Gulf, Erich Würdemann had sunk or damaged seven ships, and the more time he had to hone his hunting skills, the higher the body count. The first ship he attacked, the *Sama*, did not suffer any deaths, and the second, the *Aurora*, only one. But his last four attacks averaged fourteen sailors killed per ship. In total, Würdemann's torpedoes had cost seventy sailors their lives—and, unlike Schacht, the young commander still had multiple eels left.

While the section of ocean off the Mississippi was now buzzing with aircraft searching for the elusive subs, Würdemann could have moved to the less "hot" area of Texas or Alabama. But Dönitz had specifically wanted the young Kapitänleutnant to focus on the New Orleans area, and Würdemann decided he would stay for at least one more ship.

CHAPTER SEVEN

DENIED A SAFE PORT

"It was the worst defeat ever suffered by the U.S. Navy, because unlike Pearl Harbor, it was not a surprise attack."
—Nathan Miller, author of *War at Sea*
(referring to the number of ships sunk off
the U.S. coast from January to July 1942)

Every day on the *Heredia* was a new adventure for Sonny. The cook surprised him with new snacks and he now knew some of the crew by name, many of them taking the time to explain the functions of different equipment. He and Lucille raced on the long, empty decks, even though Lucille always won. Sonny fared little better when he and Lucille played shuffleboard, and occasionally their dad joined in the competition. But the absence of other children on the boat meant games with Lucille wore thin after a few days. He really missed his brother Terry and his dog Boy, and he looked forward to going back to school and playing with friends in his neighborhood the way they had before moving to South America.

58

On his fifth day at sea, Sonny led the family to their lifeboat station for the daily drill. He and Lucille put on their own life jackets, but Ray insisted on tying the knot and pulling hard on it to make sure it held.

"I can do it myself, Dad," Sonny protested.

"I know you can, but my job is to make *sure* it's done right. In a real emergency, we only get one chance to tie it and it has to stay put," his father said.

Sonny often found his father and mother talking in hushed tones on deck chairs, the books they had borrowed from the ship's small library set aside. They spent long periods looking out at the horizon and didn't want to play checkers much. Sonny heard Ina say more than once that she wished the ship could go a lot faster. She sighed loudly when the ship changed course to zigzag evasively, throwing a shadow across her chair.

When crewmen passed the family, they were polite, but there was a definite air of business and efficiency about them, much more so than in the early days of the voyage. Once in a while, Sonny tried to talk to sailors looking out to sea with binoculars, but those were the ones who were too busy to show him around. He knew they were looking for subs and sometimes he tried to help, but he found it boring after a moment or two.

Captain Colburn walked by and exchanged pleasantries with Ray, Ina, and Sonny. He paused long enough to answer Sonny's questions, including why they had not seen more than one or two passing vessels. "Well, Sonny," said the captain, "it won't be long before we approach the shipping lanes outside New Orleans. There I expect you'll see your fair share of ships."

"Captain," Ray asked, "any new activity around here in the water?"

Colburn raised his eyebrows and turned a little to face the railing, perhaps hoping the children wouldn't be scared by what he had to say. "We get bulletins, Mr. Downs, and we study them to ensure that the crew is aware of the latest safety precautions. But submarines being what they are, yesterday's news doesn't matter much in today's waters, if you know what I mean."

"So they could be anywhere?" asked Ina.

"Yes, ma'am, Mrs. Downs. Anywhere," the captain answered.

"But we're through the worst part, aren't we?" Ray pressed the captain. "There should be anti-sub planes patrolling."

"Yes, Mr. Downs," the captain answered. "Every day brings us a little closer to complete safety. Until we're at the dock, we rely on these fine seamen to keep watch."

"And prayers to the Lord above," added Ina.

When the captain left, Sonny wanted to know more, but his dad just put one arm around him and the other around Ina as they looked out at the darkening sea.

"Two more days," Ina murmured. "Two more days and we'll be home safe."

That evening, May 17, the family elected not to sleep on the deck because the seas were building, causing the *Heredia* to sway from side to side in a stiffening wind. Ina thought it best to avoid lying on the reclining deck chairs, worrying that one of the kids might roll right off. Clouds had moved in, making for a beautiful sunset but perhaps a rainy night. Better to be ensconced below, where the ship's motion would not be as pronounced.

Ina's decision was a good one. Several times she was awakened during the night when a wave bigger than those that had preceded it rocked the *Heredia* with a sudden jolt. At dawn, the family climbed the mahogany stairs to the deck and were greeted by howling wind, driving rain, and waves cresting at twenty-five feet. The Downses huddled together and watched wind-whipped spray lash the ship while plumes of foam streaked by. The air temperature had dropped to sixty-five degrees, and they felt cold after all the time spent in the tropics of South America. Surprisingly, none of the family was seasick, and all went down to the galley for breakfast, where the conversation was about how quickly the storm had risen and the lack of accurate weather forecasting. Part of the reason for the lack of the storm warning had to do with the war. Weather advisories had to be censored and cleared through the Weather Bureau Office in New Orleans, causing delays in the forecasts. In addition, the Weather Bureau relied on observation reports from ships scattered over hundreds of miles; but because of the presence of U-boats, the ships were under orders not to transmit. (In July 1943, these factors caused a lack of preparedness when the "Surprise Hurricane of '43" careened into the Gulf, killing nineteen people.)

———

Later that day, the lumbering waves subsided to fifteen to twenty feet, but the ship still rolled heavily in the turbulent seas. From a passageway, Sonny and Ray watched whenever a crew member or one of the Naval Armed Guard had to cross the deck, and how they wore a safety harness with a tether clipped to a cable that ran from the bridge to the bow. The *Heredia* sailors seemed right at home walking through the blasting wind and pelting rain, but Sonny noticed that one of the Armed Guard men seemed a bit unsteady on his feet. Sonny thought the Navy man looked like he should still be in high school, and he may have been right.

Most of the Armed Guards aboard ships in 1942 were from eighteen to twenty years of age, and some were as young as sixteen. Many had enlisted in the Navy with aspirations to serve aboard a fighting ship, such as a destroyer or aircraft carrier, with the idea of striking back at the Japanese. Instead, after boot camp, a handful were selected to serve aboard merchant ships—a less glamorous job in the minds of most, because they were not attacking, but defending. After a hasty three weeks of training involving the deck guns they would be operating, the men were sent off to one of three Armed Guard Centers where they were then formed into teams and assigned to ships. While the young men may have longed for offensive action aboard destroyers, being in the Naval Armed Guard was by no means a safe or cushy position. During World War II, 1,810 of these young men were killed or went missing.

———

"Can I go out on the deck, like the sailors?" asked Sonny. "I'll wear a harness."

Ray thought for a moment and surprised Sonny, saying, "If your mother says it's okay and I can find a sailor to go with you, I don't see why not."

Sonny didn't give his father a chance to change his mind and raced below to find his mother.

Ina could see the excitement in Sonny's eyes as he described what he wanted to do. She knew the trip was near its end, and she knew that Sonny would have a story he could tell over and over. "Let's go up to where your father is, I want to talk to him, but if he thinks it is safe and you are right next to a sailor, I think it would be okay."

Sonny could not believe his good fortune. He grabbed his mother's hand and together they joined Ray at the passageway. Ray had already recruited a sailor for the job, and after they explained to Ina how safe it would be, she agreed.

The sailor fastened a harness on Sonny, clipped him to the cable, and then did the same for himself. Together they stepped out into the driving rain and began slowly walking toward the bow.

Ina had second thoughts when she saw Sonny hunched over, struggling against the whipping wind and rain. She worried one strong gust might lift her boy into the air like a kite. But Sonny and the sailor safely reached the bow, and when they turned around Sonny waved at her. Ina took a half step toward him, thinking that he was crying, but while shielding her eyes from the rain she realized it was laughter coming from her son's mouth. He was having a ball, and when he came back to the passageway, Ina scooped him into her arms.

"Can I go again?" Sonny shouted, rubbing the burning salt spray from his eyes.

Ina laughed and shook her head. "Once is enough. You've got quite a story to tell Terry when you get home."

By the next day, the storm had long since moved to the east and the air became still and sticky. Around noon, a crew member reported seeing something unusual in the ocean, far off the stern. This caused quite a commotion, and the passengers and crew alike all scanned the seas, wondering if the sighting could have been a U-boat. The men of the Naval Armed Guards did the same, using their binoculars. Although there were no further sightings, Captain Colburn took the potential threat seriously enough to change course for the closest harbor, which was Corpus Christi, Texas. Once there, the captain would go ashore and get a feel for the situation, and find out if the ship should stay in Corpus Christi Bay or Nueces Bay for the night.

Ina and Ray welcomed the change of course. They not only worried about the U-boat danger, but they were ready to move on with the next phase of their life, and Corpus Christi was closer to home than New Orleans. They asked Captain Colburn if they could disembark there, and he said he'd see what he could do.

Upon reaching the outside of the bay, *Heredia*'s anchor was lowered, and Captain Colburn was taken ashore in a pilot boat.

The Downs family stood at the rail and watched the captain leave, hoping he'd return with good news. They also noted that the entire bay was full of ships at anchor. It was May 18, and this was the first time they could actually see the shore of their home country since they'd left for South America almost a year earlier.

Ray was becoming edgy from so much inactivity, and Ina wanted to get off the ship. Sonny could hear his parents talking, already making plans for reuniting with Terry and searching for a place to live. Lucille too was ready to be back on land and to see her brother and grandparents. Only Sonny was sad to see the voyage come to an end. He was hoping for one last storm so he could go back out on deck with the harness and cable to enjoy the wind and plumes of spray.

Captain Colburn returned in an hour, and he climbed the Jacob's ladder with a serious expression as the Downs family, along with a couple of other passengers, waited expectantly by the rail.

"Sorry, folks," said the captain when he was on the deck. "They won't let you off here. Too much paperwork and not enough time to get the necessary permission. But the officials say we should be fine steaming on toward New Orleans tonight." Then the captain surprised the passengers by reaching into a bag and passing out magazines and cigarettes to the adults, and candy to the children.

"Was it a U-boat out there?" Ray asked. "Did the harbormaster tell you if others have seen it? Why are so many ships anchored in the bay?"

"Mr. Downs, due to wartime restrictions, including radio silence, there is little communication between ships and shore until a ship arrives in port," said the captain. He wore a stern expression and seemed exhausted by the trip.

"I really want my family to get off the boat here, Captain," Ray said.

"We're uncomfortable going back out to sea," added Ina. "What about our children?"

"I'm terribly sorry," the captain said. "We cannot de-board you here. Harbormaster's orders. I wish we could. I would not worry too much about something somebody might have seen hours ago. As I said before, if there's a submarine out there—and I said *if*—he could be anywhere. It's a big ocean and there are a lot of boats in it. Chances are we'll be in New Orleans safely in no time."

"Looks like most of the boats are at anchor here, Captain," Ray pointed out, motioning toward the packed waterfront. "They're safely in the harbor."

A half hour later, the *Heredia* was plowing east toward New Orleans. The cigarettes and magazines did little to lift Ina's mood. With a heavy heart, she watched the coast of Texas disappear.

A spectacular sunset with streaks of gold—the best of the voyage—briefly occupied Ina's attention; but after the sun dipped below the horizon and dusk darkened the ocean, she returned to her brooding over U-boats. *If only we could have left the ship in Corpus Christi. . . .*

That evening, the *Heredia* was blacked out, but small flashlights were allowed when passengers or sailors moved around. The Naval Armed Guards were at their lookout stations, enjoying the slight breeze but having difficulty seeing through a haze that hung over the ocean. Two of the Armed Guards were at the aft gun, two more were in the forecastle, and a fifth was on the bridge. The sixth serviceman was resting below.

The Downs family was sitting together on deck chairs, quietly enjoying temperatures a bit more refreshing than the oppressive humidity of the day. They watched phosphorescence glimmer in the wake of the ship, and they talked in hushed voices. Sonny enjoyed the pauses in the conversation, when all was silent except the constant whooshing sound the ship made as it cut through the ocean. It looked like it was going to be a beautiful moonlit night.

A fellow passenger named Robert Beach paced the deck nearby, and when he walked by the Downs family, Ina said "Good evening, Mr. Beach."

Beach turned to Ina and gave a curt nod.

Ina saw the worried look on his face and said, "We'll be in port first thing in the morning."

"Not soon enough," said Beach as he walked away.

Sonny looked at his mother and asked "Is he always so mean?"

Ina hesitated and replied, "He's just anxious to get home. He's been in South America for three years." She didn't tell Sonny that she suspected that Mr. Beach was especially nervous because earlier in the voyage Beach had said he had spent a good deal of his income buying expensive jewelry in Panama, some of which he would give to his wife and the remainder sell at a profit. Beach was not just worried about his own physical welfare if a U-boat struck, but also the potential loss of his investment.

Sonny watched Mr. Beach scuttle away into the shadows. The boy switched subjects: "Can Lucille and I sleep on deck tonight?"

"Not tonight," answered Ray. "It's our last night and we've got to get our things organized, so we'll sleep in our staterooms."

Sonny knew better than to ask again, so he made a different request. "Because it's the last night, can you sleep in my room and Lucille can sleep with Mom?"

"Okay," said Ray.

"And can I sleep in my shorts just like you?"

"Sure."

Sonny grinned, glad for one last night out of the ordinary.

A few minutes later, Captain Colburn, in his dress whites, strolled up and said good evening. The captain tousled Sonny's hair and said, "Well, young Downs, by 6:30 in the morning we'll be docking in New Orleans."

"Yes, sir," said Sonny, "my dad told me. He and I are going to sleep in the same room for our last night."

Captain Colburn forced a smile. Ray stood up, and he and the captain moved out of earshot of the family. "Any more news about U-boats?" asked Ray.

"No, sir. We should be fine."

"How about news about the war?"

Colburn shook his head. "Didn't have time to even ask when I was ashore. Guess we'll both learn more tomorrow morning when we are in New Orleans."

CHAPTER EIGHT

AN UNEASY FEELING

"The Americans, apparently, had not anticipated the appearance of U-boats in such far distant parts of the Caribbean as the Gulf of Mexico. Once again we had struck them in a soft spot."
—Admiral Dönitz, writing in his memoirs

While Captain Colburn continued on his rounds, Ray wondered about distant battlefronts. Several times during the voyage, he had asked the ship's radioman what he might have heard about the War, but only got a vague response of "nothing new."

In fact, there was a lot that had happened in the week the Downs family had been at sea. Much of the war news revolved around battles for oil fields abroad and the oil/gasoline shortages at home. The Associated Press ran an article about Hitler's eastern campaign against Russia, saying "A fateful test [is] approaching along the Southern Russian battle line, where Hitler had opened a great gamble in a desperate effort to get at the Caucasus and its oil, and a sense of approaching a grand crisis was spreading to the whole global arena of the war." Experts predicted

Hitler would "throw two million men in grand assaults" on the Russian positions that included oilfields.

On the home front, the attacks by U-boats were especially effective at interrupting the delivery of gasoline at a time when the product was already in short supply due to military needs. Gasoline rationing began when the U.S. Office of Price Administration announced that motorists whose autos were classified as non-essential would be limited to three gallons of gasoline a week in Eastern Seaboard states. Several articles in the New Orleans *Times-Picayune* discussed the need for an inland oil pipeline, and one article's headline read: PLEA REPEATED FOR PIPELINE TO GET GAS EAST. President Roosevelt met with Congressional leaders to begin a feasibility study regarding construction of a pipeline from the southwest to bring oil to the east coast. Ironically, despite this crisis, caused in part because of U-boats, the *Times-Picayune* reported that the CITY STILL GLOWS IN HAZE OF LIGHT UNDER NEW DIMOUT, which was ordered to make it harder for U-boats to see the silhouettes of ships.

Other news of the period focused on the war against the Japanese. The AP reported that "The Navy produced the missing clue to one of the war's most fascinating mysteries and thereby let it be known that an American submarine was the vessel which braved bombs and shore batteries to bring a vast amount of gold, silver, and securities out of the Philippines before the Japanese could get their hands on it." The Japanese, however, had their own daring submarine ventures, including an attack on the U.S. mainland. The sub fired seventeen shells at the Richfield aviation fuel depot not far from Santa Barbara, California, triggering an invasion scare in Los Angeles. This attack occurred in February 1942, and was later followed up in June 1942 when sub I-25 arrived at the Columbia River in Oregon and followed fishing boats to bypass minefields so it could position itself not far from Fort Stevens. It fired shells in the direction of the military base, expecting the Americans to fire back and more clearly reveal the American position. But the commander of the fort held fire, and most of the Japanese shells landed in a nearby ball field.

The most successful raid during the first half of 1942, however, did not involve submarines, but instead involved sixteen American B-25 bombers sweeping over Tokyo: the Doolittle Raid. The attack occurred on April 18, but the *Times-Picayune* expanded on the story in mid-May when additional details were released. "New Orleanians learned that Brigadier General James 'Jimmy' Doolittle, a frequent visitor to this city, led the recent destructive first American air raid of the war on Tokyo." The article went on to discuss how the intrepid flyer "unloaded bombs within plain sight of Emperor Hirohito's palace." After unloading their bombs, fifteen of the aircraft landed in China and one in Russia. While the damage caused by the bombers was relatively light, the morale boost for the American public was significant, as evidenced in a follow-up article titled JAPS DIDN'T BAG SINGLE AMERICAN PLANE—DOOLITTLE.

On May 15, the newspaper also ran an article designed to uplift the public, titled GREATEST BOOM TO FOLLOW WAR, BANKER BELIEVES. The piece explained how an economist for the American Bankers Association spoke at a meeting explaining that after the war "there is a good deal of evidence that we may enjoy the period of our greatest economic development, our greatest world influence, and our greatest social gains." Articles like this and the exploits of the Doolittle Raid were sorely needed after Pearl Harbor, the Japanese submarine attack on Santa Barbara, and the seemingly unending success of U-boats along the Eastern Seaboard and in the Gulf. The *Times-Picayune* reporting of the ships being torpedoed in the Gulf and the Caribbean Sea and off Florida was becoming a daily occurrence. In fact, the Downses were quite lucky to have escaped unscathed when they earlier steamed through the Yucatan Channel, which lay between the western end of Cuba and the Yucatan Peninsula. Commander Ulrich Folkers in U-125 patrolled a relatively small patch of water south of the Yucatan Channel and sank seven ships in a two-week period, both before and after the *Heredia* somehow steamed through unharmed!

The *Heredia* had been lucky indeed, because Allied defenses against U-boats in the "Gulf Sea Frontier" (designated by the U.S. Navy to include the Gulf of Mexico, the Yucatan Channel, the Bahamas, the northwestern Caribbean, and coastal Florida) were even weaker than the Eastern Sea Frontier (from Jacksonville, Florida northward to Canada). By May 1942, the Eastern Sea Frontier had finally begun using convoys; but in the Gulf Frontier (where officials were surprised by the U-boats' arrival), ships were still traveling alone. Lack of resources was the major problem: most naval ships had been diverted to the Pacific and to convoys crossing the Atlantic. To cover the Gulf Sea Frontier area, Commander Russell Crenshaw only had a couple of old destroyers, five cutters, an assortment of smaller craft, and thirty-five aircraft. It was difficult enough to find a U-boat in the daytime in this nearly 618,000-square-mile area, and downright impossible to locate one after sundown. Without radar on the planes, the U-boats owned the night. Even in the rare instances when a U-boat was on the surface in daylight, inexperienced U.S. sailors and pilots sometimes overlooked them. U-boat crews were astounded when aircraft flew directly over them and nothing happened, or when patrol boats motored close by but continued patrolling. Sonar had been invented by the British, which they called ASDIC (named after the Anti Submarine Detection Investigation Committee), and the U.S. had it installed on some sub-hunting vessels, but it took expertise, and the sub had to be relatively close by for it to be effective. While some U-boat crews in the Gulf said they heard the distinctive "ping" of the sonar, neither Würdemann or Schacht mentioned it in their War Diaries.

To compensate for the lack of defensive resources, large civilian yachts were purchased by the military and converted to patrol boats equipped with depth charges and at least one .50-caliber machine gun. Coast Guard personnel usually operated these armed vessels, and strict instructions were given on operating the depth charges. (If a small-boat crew dropped a depth charge too near their vessel, they could sink themselves!) These vessels rarely engaged the enemy, but they were effective at patrolling and rescue.

The Navy and Coast Guard also reached out to commercial fishing vessels and civilian yacht clubs and power squadrons, and they responded. Volunteers onboard small craft assisted the military by offshore observation—the more patrolling watercraft, the more difficult it was for U-boats to surface and recharge their batteries. Even sailboat skippers volunteered, pointing out that their vessels were silent and sailors could climb the rigging for a better vantage point to spot a U-boat or its periscope. The Coast Guard called them the "Corsair Fleet" and used them in the Coastal Picket Patrol, but the public simply referred to them as the Hooligan Navy. (The British wondered what took us so long to use the services of civilian vessels: after all, they had employed them during the 1940 evacuation of Dunkirk with great success.)

Other experiments also held promise, such as using blimps to hover over merchant ships. The helium-filled blimps, about a quarter of the size of the dirigible *Hindenburg*, could cruise along at fifty miles an hour. Incredibly, the blimps were armed with depth charges, and a United Press article extolled the young men who manned them: "they were itching to pull the lever that would send depth charges hurtling from the bomb bay down on one of the many U-boats marauding off the coast." That was easier said than done, because even if the blimp should catch a sub on the surface in daytime, they often had only thirty seconds to get into position directly above the sub before it completed its crash dive. The blimps' real value was in deterring submarines from surfacing. Catalina flying boats (the Consolidated PBY Catalina) were also used successfully as "protecting eyes" over merchant ships. Because they could land and take off from the water, they were especially useful in search and rescue.

These various resources became increasingly effective in the second half of 1942. But now, in May 1942, when the *Heredia* was almost at safe port in New Orleans, effective defensive measures were few and far between. Schacht and Würdemann, being the first U-boat captains to enter the Gulf of Mexico, enjoyed the element of surprise. The *Times-Picayune* hinted at the frustration of the public in a May 13 article where they discussed a sinking off Florida and commented that the Navy "has let out few facts about the counteroffensive being waged against Axis submarines. There has been no public statement about the Navy's success about meeting the undersea challenges."

Although the Navy was silent on many of its countermeasures, it did make public shipping losses and casualties (after a brief delay) but withheld the name of the ship, its size, and its cargo, which might have been of value to the enemy. Newspaper reporting itself showed an unfamiliarity with submarine warfare, frequently beginning an article about a torpedoed ship with the words "torpedoes hit without warning" or "attacked without warning," as if they thought there should be more civil rules of engagement.

One response to this springtime carnage was to build more ships at a quicker pace. The May 14 *Times-Picayune* edition reported on both this plan and President Roosevelt's submarine bill which initiated "construction of 200,000 tons more of submarines in a move to beat the Axis at its own game." All this was good news for a public who had endured five months of maritime losses, but it did nothing for those currently out at sea like the Downs family.

In some respects, the U-boats were too successful and aggressive. On May 14, the neutral Mexican tanker *Potrero del Llano* was sunk off Miami by U-564 commanded by Reinhard Suhren. It is unclear if commander Suhren knew the ship was Mexican, because the German government claimed the ship was traveling at night and did not have its national flag illuminated. However, survivors and the American press said the ship was fully illuminated. *Potrero del Llano* Quartermaster Edwardo Sibaja Rameriz recalled how one of his crewmen burst into his quarters shouting "we're being followed!" He went on to shout that it was "a big animal" trailing the ship. The quartermaster ran toward the bridge just as the torpedo hit, later saying "the bridge went to pieces before my eyes." An article written by the Associated Press which ran in the *Times-Picayune* said that "the blazing ship, on which thirteen men were killed, floated for hours past Miami Beach and thousands of persons gathered on the seashore to watch the burning vessel." A Coast Guard ship rescued twenty-two from the "fire-drenched sea."

The Mexican government, in a statement addressed to Germany, demanded complete satisfaction and a guarantee of damage reparations or they would "take a position in accordance with Mexican honor." Instead, a few days later, another Mexican tanker, *Faja de Oro*, was torpedoed at night by a different U-boat off the western end of Cuba. The tanker sank and ten sailors were killed. Mexican citizens demanded that their government declare war on Germany, and the Mexican Senate quickly voted unanimously to do just that. Germany now had yet another foe.

After Ray's conversation with Captain Colburn inquiring about the latest War news, the Downs family soon retired to their berths at 9 P.M. Sonny, thrilled to be sleeping with his father, climbed up to the top bunk while his father lay down in the bottom bunk. Each of them checked that their life jackets—grey canvas covering balsa wood strands—were hanging on a peg within reach of their bunks. They talked for a couple of minutes, but soon both were fast asleep. In the adjoining room, separated by the bathroom, Lucille had also fallen asleep, but not Ina. She simply could not shake her sense of foreboding, and she tried in vain to let the ship's rocking motion calm her.

While Ina lay awake in her berth, the *Heredia* steamed eastward at 12 knots. She realized they had stopped zigzagging and were simply plowing into the night, and she hoped it was a good sign. Perhaps the captain had been told evasive maneuvers were unnecessary because there were no submarines nearby. Still, she couldn't sleep.

The old ship was approximately forty miles to the south-southwest of New Orleans, just a few miles from Ship Shoal Buoy.

―※―

While the Downs family spent their last afternoon and evening aboard the *Heredia*, Erich Würdemann maneuvered U-506 farther out in the Gulf and away from the Mississippi. He and his men had a dangerous job to perform: moving torpedoes from the deck down into the firing tubes. To do the job, the U-boat had to remain on the surface, a vulnerable position should U.S. aircraft spot it. Using cables, a winch, pulleys, and considerable manpower, the first 23-foot-long, 3,600-pound eel was wrestled from its deck housing and slowly lowered on a rail through an open hatch into a torpedo tube. Then the process was repeated with the other deck torpedo, as crewmen anxiously kept an eye on the sky, hoping no planes would appear.

Once the torpedoes were safely in their firing tubes, Würdemann ordered U-506 submerged and set a course for Ship Shoal Buoy. Every now and again, the commander had the sub climb to a position just below the ocean's surface, where he could scan the seas through the periscope. He spotted several fishing boats and one unloaded tanker that was so far away he declined to chase it, surmising that more ships would soon come along.

As darkness fell, the young commander ordered the submarine back up to the surface and continued hunting, now just a few miles from Ship Shoal Buoy.

At approximately one in the morning, Würdemann noted in his War Diary that a shadow could be seen bearing 260 degrees. He ordered U-506 to change course slightly, so that his sub could get ahead of the ship and lie in wait for it. Commander Würdemann's confidence was sky-high; he knew that at night he could operate without the slightest risk of being detected and he'd be able to maneuver so close to the ship that his torpedoes were almost guaranteed to find their mark.

U-506 cruised along the ocean's black surface at its maximum speed of 18 knots, its crew excited with the anticipation of unleashing their torpedoes.

PART II

CHAPTER NINE

TORPEDOES IN
THE NIGHT

"Don't come down here! Take the stairs to the deck! We've been torpedoed!"

—*Heredia* sailor

The first torpedo tore into the *Heredia* with a tremendous explosion, causing the old ship to shudder. Sonny struggled to sit up in the top bunk of the cramped, dark cabin. *Did we hit the pier in New Orleans?*

Then, BOOM! The second torpedo rocked the boat so hard, he almost fell to the floor.

Ray turned on the cabin light, and it flickered, casting an eerie glow on the father's ashen face. He was now standing next to the bunk bed.

Sonny felt his father's hands on his shoulders.

"Put on your life preserver," Ray barked. "Tie it tight and stay right here."

Disoriented and afraid, Sonny could see water eddying around his father's ankles as his dad opened the door to his mother's adjoining cabin and disappeared.

Snatching his life jacket from the peg next to his bunk, Sonny fumbled with the straps. The life jacket's bulk pushed awkwardly against his ears as he pulled the ties together across his chest. *Is Dad coming back?* Sonny wondered, his fear growing as more water swirled into the cabin. *The ship must be sinking!* He could hear shouting outside in the hallway, and he considered hopping off the bunk and running for the lifeboats like he had done in the drills.

He was about to holler for his father when Ray burst back into the room, followed by Ina and Lucille. Lucille's life vest was secured over her nightclothes, while Ina, her face stricken, had grabbed a coat to put over her night gown and put a life vest over it.

Ray lifted Sonny off the top bunk and tugged at his son's life jacket to be sure it was secure. "You did a good job. Now hold my hand and don't let go!"

The family, hand in hand, left the cabin and entered the corridor. Pale blue lights lining the passageway flickered, and they briefly saw Mr. Beach standing up ahead just outside his cabin door, heading back inside rather than going to the lifeboat station. Ray shouted, "What are you doing? Head up on deck! We've been torpedoed!"

"Got to get my suitcases!" shouted Mr. Beach. Just as he ducked back inside his cabin, the lights went out for good.

Sonny felt like everything was in slow motion. His father gripped his small fingers so tightly it hurt, but it gave the boy a measure of comfort knowing his dad was right next to him.

At the end of the corridor, toward the stern of the ship, a sailor swung two flashlights in wide arcs, and the family sloshed that way, the water now up to Sonny's thighs.

"Don't come down here! Take the stairs to the deck!" the sailor shouted. "We've been torpedoed!"

Sonny was confused: this was not the usual route to their lifeboat station. And how did the ship get torpedoed with all those guards standing watch? But he had all he could do to keep up with his dad's long strides.

With his father half dragging him up the steps, Sonny looked up and saw that there was a bit of light coming from the deck above. It seemed to take forever to climb those stairs and escape the rushing water below. People were shouting up on deck, and Sonny wondered if the *Heredia* might be on fire.

Just as the family reached the last couple of steps, disaster struck.

The ship suddenly lurched to starboard, and the entire family was slammed by an avalanche of churning water. So much water rushed by Sonny that he was torn from his father's grasp. The boy felt himself tumbling underwater as if inside a washing machine, not sure which way the surface was. He opened his eyes but saw only blackness, adding to his disorientation and fear. Someone grabbed one of his legs, and, terrified, he instinctively kicked away. His lungs screamed for air as he thrashed wildly. Using what little strength he had left, he clawed at the water, panicked by the sense that the ocean would never let him go.

Ten seconds later, his head broke the surface and Sonny came up gasping for air, then coughing up seawater. He swiveled around, desperately looking for his parents and sister. They were gone. He was alone in the ocean alongside the ship, terrified.

Sonny tried to scream, but a wave slapped him in the face and he ingested more seawater.

Now he wondered if he was dreaming, because it was so bright around him that he thought it was daylight. *Am I dead? Is this a nightmare?* The eight-year-old had no way of knowing that the brilliant light was from the powerful searchlight on the conning tower of U-506.

Sonny tried to make sense of what he could see. He knew he was in the ocean—could see the swells rising and falling—but he also heard voices coming from somewhere above him. He looked toward the sound and saw what he thought was the center of the *Heredia*, the uppermost deck above the bridge, where the machine guns were mounted. But everything was at a crazy angle, and it took him a moment to process it. Then he understood: the ship was listing badly to starboard and the entire stern was underwater, causing the rest of the ship to stick out of the ocean at a forty-five-degree angle.

In an incredible stroke of luck Sonny surfaced just a few feet from a short steel ladder leading to the upper deck. Sonny swam to it and tried to climb its five or six steps. The boy had no way of knowing that just behind the ladder, only a few feet away, his mother was pinned by rushing water between the ladder and a steel bulkhead.

Sonny only managed to scale a couple of steps before sliding back down. The angle of the ship made climbing the ladder almost impossible. Holding on to the ladder, the boy shouted for help, but only a faint croak came from his mouth. *Where's Dad? I need him now.*

Again he attempted to ascend the ladder, and this time when he fell off, he landed right on top of another man. His silent prayer was answered, but it wasn't Ray who came to the rescue, but rather a thin, gawky, balding man named George Conyea, a fellow passenger from New Orleans.

"We gotta get up there!" shouted Conyea. "You try again, and I'll be right behind you!"

This time the boy made it to the top, with Conyea right behind him.

"You stand by the wire rail," Conyea shouted, "and hold on to it!"

Sonny could only nod; too much was happening and he was shaking from a combination of cold, exhaustion, and fear.

Conyea pointed to the wire cable supported by stanchions that encircled the upper deck. That's when Sonny realized there was another man standing on the top deck, someone he had gotten to know quite well on the voyage, Captain Erwin Colburn. The captain, still wearing his white uniform, was struggling to free a life raft from its brackets. Binoculars dangled from the captain's neck as he cursed at the stubborn raft.

"Where's my family?" Sonny shouted. Silence. Neither Conyea or the captain said a word, nor did they even meet Sonny's eyes. It was a crushing blow for the boy. He choked back a sob, thinking his mother, father, and Lucille had all been swallowed by the ocean.

Conyea and the captain both stooped down and resumed pulling on the raft, even kicking at the brackets that held it in place.

Sonny looked down at the black five-foot swells sliding beneath the ship, searching for any sign of his family. From the vantage point of the upper deck, the boy now realized just how desperate his own situation was. The entire stern of the ship was submerged, the radio shack and lifeboats had been obliterated, and jagged pieces of metal protruded from the lower deck just aft of where he stood. It looked as if the *Heredia* would break in two at any minute. He also saw the source of the light. About two hundred yards away, the searchlight from the sub cut through the darkness, seeming to point directly at Sonny. He wasn't sure what the sub might do next; but he was thankful for the light, as it allowed him to continue scanning the ocean's surface for any signs of his family. Although he could hear distant shouts for help, he couldn't see another soul, nor did the shouts sound like anyone in his family. *Are these two men and I the only ones left on the ship?* He shivered in the cool night air. His only clothing was his wet shorts, and he felt colder now than he had in the water.

Sonny watched Conyea and Captain Colburn move to the same side of the raft and pull together, still without result. The raft was small, just a simple four-foot-by-four-foot balsa wood frame. Grey canvas was wrapped around the balsa wood but did not cover the middle. It reminded Sonny of a sandbox with no bottom, and he realized that even if they got it free, there would be no place to sit, just the frame to hold on to. But no raft at all meant a death sentence, and even the eight-year-old boy knew that—the ocean was clearly pulling the ship down. More of the ship was under water now than just a minute earlier when Sonny had first stood on the gun deck.

Still clutching the wire cable, Sonny noticed movement where the ocean covered the submerged part of the ship on the starboard side. A man burst from the water and swam toward the gun deck where Sonny stood transfixed. The man was his father!

Commander Erich Würdemann stood on the bridge with some of his men and quietly watched the stricken *Heredia* wallowing in its death throes. He would have preferred it if his prey had been an oil tanker rather than a merchant ship. Still, he was satisfied that the *Heredia* was another kill, adding to his tonnage, just as Admiral Dönitz had instructed. Having already expended multiple torpedoes on this ship, he did not want to use another, and instead would wait a few minutes to make sure the *Heredia* went to the bottom of the sea. If needed, he'd use his guns to put holes near the water line of the vessel and speed the process.

The commander watched small figures moving on the ship's uppermost deck where machine guns were mounted, but he was unconcerned. The bow section of the ship extended from the sea at such a steep angle that he surmised the guns would be useless, and none of the people on the deck was even manning the guns. He was also unconcerned about aircraft. Even if the radio operator had sent out an SOS, it would take an aircraft at least a half hour to arrive on the scene, and when and if it did, he'd simply shut off his light and move off. And should another ship come to pick up survivors, he'd submerge to periscope depth and torpedo that ship as well. Efficiency, that's what Dönitz's training was all about, and Würdemann lived it. He watched the men on the upper deck struggling with what was probably the life raft, and he could see a child standing behind them. Someone else was in the water, swimming toward the group on the deck. Unlike fellow commander Schacht, Erich Würdemann had no plans to talk to any survivors to learn more about the ship or to wish them luck. He could estimate the tonnage of the ship, and now all he really cared about was seeing it sink with his own eyes. But if the group on the ship's upper deck did not leave the vessel soon, he might fire a warning shot to indicate that they'd best get in the water immediately. It was ships he was after, not human lives.

CHAPTER TEN

THE RAFT

"I can't swim!"
—Captain Erwin Colburn

S onny could not believe his eyes. It was as if his father had risen from the dead, the way he burst from the water.

When the boat initially lurched to starboard and the family became separated, the avalanching water pushed Ray back down the staircase and washed him around like a matchstick. Several times he found air pockets, only to be pulled back under the swirling water. Somehow, by swimming and being pushed by the water, Ray found himself in the flooded galley. He hollered for Sonny, Ina, and Lucille, but no one answered.

Ray repeatedly dove down into the black water, frantically groping around. He was feeling for a body in case one of his family members had also been washed into the room and was trapped. *Where are they?* They could be on the outside of the ship in the ocean. They could have been flushed to the bottom of the mahogany staircase and unable to get back up. The ship was making terrible groaning noises from metal being twisted by intense water pressure and loud hissing sounds from escaping air. Time was running out. He was afraid the *Heredia* would plunge to the seabed at any moment.

Seeing light coming from a window, he swam to it and used his legs to break the glass, slashing his right leg just above the knee.

Ray swam through the glass, kicked to the surface, and the first thing he saw was the tiny upper gun deck illuminated as if were a sunny day. He was confused, but didn't waste any time, swimming to the deck and scrambling aboard. The first word he heard was "Dad!"

Ray hugged his son, and then assessed the situation, noting that the captain and Conyea were the only other people on the deck. The U-boat was just 200 yards away, off the stern, and Ray thought the Germans might open fire with their machine gun at any second. He turned to the captain and Conyea.

"What the hell is the matter with you guys, we gotta get off this ship!"

Captain Colburn responded, "We can't get the raft out of the mounts."

Ray pushed the captain aside, yelling "You jackasses!" Next, he took a quick look at the way the raft was mounted. He squatted down, putting both hands under one side of the balsa wood, and in a single quick motion wrenched it free of the brackets.

Ray turned back to the captain. "I'm going to have Sonny lay on top of one side of the raft, and while he's holding on, slide it into the water. Then we'll jump in the water and swim to it."

"I need to be on it when you slide it off!" shouted the captain, adding, "I can't swim."

Ray jabbed a fist into Captain Colburn's chest, roaring, "Well, you're going to learn real quick, because my son goes first!"

Sonny, watching this exchange, was as stunned as Colburn. He had viewed the captain as the ultimate authority, like a school principal, but now there was a clear shift in who was in charge. And he intuitively sensed that the change was permanent. He knew what his father was like when he was riled and things had to be done in a hurry.

Ray felt a sense of urgency beyond the threat of the ship sinking, beyond the possibility of the U-boat's machine guns opening up, and even beyond the chance of the ship's boiler exploding and blowing the *Heredia* to smithereens.

He wanted to get that raft in the water immediately and start searching for his wife and daughter. His bleeding knee throbbed, but he ignored it and stepped toward the raft.

"Get out of the way!" Ray shouted at the captain.

Colburn moved aside.

Ray positioned the raft at the aft section of the deck where the drop to the water would only be about four feet. Then he lifted Sonny and put him on top, saying "Just hold on tight. As soon as I slide you down, I'm jumping off and I'll climb on the raft right next to you. We're going to be all right."

Sonny hugged one side of the hollow square, his fingers digging into the canvas. Terrified of going back down into the dark ocean, he closed his eyes. Then he felt his father slide the raft a foot or two and shove it over the side.

The raft splashed into the water with a jolt, and Sonny lost his grip but managed to stay onboard. He lifted his head and saw his father, Conyea, and the captain leap off the deck and into the sea, landing just a couple of feet away amid floating debris. The three men scrambled aboard, and Ray immediately lay on top of Sonny, trying to protect the boy, worried that the Germans might fire their machine gun at them. The three adults used their hands to begin paddling the raft away from the crippled ship.

Ray's weight was pushing Sonny so low that he swallowed seawater and tried to squirm out from under his father, his lungs screaming for air.

⸻

Commander Würdemann watched the boy and men escape the ship, but he kept his searchlight on the *Heredia*. He stayed on scene (28.53°N, 91.03°W, 16 fathoms of water) to make sure the vessel sank.

Würdemann and the other Germans on the conning tower were amazed that part of the *Heredia* was still floating after taking multiple torpedoes in its hull. He could hear people shouting for help in the water, but that was of no concern to him. The commander kept his searchlight on the stricken ship, thinking the time had come to blast it with its deck gun. As he watched the men on the raft furiously paddling and kicking away with their arms and legs, he decided to give the ship one more minute.

Ray's fear that the U-boat would shoot them with the machine gun was unfounded. Throughout World War II, there was only one documented case of a German U-boat commander ordering his men to open fire on survivors in the water or on life rafts. Commander Heinz-Wilhelm Eck was found guilty in post-war trials of machine-gunning survivors of the Greek ship SS *Peleus*. In the hundreds of other sinkings by U-boats, there was not a single case or accusation of this kind of behavior. In fact, just two days before the *Heredia* attack, a U-boat commander went out of his way to help a survivor, and the *Times-Picayune* later ran an article with the headline INJURED SEAMAN SAVED BY U-BOAT AS VESSEL SINKS. The seaman, with a shattered elbow, was struggling to stay afloat in the ocean and unable to reach a life raft where other survivors had found refuge. The U-boat commander saw his plight and "scooped him up with the bow" of his submarine and in broken English called to the lifeboat to "come on over and get this man." After the men in the lifeboat picked up the injured man, one shouted to the U-boat commander that they wanted cigarettes. The commander threw over two packs and said, referring to the attack, "You can thank Mr. Roosevelt for this, I am sorry."

German U-boat men, from Dönitz all the way down to the lowest-ranking sailor, kept a code of conduct that did not allow killing of survivors in the water. However, in the Pacific, it was a very different scenario, and Japanese submarine commanders routinely tried to kill anyone who didn't go down with the ship.

One of the Japanese atrocities involved the U.S. Liberty ship *Jean Nicolet*, which was carrying military supplies from Australia to Ceylon. A hundred men were aboard, a mix of merchant crewmen, Naval Armed Guard, various military personnel, and four civilians. On the night of July 2, 1944, a Japanese sub, I-8, commanded by Tatsunoke Ariizumi, sent two torpedoes into the ship. All of the people on the *Jean Nicolet* were able to safely abandon the sinking ship and board life rafts and lifeboats. That's when the sub surfaced and an English-speaking Japanese sailor ordered the survivors to come alongside the sub or they would be shot with machine guns. A few lucky survivors, using cover of darkness, slipped off the lifeboats and rafts to hide among the debris. The others paddled their vessels to the sub, where most were ordered onto the bow of I-8. That's when the killing began, with some men bayonetted, some shot, and others beheaded. The majority, however, had their hands tied, and then one by one they were ordered to the rear deck of the sub, where a gauntlet of approximately fifteen Japanese crewmen were waiting with steel pipes, bayonets, and swords. The slaughter was in its full bloodletting when the Japanese saw an approaching aircraft on their radar. The sub immediately crash-dived, and those survivors on the bow with their hands tied found themselves in the sea unable to swim. Some were ripped to pieces by sharks, others quickly drowned, but incredibly a few managed to make it through the night and were rescued. Of the one hundred men who evacuated the sinking ship, twenty-four survived. For submarine commander Ariizumi, this was not his only atrocity; a similar crime was committed by him against the sailors aboard the Dutch vessel SS *Tjisalak*.

Another case of Japanese killing survivors who abandoned ship occurred when the commander of sub I-12 intentionally steered into the lifeboats and rafts holding survivors from the sinking SS *John A. Johnson*. The survivors spilled into the sea and became target practice for Japanese with pistols and machine guns. Five Americans were killed before the sub appeared to move on, and the remaining survivors thought they had seen the last of the Japanese. But the sub turned back and tried to kill the men in the water with its propeller, then opened fire again with machine guns. Five more were killed before the nightmare was over when the sub submerged and disappeared.

Japanese aircraft crews were just as heartless as their submarine counterparts. Louis Zamperini, whose tale was so memorably told in *Unbroken*, is the best-known survivor of an attack from the air while he and his mates were adrift in the Pacific on two tiny life rafts. The Japanese bomber didn't just pass by and take a few shots while continuing on its mission; instead, it circled back, making several passes as it sprayed bullets at the men. Louis was in the water, and his two fellow survivors were in the raft, and incredibly, although bullets hit within an inch or two of each man, not a single bullet hit any of them. The bomber still didn't give up, and made one final pass where it dropped a depth charge! Again the men had luck on their side—the bomb was a dud. The two rafts the men were in, however, were riddled with bullet holes, but the survivors were able to patch one raft as sharks circled them.

Würdemann stood by the *Heredia* for a couple more minutes, and then saw what he'd been waiting for. The bow of the ship finally gave up the fight and followed the stern into the sea. The commander later recorded the following in his War Diary: "Steamer settles astern quickly. Stern rests on the bottom (water depth 25–30 meters). Initially the foreship protrudes up to the bridge, later however that sinks also. . . . Accepted size: 5,200 gross registered tons."

Würdemann ordered the sub to move away, to see if he could find and bag another ship in the same night.

CHAPTER ELEVEN

A MOST HOPELESS NIGHT

"Off Mississippi continuous heavy independent traffic. Certainly worthwhile for other boats. Constant air, however no sea patrol determined."

—Erich Würdemann's message to
Lorient suggesting that more
U-boats be sent to the Gulf

T he raft's square shape didn't help, but Ray, Conyea, and the captain were able to gain distance from the sinking ship. At any minute they expected disaster to strike in the form of bullets from the submarine, an explosion from the *Heredia*'s boiler, or a whirlpool of suction if the ship suddenly went down. Bits of debris floated all around them, but not a single other survivor could be seen. Sonny had managed to squirm out from under his father, and he was now in the middle of the raft, his arms clutching the raft's edge and his legs dangling in the ocean. The three adults were in similar positions, either on the middle or outside edge of the raft.

Conyea started to say something, but Ray suddenly yelled, "I can hear Ina shouting! I'm going back!"

"You can't go back," hollered Captain Colburn. "You'll never make it!"

Conyea too shouted at Ray, "The ship is going to sink any minute! The sub is still there, I can see its light!"

"I don't care," boomed Ray, "I heard Ina!"

"You can't be sure it was her!" pleaded the captain.

Sonny was terrified that his father would leave him and never make it back. He watched in fear as his dad moved from the middle of the raft to the outer edge. Conyea positioned himself next to Ray, grabbing Ray's life jacket. "Your son needs you here!"

Ray swatted Conyea's arm away, then looked back at Sonny. He was torn between keeping his son alive and making a dash for the voice that he was sure was Ina's.

"Let's listen," reasoned Captain Colburn, "and see if we hear another shout."

Ray moved back toward Sonny.

The four survivors didn't speak as the raft drifted farther from the death throes of the *Heredia*, which continued to emit loud bubbling and gurgling noises as it settled lower in the water.

Finally the captain broke the silence. "The sub has moved off. I can't see its light."

"Can anyone see the ship?" asked Conyea.

Without the light from the sub, none of the survivors could see the vessel, nor could they hear the noises it had made just minutes earlier. Ray tried to put Ina out of his mind and focus on saving his son.

"We can sit on the edge of the raft," said Ray to the others, "but we gotta spread out."

Conyea took two strokes and perched on the edge opposite Ray, while the captain, his face in a tense grimace because he didn't know how to swim, slowly inched to the side just to the right of Ray and carefully pulled himself up. Sonny, who fortunately had just learned to swim in Costa Rica, went to the side of the square to the left of his father, pulling himself up and into a sitting position. Because Sonny only weighed a third as much as the other men, his side of the raft rode out of the water, while the captain's end rode so low that the water almost reached his neck.

"This won't do!" bellowed Ray. "One wave and we're going over. Mr. Conyea, you and I gotta scoot over closer to Sonny's side."

This simple move helped balance the raft. However the weight of the three men plus Sonny was enough to submerge the raft a few inches, so that from the waist down the survivor's bodies were underwater. It was a delicate balancing act, but at least they had their upper torsos relatively dry, which would help ward off hypothermia.

Ray glanced at Sonny, worried sick that the boy would be the first victim of the ocean because of his small size.

"Are you cold, son?"

"I'm okay, Dad."

"Well, if you get really cold, just tell me, and you can sit on my lap and I'll wrap my arms around you."

The air temperature was in the upper 60's and the water temperature about 75 degrees Fahrenheit. The relatively warm temperature of the ocean may not sound dangerous, but it is far short of the 98.6-degree optimal body temperature; and, making matters worse, water draws off a person's heat about twenty-five times faster than the same air temperature. If Sonny's core temperature dropped to 95 degrees, he'd start shivering, and soon his extremities would start to feel numb, as the blood vessels constricted. That is the body's way of minimizing the amount of cold blood that would flow to the vital organs. Layers of fat would also slow the cooling of the blood, but eight-year-old Sonny was as thin as a sapling.

Ray vowed to himself that he'd do whatever it took to keep the boy warm, even if it meant hoisting him out of the water and somehow putting him on his shoulders.

In the darkness, Ray could faintly see Sonny's shape but not the features of his face because high thin clouds blocked out most of the light from the stars and moon. Ray stared toward Sonny and thought *this is all my fault. I should have known the full danger when they made me sign the release papers before we boarded the ship.* He shook his head, realizing this kind of thinking was torture. *Stop. Just focus on Sonny.*

A minute later Sonny, as if reading his father's thoughts, asked, "Will Mom and Lucille be all right?"

"They should be fine," lied Ray. "They are probably floating on a raft just like us."

"That's right," said Captain Colburn, "the ship had three rafts."

"Where were we when the ship was torpedoed? How far from port?" asked Conyea of the captain.

"About forty miles out from New Orleans. To the southwest."

Ray turned his head in the direction of the captain and asked, "When do you think help will come?"

Captain Colburn hesitated before answering, concerned about saying anything negative in front of Sonny.

"Just tell us the truth," said Ray. "We're going to be fine no matter how long we have to sit on this raft."

"Okay," said Colburn. "We were operating on radio silence, but that doesn't really matter because I think the section of the ship where the radio was took a direct hit from one of the torpedoes. So the authorities on shore only know that we were scheduled to reach New Orleans about 6 A.M. I'm guessing that by 8 A.M. they will become concerned. One of the patrol planes will start looking for us."

Conyea, who was from New Orleans, added, "and we might get lucky. There are probably several Coast Guard and shrimp boats in the area, and one of them may find us at dawn."

"You're right, Mr. Conyea," said Ray, "just gotta sit here patiently until the sun comes up."

"Call me George," said Conyea.

Ray nodded. Then each survivor settled in for a long night, lost in their own thoughts. Ray tried to make an honest assessment of their situation. They had no food or water. Once the sun came up, their thirst would increase, and dehydration would wear them down with each passing hour. The weather was calm, with just a light breeze, and for that Ray was thankful. If the seas had been up like the day before, none of the four survivors would have been able to hang on to the flimsy raft. They were lucky indeed to be in gentle swells rather than breaking waves. However, they had no flares should a plane or patrol boat appear on the horizon.

After days of sailing from South America, Ray had an appreciation for the vastness of the ocean, and he felt the little raft was like the proverbial needle in a haystack: it was going to be difficult to find. And a person in the water without a raft would be damn near impossible to locate. Ray said a silent prayer that Ina and Lucille were together on a raft and not alone in the endless void of the sea.

May 18 and 19 were particularly bad days for freighters and tankers in the Gulf. Not long after Würdemann sank the *Heredia*, another U-boat—which had just recently entered the Gulf via the Yucatan Channel—added to the carnage. U-103, commanded by Werner Winter, a veteran U-boat ace, sneaked up on the freighter *Ogontz* loaded with nitrate in the southern section of the Gulf. Winter sent an eel slicing into the vessel, and the ship's captain, Adolph Wennerlund, ordered the crew to evacuate the *Ogontz* and board the lifeboats and rafts. Two Naval Armed Guards clung to their guns and just as the ship started to roll, they got off a shot that went wide of U-103.

As the ship rolled, its mast landed squarely on one of the lifeboats, killing Captain Wennerlund and eighteen others. Two survivors, however, surfaced near the U-boat, and Commander Winter decided to help them. His crew hauled them onto the U-boat, and Winter treated one man's wounds with alcohol as the U-boat transported them over to the nearest lifeboat. Winter, wearing shorts and deeply tanned, asked the sailors if they were Americans. When they responded in the affirmative, he replied in perfect English, "Sorry we had to do this, but this is war." He gave the men some cigarettes and food, watched them safely board the lifeboat, and then ordered U-103 down into the depths.

Commander Erich Würdemann was not in the business of helping the enemy or offering apologies; he was after more ships. The same night that he torpedoed the *Heredia*, Würdemann later saw a small freighter on an easterly course in shallow water of just fifteen meters. This ship was lucky. The young commander estimated that he could not get in position before daylight, and let the ship sail away. U-506 submerged. Würdemann was content with the prize of sinking the *Heredia* . . . for now. He still had more torpedoes.

U-506 glided to the west a few miles and later, after the sun was down, resurfaced for more hunting. The commander didn't have to wait long for his next target. The *Halo*, a 7,000-ton tanker loaded with oil, was zigzagging in a rapidly changing pattern, making it a much more difficult target than the *Heredia*. But Würdemann knew this was a loaded tanker, a real prize, and although the ship came in and out of sight, he doggedly pursued it. When he finally was within 450 meters, he ordered the firing of two torpedoes. "After twenty-one seconds," the commander wrote, "[the torpedoes] hit forward edge of the bridge and center. Tanker bursts into flames and in just a moment is a torch. A heavy internal explosion follows. Apparently the tanker is torn apart in the middle. Details cannot be distinguished in the bright fiery flare." Würdemann watched his prize burn for a few minutes, then "dived, ran off." But an hour later his curiosity got the better of him, and he surfaced in a different location, farther away, and confirmed that the ship had indeed sunk, and that "burning oil can still be seen some time on the water."

While most of the *Halo*'s sailors survived the initial explosion by jumping into the sea, help was slow in coming, as the ship did not get off an SOS. Over the next few days, the men began dying of exposure. Of the forty-two crew members, one was rescued after five days and two were picked up after seven days of clinging to a half-burned raft. The other thirty-nine crew members perished.

Within hours of sinking the *Halo*, Würdemann spotted two freighters, and used his last three torpedoes in a vain attempt to sink them. With the first freighter, Würdemann thought he had miscalculated the freighter's speed, but the second left him scratching his head. "Both [torpedoes] missed, unexplained with low range and good data. From sound, both torpedoes ran perfectly."

While the commander was miffed at this waste of torpedoes, the crew was likely thinking of home. They had been at sea for forty-five days, and their time in the Gulf was especially difficult because of the intense heat, making them feel like they were in the mouth of a dragon. No one had bathed during the trip, and condensation formed on the inside of the sub, adding a clammy feeling to the men's stinking bodies. Fresh food had long since all been consumed, and the crew was living on rice and "gruel." They had survived depth charges dropped by enemy aircraft and a near-grounding off the mouth of the Mississippi, but it was the day-to-day grind of being locked inside a steel tube that could wear even the most gung-ho sailor down, except perhaps for Würdemann himself. He had used up all his torpedoes and set a course to exit the Gulf and return to Lorient, still hoping to bag yet another ship using his deck guns. As U-506 plowed eastward, the commander sent a short message to Lorient, encouraging his superiors to send more U-boats to the area. "Off Mississippi continuous heavy independent traffic. Certainly worthwhile for other boats. Constant air, however no sea patrol determined."

CHAPTER TWELVE

DAWN

"How bad does it hurt, Dad?"
—Sonny

Around four in the morning, Sonny was shivering slightly. He could hardly believe how slowly the night was passing, as it seemed like it had been days ago that the *Heredia* was torpedoed. He knew he was supposed to tell his father if he was cold, but he thought it best not to say anything for a while. The grown-ups had stopped talking, but every now and then Sonny's dad would ask how he was doing.

"Sonny, it will be dawn soon, and we'll all get a chance to warm up in the sun."

"Yes, Dad, I, I . . . know."

Ray picked up the hesitation in the boy's voice and he could tell Sonny was shaking.

"Mr. Conyea, I mean George," said Ray, "I'm going to have Sonny come sit with me, so you may need to shift position slightly."

"Okay, it will be good to move. My back is as stiff as can be."

Ray slid down to the end of his side of the raft closest to Sonny's side, and then said, "Sonny, you can scoot over to me, now."

The boy had no trouble sliding to his father. It was wonderful to feel his dad's muscular arm pull him in tight so that he was leaning into his dad's chest. Sonny could feel himself relax, and began to examine the luminescent light where the gentle swells swirled around the raft. On board the ship, his father had called the eerie light phosphorescence, and Sonny was fascinated by the glowing plankton that shimmered in the night.

Feeling secure in his father's embrace, the boy closed his eyes for the first time since the ship was torpedoed. He must have dozed for a few minutes, but was awakened by a commotion.

"I've got it," said Captain Colburn.

Sonny could see that the captain had something large in his hands but had no idea what it was.

"What's happening, Dad?"

"We saw a board floating on the water, and the Captain was able to grab it. Might come in handy in the morning. Maybe use it as a paddle."

A faint hint of dawn allowed the red-haired captain to better see his bleak surroundings. The grey canvas-covered raft seemed minuscule and so flimsy that he wondered how long it would take for the fabric to rip and the balsa wood to float free. He glanced at his shipwrecked mates. George Conyea appeared exhausted, and he had said very little during the course of the night. The boy Sonny hadn't cried once, but he looked so small and skinny that the captain knew he must be extremely cold. His father Ray had calmed down since he thought he heard his wife shouting, and he was now holding the boy close to his chest.

It crossed the captain's mind that the four of them might be the only survivors of the ship; and if that were true, his own survival might become a lifelong burden and source of shame rather than a blessing. He could just imagine what the newspapers would say and what other mariners would think when they learned that of the entire list of working crewmembers on the *Heredia*, he, the captain, was the only one that lived. That would mean forty-eight of his crew had perished, six of the Navy Armed Guard, and five out of the eight passengers had perished—all on his ship, on his watch, during his leadership. He knew the notion that the captain should go down with the ship was still a strong one. But, he thought, at least these three civilians on the raft with me can testify that we were the very last ones off the ship. It didn't ease his anguish, but it was something. . . .

Colburn had also been thinking about sharks on and off all night, doing his best to put the predators out of his mind. But when Ray Downs shifted positions slightly, the captain's eyes widened. In the gloom he saw a dark smudge on Ray Downs's knee.

"Is that blood or oil on your leg?" asked the captain.

"Blood," said Ray. "I cut myself trying to break through the window."

"Let me help you cover the wound. I can rip a piece of my shirt off."

"I can get it," answered Ray. "We've got the raft pretty well balanced, and the less moving around, the better."

Ray wore only a sleeveless T-shirt and his boxer shorts. He ripped a small patch of cloth from his T-shirt to tie around the cut.

Sonny watched his father's hands work. The gash looked deep and, even after more than three hours in the ocean, it was still trickling blood.

"How bad does it hurt, Dad?"

"Can barely feel it. Salt water stings a bit. This bulky life jacket bothers me as much as the cut, the way it's rubbing against my skin. I'll bet your life jacket is doing the same."

"I don't mind. I'm sure glad I had it on when we were climbing up the stairway from our cabin. I felt like I was being dragged to the bottom of the sea."

"Me, too," said Ray. "I tried to hold on to you, but the water just yanked you away."

"Did you try and grab my leg?"

"Don't remember, everything happened so fast."

"Something grabbed my leg and scared me so I kicked at it. Hope it wasn't you. Hope it wasn't Mom or Lucille."

Ray winced. The thought of Ina and Lucille being pulled to the depths was more than he could bear. He had never been religious like his wife, but now he said a silent prayer. He thought it was a miracle that he had escaped the sinking ship, and maybe God did have a hand in his survival so he could be here with his son. Mixed with these thoughts of God was a brooding anger that bubbled to his consciousness periodically. His most intense fury was directed at the Germans on the submarine who had crossed an entire ocean and most of the Gulf to hunt down and torpedo a ship that wasn't even part of the military. *They will pay for this*, he thought; *nobody hurts my family and gets away with it.* While the adrenaline prompted by thoughts of revenge coursed through his veins, he also felt rage toward another group: the nameless bureaucrats sitting safely in Corpus Christi who wouldn't let his family leave the *Heredia* when anchored outside the bay. He wondered if the captain had really made a strong effort to persuade those same authorities to let the family de-board. Now, sitting on this floating sandbox just four feet from the captain, it took a supreme effort not to tell him exactly what he was thinking.

Ray looked down at the top of his son's head and held him tighter. As much for himself as for Sonny, Ray corralled his emotions and said, "Your mom and Lucille are probably floating with a bunch of the ship's sailors. They might even have been rescued by now."

With the innocence of an eight-year-old, Sonny believed his father. *Lucille is probably having breakfast on board a rescue boat and she's worried about me. And Mom's likely right by her side, just the way Dad is with me.*

But a few minutes later, Sonny remembered that his Dad thought he had heard his mother shouting when they were still near the sinking ship. *Maybe they are not with sailors or rescued.* He was about to say something, to remind his father about his mother shouting for help, but decided it was best to let it go. *Don't upset him.*

Sonny wanted his father to be proud of what he said and did while on the raft.

Now that the boy could actually see the vastness of the ocean and their own insignificance, he felt a sense of fear and dread almost equal to when he had been washed from his father's grip when the ship lurched. He didn't want his father to know that the only thing keeping him from crying was his dad's presence.

Captain Colburn admired the way the boy and his father interacted. He wasn't so sure about how he and Ray would sort things out when and if a major decision needed to be made on the raft. He was still smarting from the exchange with Ray when they were launching the raft, how the man had poked him in the chest and shouted he'd have to learn to swim real fast. He wasn't about to start a fight earlier with the *Heredia* in the process of sinking, but now adrift on the raft, where minutes felt like hours, he wondered if they'd have another disagreement. His ship might be at the bottom of the ocean, but he was still the captain.

CHAPTER THIRTEEN

DESPERATION

"At sea a fellow comes out. Salt water is like wine in that respect."
—Herman Melville

When dawn broke at the busy shipping port of New Orleans and the *Heredia* did not appear at its estimated time, there was no sense of alarm. The port officials knew that a vessel could be late for a variety of reasons, and under the restrictions of radio silence the captain had no way to update them on his progress. While there had been U-boat attacks on ships in the Gulf almost daily, the *Heredia* did not send out a mayday and no other vessels nearby had broken the radio silence with either a report of a ship in distress or an explosion.

———

The grey life raft and the four survivors rose and fell with the endless swells. Each time it reached the crest, the three adult men would scan the ocean in all directions, hoping against all odds that they might spot a ship. The captain had managed to retain his binoculars through the tumultuous night, but they were of limited use as the horizon remained empty of ships. As the sun's rays gained strength, Sonny was able to leave his father's arms and perch on the edge of the raft with his legs dangling underwater in the raft's middle.

"The sun feels good," said Ray. "I don't care what people say about the warmth of the Gulf Stream, this water is cold."

George Conyea agreed. "If and when I warm up, I'm going to slip into the water just so I can stretch my back. Can only sit for so long."

Sonny too felt stiff, but was too cold to even think about floating in the water. Instead, he thought of what he'd be doing if it were a normal day on the ship. Soon he and Lucille would be having flapjacks, followed by their usual race or hide-and-go-seek on the deck. *Lucille*. He could not imagine life without her or his mom. Where were they? He retraced the family's steps after the first torpedo hit. They had all been together in the hallway, and he remembered Mr. Beach going back to his cabin and wondered if he'd made it out of the ship. Then he recalled the sailor swinging the light directing them to head up the mahogany stairs. As they climbed the steps, Lucille and his mother had been directly behind him. Then the ship had lurched and the family was torn apart. *How did he and his father somehow manage to escape the swirling water, but maybe not his sister and mom? Where were they now?* His thoughts went back to whatever had grabbed his ankle, and he felt a wave of guilt wash over him. *What if it was Lucille? Why did I have to kick away?*

Captain Colburn's voice brought him out of his gloomy thoughts.

"Way off to the east, I think I see a plane. It's hard to see with the sun, but I think it's coming this way."

Everyone immediately looked east, squinting into the sun's glare. "Yes! Yes!" shouted Ray. "I can see it. Quick," he barked, looking at the captain, "give me your coat! Let's get it on the board!"

The captain's white jacket was draped over the board, and Ray held the makeshift flag as high as he could and then waved it back and forth.

Sonny thought for sure that the pilot, far off in that plane, would easily see it.

The plane was over a mile away. Sonny held his hand over his eyes to block the sun. He was literally holding his breath. He stared until he could no longer see the speck in the blue sky.

Ray slowly lowered the board.

George Conyea broke the silence. "Maybe there'll be others. That one was just too far away."

Ray and the captain nodded, but neither spoke.

Conyea continued, "Sure wish we had a flare."

Sonny figured that, now that it was daylight, another plane would come by in a few minutes. The boy didn't really realize the danger he was in. His father was with him and that would ensure his safety. He worried about Lucille and his mother, but for Sonny this was an adventure, a test . . . that would end any minute. Yes, he was cold, thirsty, and hungry, but it was nothing that he couldn't handle for a few more minutes. His father didn't show a trace of fear, so Sonny assumed he had the situation under control and it would all work out.

Later in the morning, the group spied a ship in the distance, and the captain took his coat off, placed it on the board, and kept it ready to wave when the ship got closer.

Sonny got a glimpse of the ship whenever the raft crested a swell, and then it was blocked from view by the water. Each time the raft rose to the top of the swell, he spotted the ship but couldn't tell if it was steaming toward them: it was just a little bump on the horizon. Eventually he tired of looking at it.

A few minutes later, the captain took his jacket off the plank and draped it over his head to protect his fair, freckled face and neck from the sun's damaging brilliance. No one needed to say the ship was moving in the wrong direction, and the group remained silent. The ocean, taking on a grey-green hue under the climbing sun, stretched out as empty as a desert. Their only salvation would be from either a ship or a plane. (Offshore oil rigs were not built in the Gulf until 1947.) Ray cursed the designers of the life raft. Why did they not dye the grey canvas a brighter color so they could more easily be spotted? He imagined himself on a passing ship far off in the distance and knew it would be virtually impossible to see this tiny raft. Half the time it would be hidden from view by the swells. He reckoned a ship would need to be within a quarter mile for any crewmember to have a shot at spotting the captain's white coat on the board. And even if someone did see it, they might think it was flotsam drifting up and over the swells.

Sonny asked his father if he could move off his lap and back to his original side of the raft. He needed to stretch and didn't feel quite so cold anymore.

A couple more hours passed in silence. Eventually Captain Colburn muttered, "We'd better be rescued before dark, because we're drifting into the shipping lanes where there's a good chance we'll be run down."

Ray shot a piercing glance at Colburn, jerking his head toward his son. He didn't want the boy to hear any of this talk about being run over by a ship.

It was almost noon and the sun was blazing hot, its rays amplified by bouncing off the water back onto Sonny's bare skin. He no longer felt quite as cold, but his little body had used considerable amounts of energy through the endless night just trying to keep warm. Simply shivering was consuming his limited supply of reserve strength. Of course he knew nothing about the body's response to hypothermia, but was well aware of how tired and weak he felt, similar to the way he did when he had been sick with the flu. Sonny didn't tell his father because he was determined to be as tough as his dad. Instead he simply asked if he could move back to sitting next to his father so he could lean against him.

"Yes, and lay your head against my side and maybe you can doze."

Sonny craved water, just a sip, and earlier had asked his father about taking in a mouthful from the ocean. Ray told him not to, that it would make him sick and that he'd have all the water he wanted when a rescue boat came. But Ray still kept a wary eye on his son, afraid he might take a small sip from the ocean when he wasn't looking. It was an overwhelming, constant temptation for all four of the survivors, but drinking seawater would have the opposite effect intended. The high sodium content meant that the seawater would dehydrate the castaways even quicker than having no water at all by causing the body to try to expel the sodium. That meant precious fluids from the muscles, tissues, and organs would be drawn off to produce urine. This includes brain tissue, and the resulting loss of moisture often causes delirium and hallucinations within an hour or two of drinking seawater. This altered mental state has caused more than one shipwrecked person who succumbed to sipping sea water to do the unthinkable—climb out of the life raft and start swimming toward an object that only they could see.

Shortly after noon, Sonny felt something brush up against his leg, and he looked down to find a banana floating next to him. He grabbed the banana. "Look what I found," he exclaimed to his father.

"Good job. Better hang on to that in case we need it."

Sonny smiled. He was contributing.

The motion of the waves and the lack of conversation lulled the boy to sleep. The slumber didn't last long, because even in the sun he was chilled and his muscles cramped. When he awoke a half hour later, he realized he had dropped the banana, and felt devastated.

"Dad, I dropped the banana."

"Don't worry. You'll find it—or another one."

Sonny didn't think so. He could see absolutely nothing on the ocean's surface and knew that the only reason he'd found the banana in the first place was because it had bumped into his leg. Under the circumstances, it was more than a piece of fruit; Sonny imagined it as evidence that he was doing his part to keep everyone alive, making losing it a terrible mistake. He fought to restrain his emotions.

Ray tried to cheer him up. "A while back while we were on the top of a swell, I thought I saw a couple of little specks on the horizon."

The captain joined in. "I'll bet they were shrimp boats and one of them is bound to head our way."

Sonny wasn't so sure. Despite the sun burning his skin, he was cold again and he felt weaker than ever.

———

By 3 P.M., all three adults on the raft were concerned that they wouldn't be found before sundown. The specks on the horizon were gone and no more planes came out of the cloudless sky. The landscape of ocean and sky was so bleak and empty, they felt like the only living things on the planet. Their thirst had reached an unbearable level, and talking was now at a minimum. Parched mouths and throats made speaking difficult, and each survivor had turned inward. Ray knew he could get through another night, but he wasn't so sure about Sonny. He worried that as the night wore on, the combination of dehydration and hypothermia would take its toll on the boy and he might not be conscious by morning. Rescue, if it were coming at all, had to come soon.

The men took turns being on lookout so the other two could close their eyes against the sun's burning glare. Sonny, too, kept his eyes closed but could not sleep. His skin felt like it was on fire, and his father did his best to use his own body to shield his son.

"Captain," said Ray, "my son needs your coat. His skin is burning."

Captain Colburn looked at the boy's skin and it did not look red. Then he glanced at the boy's dark hair. "But I'm so fair-skinned, I really need it," Colburn replied.

There was an awkward silence. Sonny had heard the exchange, felt his father's body tense, and the boy sat up.

His father spoke in a tone he had not heard before: slow, measured, and very soft.

"Give him the coat," said Ray, "or I will throw you off this raft."

The captain looked like he'd been punched in the stomach. He started to say something, then stopped, took the jacket off, and tossed it to Ray.

A tense silence descended on the life raft. George Conyea averted his eyes from both Ray and the captain, and simply stared at the horizon. He hadn't said a word since the morning, and he wanted no part in the mounting animosity between the captain and Ray. Conyea was dealing with his own pain. His bald head had been burned by the morning sun, so he had taken off his shirt and covered his head with it. But now his bare back was as red as a tomato.

Ray felt like he was going to jump out of his skin. His mind kept circling back to Ina and Lucille, and the helplessness he felt ate away at him like acid. He had never sat in one place as long as he'd done on the raft and he needed to be doing something, doing anything to keep busy to take his mind off his wife and daughter. Minutes dragged by like hours. He felt that if the captain said one more word about anything at all, he'd erupt like a volcano.

CHAPTER FOURTEEN

RUNNING OUT OF TIME

"O Lord, have mercy, Thy sea is so large, and my boat is so small."
—Breton Fisherman's Prayer

round four in the afternoon, Ray's back was aching so badly that he needed to straighten it. He told the others he was going to slip in the water the way George Conyea had done earlier, and asked the group to steady themselves and do their best to keep the raft balanced. He inched forward and lowered his body into the middle of the raft and turned so that only his arms were draped across the canvas and balsa wood on his side of the square. The cool water and a straightened back felt wonderful, and he floated in that position for several minutes before climbing back into the sitting position.

He asked Sonny if he wanted to do the same thing, but the boy said no. Sitting with the captain's jacket on had helped with the sun, and he was lost in his own exhausted stupor. Then he felt something against his leg. He glanced down and could not believe what he saw: a banana, perhaps the same one he had lost earlier, was bobbing in the water.

"Dad, look!" he shouted, reaching out and snatching the green banana.

"I knew you'd find it. I think that banana is really going to help us. Why don't you unpeel it and take a big bite and then pass it around for all of us to share?"

Sonny did as he was told. It was a struggle to swallow his piece of the banana with his mouth and throat so dry. Twenty seconds later, he felt nauseous and vomited the banana bite back into the sea.

"Well, that didn't work so well," Ray said. "The banana wasn't ripe anyway."

Sonny only nodded. He was slumped forward with his head hanging so low that it almost reached his knees.

A few minutes later, Sonny said, "Dad, can we go in now?" He said it as if they were on a fishing trip and it was up to his father when to call it quits.

Rather than try to explain the situation, his father answered, "Soon, son, soon."

Sonny looked up at his father and just nodded.

It wasn't long after this exchange that Ray noticed Conyea staring at something directly behind where Ray was sitting. Ray turned his head and saw not one but four grey shark fins lazily cutting through the sea just five feet away from the raft. When he looked over at Conyea and the captain, he saw another couple of fins. By now, all four of the survivors could see the sharks. No one said a word.

One shark turned toward the raft and then glided directly under it. The group could see the outline of its body as it passed directly beneath them. It looked to be about five to six feet long.

Sonny quickly pulled his feet out of the water.

"Take it easy, Sonny, don't thrash around," said his dad. "They'll move on."

But they didn't move on.

The four survivors now counted seven different sharks making slow half-loops around the raft before making a pass directly underneath it. This was by far the most terrifying experience of the ordeal for both Sonny and the three adults. The raft was too small for the men to try and get their legs on top of the balsa wood. Ray was right: their best defense was not to make a commotion.

The men did not know what kind of sharks they were, only that they were as big as themselves. The Gulf of Mexico has over forty different species of shark, but the ones the group should have been most worried about were bull sharks, hammerhead sharks, tiger sharks, oceanic white tip sharks, dusky sharks, and of course great white sharks. Because of the shape of the shark, the hammerhead could be ruled out, as could the great white, bull shark, and tiger shark because they are usually solitary hunters. It's also probable that the sharks were not the oceanic white tip, because the dorsal fin the survivors saw was a solid grey color.

The sharks circling the raft might have been dusky sharks because they are known to hunt in packs, often corralling their prey and then taking turns darting in to take a bite. And their bite is among the strongest of any shark on the planet. While not as aggressive as the bull shark, tiger shark, or great white shark, they have attacked and killed humans, and are considered among the most dangerous to man.

The life raft probably acted like a magnet for sharks, attracting their interest simply because it was a floating object, and the sharks, with their keen sense of smell, could also have been drawn in by the scent of the blood from Ray's wound. And any movement the group made, such as switching position, would have caused a vibration in the water, and that too would attract sharks. It's also possible that smaller fish were holding position under the shade of the raft, and the sharks came in to investigate this potential prey, and then became inquisitive about the humans.

Several castaways have reported that circling sharks will slowly move closer and then bump and nudge a raft, perhaps to see if the raft was a living thing. Over time, the sharks become more aggressive and, instead of a gentle bump, they'd slam into the raft. It's been reported that once sharks realize there is something living on the raft, they will try to flip the vessel to get at its occupants.

Whatever kind of sharks were circling the *Heredia* survivors, they were curious and gradually moved in closer to the life raft, making their lazy half-loops just a couple of feet off the side of the raft before they submerged and swam directly under it. One shark, when passing under the raft, rolled on its back, and an anxious Sonny could see its half-opened mouth. The boy almost let out a scream, but his dad, who had seen the same thing, reached over and put his hand on Sonny's shoulder.

"Don't worry, they are just checking us out. We are something new to them."

Ray had no idea if what he was saying was true or not, but the last thing he needed was for his son to go into a panic. He also hoped his words calmed the captain and George Conyea, because they were as wide-eyed as Sonny, watching every move their new visitors made.

Ray felt despair like he had never known. Sundown was just three and a half hours away, and the thought of the sharks gliding beneath them at night was too terrible to contemplate. He felt absolutely helpless.

Minutes crawled by and the four survivors kept still, eyes glued on the fins lazily cutting through the water on all sides of the raft. The behavior of the sharks stayed the same; they came within a foot or two of the castaways but there was no direct contact with either the raft or the group's legs or feet.

"How long will they stay?" asked Sonny, looking at his father.

"Don't know, Sonny; but like I said, they are just curious." Ray paused and continued his calming words: "If we don't bother them, they won't bother us."

George Conyea spoke up for the first time in quite a while. "Do you know what kind they are?"

"Probably harmless sand sharks," Ray responded. In reality he still did not know. Ray had spent little time on the ocean and this was an entirely new experience. If the captain knew more than Ray, he didn't say so.

An hour went by and the group tried to ignore the sharks, but with little success. There was nothing else to look at, nothing else to take their mind off the seven fins circling them.

About two hours after the sharks first arrived, more fins appeared in the water not far from the raft. Sonny was terrified, thinking, *not more sharks.* . . .

Captain Colburn spoke up. "Hey, those are dolphins."

Like the U-boat that had caused their ordeal, the sharks submerged and were not seen again.

Sonny experienced an incredible sense of relief and joy with the dolphins' arrival and the sharks' departure. He felt as if he had been holding his breath for the past two hours, afraid to move a muscle. There was no doubt in his mind that the dolphins had driven the sharks off to help him.

It's doubtful that the dolphins were intentionally trying to save the lives of the humans, but that rather, like the sharks, they were curious about the raft, and for whatever reason their presence caused the sharks to move off. Little is known about the dynamics between sharks and dolphins. Some researchers think the sound dolphins make can drive away sharks, while others think the dolphins' ability to work as a team can thwart sharks. Over the years there have been many accounts of castaways saying they were being shadowed by a shark only to have dolphins "chase the shark away." But dolphins are not always the dominant species; sharks will attack and eat a dolphin given the chance.

The dolphins' presence not only relieved Sonny's concern over the sharks, they also gave him something new to watch. Unlike the sharks, the dolphins swam quickly around the raft, their entire backs almost coming out of the water, and then briefly submerge and repeat the process. Up and down came their fins. But after just three or four minutes, they moved on and were gone from sight.

The group didn't speak. Without the fear of sharks, their minds went back to the predicament of time running out for a rescue. It would be dark within the hour. Their thirst was unbearable and all felt extremely weak. Sonny was in the worst shape because of his small body. Now that the sun was low in the sky, he was shivering again. His father noticed and had him move back on his lap where he wrapped his big arms around the boy, trying to stop his shaking.

Sonny looked up at his father. "Shouldn't a boat be here by now?" he asked.

Ray needed to keep his son's mind occupied. So instead of discussing the lack of a rescue boat, he said "Let's play a game. See those seagulls way up there? You choose one and I'll choose one and we'll count how long they go without flapping their wings. Whoever's bird flies the longest without using its wings wins."

Sonny perked up a bit. He didn't really want to play the game because he was so chilled and his mouth so parched that he'd rather not talk. But he thought maybe this game was what his father needed to do.

"Okay, I'm picking the one over there," Sonny said as he lethargically pointed at a shape off to the west.

"And I've got the one straight up," answered Ray.

With heads tilted back, father and son watched the birds they had chosen. It was easy to look up because the sun was almost touching the ocean.

"Mine just flapped," said Ray. "You win."

Sonny gave a half-hearted nod.

"Well, let's play another round," said Ray.

Again they chose birds. Sonny chose one high in the sky and way off on the eastern horizon. This time the captain and George Conyea also looked up to see which birds the father and son chose. Anything to take their minds off their body's demands for water.

Again Ray's bird flapped its wings quickly. "You win again," he said.

Sonny kept his eyes on his own bird. "Wow, Dad, mine is still going along without flapping."

Ray looked closer at the bird in the distance.

"Captain, let me use your binoculars," Ray said.

The captain removed the strap from around his neck and handed them to Ray, who hurriedly put the binoculars to his eyes. He adjusted the focus and stared intently at the bird far in the distance.

"That's no seagull, it's a plane!" he shouted.

"Yes, yes!" shouted the captain.

The survivors still could not hear its engines or tell what kind of plane it was, but there was no doubt it was a plane and that it was heading toward the raft.

"Quick, Sonny, take off the captain's coat! I've got to get it on the board."

Within seconds, Ray was waving the board with the white coat on it, and the others were waving their arms.

Ray couldn't tell if the pilot had spotted the white coat, and the tension was unbearable. *Please, please,* he said to himself. His son's very life was at stake. The boy could not make it through another cold night. He waved the white coat wildly.

As the plane drew closer, its metal skin briefly glittered when the sun's rays hit it. Now they could hear the dull drone of the engines, and Sonny shouted "Help!"

"Keep waving the flag!" shouted the captain, his excitement growing. "It's got to see us. It's our last chance. I think it's coming our way."

Ray could make out the outline of the plane and, because of its unique construction, realized it was a PBY. The single wing was elevated on a pylon above the fuselage rather than coming straight out from the sides. This allowed unobstructed visibility for its aviators to scan the ocean during either patrols for U-boats or search-and-rescue missions. Two engines with propellers were mounted on the wing, one on each side of the aircraft.

The plane came ever closer but it did not descend. Ray thought maybe it was going too fast to see them.

But Sonny's heart soared. He was certain the plane was coming for them. And he was right. In one swift motion, the PBY started descending and adjusting its course slightly so it was just fifteen feet off the ocean and heading right toward the raft, banking hard so that Sonny could actually see the pilot, who was giving a thumbs-up. The boy let out a croak of joy along with the cheers of his father, the captain, and George Conyea.

The four raft passengers watched with awe as the plane circled back toward them. Its 104-foot wingspan and sixty-three-foot length made it appear enormous so close to the water. Just as the plane was barreling over their location, they saw the pilot drop a package out the window, landing just ten feet from the raft. Using the board and their hands, all four survivors paddled furiously toward what they hoped was their salvation floating in the water.

The captain grabbed the package and ripped it open. Inside were two flares, a large container of water, and a note. The captain read the note out loud: "We will send shrimp boats to come and get you. If anyone is seriously hurt, wave me in and I'll pick them up."

Ray thought for a minute. He knew the plane was going to search for other survivors in the few minutes of daylight left and he didn't want to slow it down. Someone, maybe Lucille or Ina, might be hurt and the plane could rescue them. He thought Sonny could make it the half hour or hour that he expected the shrimp boats to take to arrive.

The plane made a broad circle above the raft and then moved off.

"We made it, son," said Ray; "we'll be on the boat in no time."

Then the captain passed the water container to Ray, saying, "Let's all take a drink. We may want to let our bodies adjust to the water before we take a second drink."

When Sonny took his gulp of water, he thought he had never tasted anything so good, so sweet. It was as if the water had magical powers, because he felt better immediately. He couldn't wait for the container to come around again for his second drink of the life-giving fluid. But the captain said again that they shouldn't drink too much all at once, and the other adults agreed.

A few minutes later the plane reappeared, then moved off. The survivors had no way of knowing that the pilot had dropped a note to shrimp boats a few miles off that said: "Watch my direction. Follow me. Pick up survivors in water."

A half hour went by and the survivors bobbed on their little raft in the darkening shadows. They all had another drink of water, and the captain said that he thought a shrimp boat could reach them within the next half hour.

Sonny shivered in his father's arms. The hydrating water had eased his thirst but did nothing for his growing hypothermia.

"That plane can land on water, right, Dad?"

"Yes."

"Then why didn't they just do that and pick us up?"

"They needed more time in the air to find others. But the boat will be here soon."

"What if the boat can't find us?"

"They will. And remember, we've got flares to use if we see a boat."

Sonny had forgotten about the flares. But he also wondered how his dad would see a boat in the distance in the pitch black of night.

More time went by. The sun had set, but the survivors could still differentiate between the horizon and the ocean in the twilight. Sonny had forgotten all about the sharks, but Ray hadn't. Ray still scanned the dark

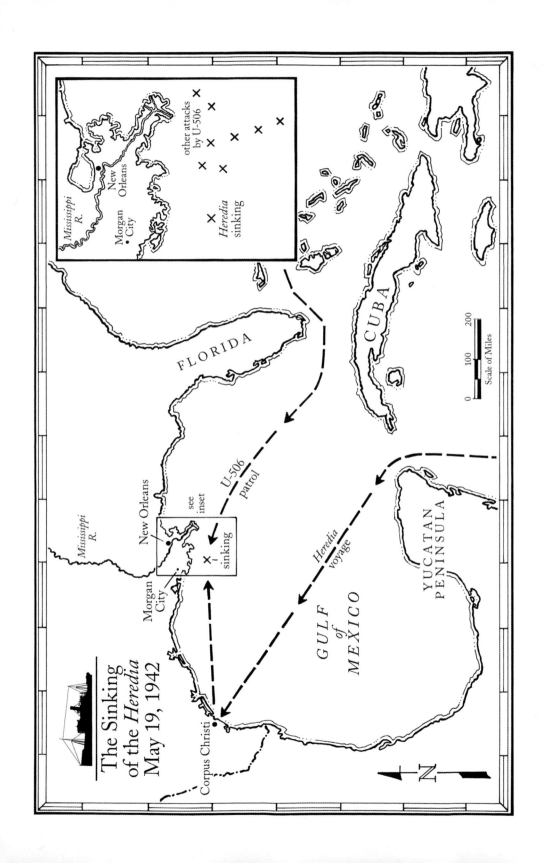

other attacks
by U-506

Heredia
sinking

*Mississippi
R.*

New
Orleans

Morgan
City

CUBA

FLORIDA

0   100   200

Scale of Miles

New Orleans

see
inset

Morgan
City

*Mississippi
R.*

U-506
patrol

×–
sinking

Heredia
voyage

YUCATAN
PENINSULA

GULF
of
MEXICO

Corpus Christi

The Sinking
of the *Heredia*
May 19, 1942

N

LEFT: Admiral Karl Dönitz, known as "The Lion" to his U-boat men, launched Operation Drumbeat against the U.S. He later achieved the rank of *Großadmiral* in 1943 and became commander in chief of the German Navy. When Hitler committed suicide near the end of the war, Dönitz became his successor.

RIGHT: Captain Harro Schacht, the colorful commander of U-507, competed with Captain Erich Würdemann on U-506 to see who could sink the most ships in the Gulf of Mexico and Caribbean. He also played a part in the rescue of survivors of the *Laconia* sinking, then terrorized Brazilian ship captains with a one-submarine campaign that took 500 lives in a brief period.

LEFT: Captain Erich Würdemann, commander of U-506, waged war successfully against ships in American waters, including the ill-fated *Heredia* that carried the Downs family. As the war went on, returning to the U-boat bunkers at Lorient became a painful reminder of the Allied advancements in submarine detection and destruction as fewer and fewer of his comrades returned to base.

Sonny and Betty Lucille were just 8 and 11 years old respectively when their family's adventure to South America turned deadly. The children were asleep aboard the *Heredia* when it was stalked and sunk just a few miles from the Ship Shoal Buoy off Louisiana in the Gulf of Mexico.

Roy Sorli was a Norwegian immigrant and Second Mate on the *Heredia* who doted on the Downs children during their voyage. He received the Merchant Marine's Meritorious Service Medal for saving Lucille Downs when the ship was torpedoed. His wife, Heddy, forbade him to return to the sea after the experience.

Once called the *General Pershing*, the *Heredia* was converted to a combination freight and passenger ship by United Fruit Company. It was successfully steered through a phalanx of aggressive U-boats on its final voyage from South America to New Orleans but was ultimately sunk by multiple torpedoes fired from U-506 on May 19, 1942. It sits in about 85 feet of water about 40 miles from Morgan City, LA.

The Morgan City waterfront on the Atchafalaya River was where four local shrimp boats discharged the living and dead from the *Heredia* sinking. The Downs family spent several weeks at Morgan City General Hospital recuperating and setting the course for the next few years of their lives. Local residents pitched in to help the small hospital cope with the sudden influx of patients.

The Downs family was a media sensation when reporters were allowed to interview them about their experience in the Gulf of Mexico after the *Heredia* was torpedoed by U-506. Many newspapers prominently ran Lucille's story about sharks tickling her feet.

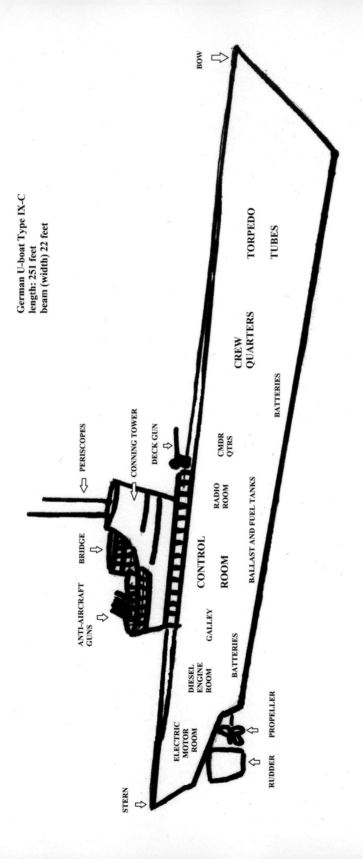

German U-boat Type IX-C
length: **251 feet**
beam (width) **22 feet**

BOW

PERISCOPES

CONNING TOWER

DECK GUN

BRIDGE

ANTI-AIRCRAFT GUNS

CONTROL ROOM

RADIO ROOM

CMDR QTRS

BALLAST AND FUEL TANKS

GALLEY

TORPEDO TUBES

CREW QUARTERS

BATTERIES

BATTERIES

DIESEL ENGINE ROOM

ELECTRIC MOTOR ROOM

PROPELLER

RUDDER

STERN

The type IX-C submarine is a primary character in *So Close to Home*, as U-506 and U-507 are this model, housing crews of about 52 men and capable of long-range travel. Oftentimes crews would sacrifice "extra" space, like the second toilet, crew quarters, and fresh water tanks, for storage of additional food, fuel, and munitions so they could stay at sea longer. The interior spaces were smaller than the exterior shell, which was called the pressure hull.

ocean around the raft for any sign of a fin. He wondered what to do if a shark appeared and thought that should one come, he could use the strong light from a flare to scare it off. But with only two flares. . . .

The prospect of another night in the water scared Ray to the core—not for himself but his concern over Sonny, who he could feel shivering in his arms. He second-guessed himself about not waving in the plane. Now there was nothing he could do to change that decision.

CHAPTER FIFTEEN

THE SHRIMP BOAT
AND A SURPRISE

"Faith is a knowledge within the heart, beyond the reach of proof."
—Khalil Gibran

Each time the raft rose up a swell, all four survivors craned their necks to get a quick look on the horizon, hoping to see a boat. The captain estimated they had another twenty minutes before darkness would obscure their vision.

The adults were discussing when and if to use the first of the two flares when Ray thought he saw a flicker of light in the distance. He didn't say anything, but instead waited for the raft to ride up the next swell so he could get another look.

At the top of the swell, he not only saw the light but could see the unmistakable silhouette of a boat!

"I see a boat! A shrimp boat is coming!"

Soon, the men could see the outlines of other fishing boats heading in their direction.

In a few moments, one of the shrimp boats arrived at the raft, and the crew helped the survivors clamber aboard.

One of the first things Sonny noticed was the smell of jambalaya, and he realized how hungry he was. The crew wrapped him in blankets while his father asked if they had any news of his wife or Lucille. Unfortunately, they had not.

The survivors were given more water and a small bowl of jambalaya, while the captain continued searching the sea, using floodlights on either side of the vessel and a third mounted on the top of the cabin aimed forward. Captain Colburn stayed by the side of the shrimp-boat captain and explained how they'd been torpedoed, how many people had been on the *Heredia*, and how quickly the ship had gone down.

Sonny and Ray began a silent vigil, hoping against the odds that they would find Lucille and Ina, even though it was now dark. Ray considered the two lucky breaks his wife and daughter would have needed to still be alive. First and foremost, they'd have had to make it out of the staircase when the *Heredia* lurched and the family was separated. Furthermore, thinking of his own struggle to break the glass and escape through a window, he knew it was essential to have been swept entirely out of the vessel for a reasonable chance at survival. And secondly, they would have needed to find a lifeboat or a raft from the ship if any had actually floated free. He recalled how quickly the ship had gone down and that the stern had been underwater almost immediately, and knew the odds were long. He didn't think anyone swimming in the cold water for more than eighteen hours would be found alive.

While Ray was on the raft, he had put all his faith for his wife's and daughter's survival into the hope that they had been rescued well before Sonny and himself. Now, the bitter reality hit him that the odds of their being alive were small indeed. If they had been in a life raft or lifeboat, surely the same plane that spotted his raft would have spotted theirs, and one of the shrimp boats in the fleet would have picked them up. The despair he felt was crushing, and while he told Sonny it was just a matter of time before the women were found, he was in fact losing hope. The waiting was agony, so he told Sonny to lie down on a bunk, and he went up to the bridge and asked the captain if he had his radio on. The captain said he did, explaining that a boat this small would not be a target for a U-boat. Ray asked if any of the other shrimp boats had picked up survivors. The captain said not yet, but that at least seven or eight boats were searching with their floodlights. Ray thanked him and returned to his son, hoping and praying for a miracle.

Sonny sat on a crewmember's top bunk and stared out a porthole, and his dad did the same from a different porthole. The side floodlights illuminated an area of the sea about twenty-five feet out from the vessel. Sonny could not rejoice over his own rescue, thinking his mom and Lucille might be floating out there in the night . . . or worse. His eyes scanned the dark water that shone under the floodlights, thinking if he remained vigilant he might be the one to spot the women. Keeping his eyes open was another matter. Except for a brief period of sleep on the raft, he'd been awake since the first torpedo hit at 2 A.M. the prior night. He pressed his head against the glass and willed himself to keep looking, knowing his dad was doing the same.

After an hour of staring out the porthole at the black sea, Ray could stand it no longer and went back up to the helm, making sure the shrimp-boat captain would search through the night. Once assured, he returned to a bunk near Sonny and continued gazing out a porthole.

Around 10 P.M., Sonny and Ray heard a commotion on deck. They abandoned their portholes and rushed topside.

Sonny could see that someone was in the water. The person was dark-skinned and wore what looked to be a pea coat.

"Dad!" Sonny shouted, "looks like they got one of the Filipino crew members."

Ray leaned as far as they could over the rail and saw a person covered in black oil whose hair was matted and thick with the gooey substance. He stared at the struggling survivor below.

Then Ray erupted. "Filipino, hell! That's your mother!"

CHAPTER SIXTEEN

INA

"Dear Lord, I don't want to wait here for the sharks to get me . . .
better to just have it over with quick."

—Ina

Ina's survival story was one fueled by luck, determination, and pure stubbornness. When the Downs family was escaping from the lower deck of the *Heredia* and climbing the mahogany stairs, the ship lurched and rushing water tore Lucille from her grip. Ina heard Lucille scream, "Mother, where are you?" Then the young mother found herself underwater, tumbling in the churning water, more terrified than she had ever been in her life.

An eddy of water pinned her against a wall, beneath a ladder to an upper deck. As the swirling black water rose, Ina felt helpless; she was trapped, unable to move and unsure where her children and husband were. Then in a split second the eddy shifted and pushed her upward so she was able to grab on to a window and perch on the sill looking out toward the sea as the ship groaned and convulsed beneath her. She looked around for her family but saw no one. Self-preservation instinctively kicked in, and she heard a voice say to her: "Jump or you'll go down with the ship."

She pushed away from the ship with her stomach in her throat, flying through the blackness of night and water and uncertainty.

When Ina's head broke the surface of the water, she felt herself covered in a warm gooey substance: oil from the ship's engines that was spreading from the sinking hulk. Gasping for air, she looked around frantically for her family, desperate for Ray and the children, while trying to clear her vision with an oil-soaked hand. There was no one around, and the only source of light was on the other side of the ship, but she didn't know what it was or how she'd reach it.

She tried to call out for help, but could only manage a low croak. The acrid smell of oil stung her throat, and panic squeezed her airway to a sliver. Oil was in her eyes and her sight was limited, but she was well aware that she was utterly alone, drifting away from the ship.

⁓

Just minutes before, Ina had been with her family. She tried to remember the sequence of events that resulted in her being here, in the oily water at night, but it seemed like a dream, or something that happened to someone else.

Before going to bed, she'd been lingering over trimming her fingernails and brushing her hair, not knowing why except that it was to be her family's last night on board. Later, unable to sleep, she thought of her family's future. She had faith that they could settle back into a productive life in Texas with Ray's newly developed skills as a locomotive mechanic. Then her quiet, pensive night was blown apart with the blast that threw Lucille out of her bunk, catapulting Ina into action.

"Oh, Mother, was that a torpedo?" Lucille cried out. Without a thought, Ina grabbed their life jackets from under the lower bunk. The lights flickered, but she still had the presence of mind to knot the ties in place as she'd been instructed, because bows might slip loose.

She couldn't remember exactly what happened next. One minute, the family had just climbed the mahogany stairs; the next, they were thrown into a river of seawater cascading over the deck and roaring down the stairway.

⁕

Now, alone in the water, she could hear horrifying sounds of people screaming and the ship breaking apart. A broken board bumped into her and she grabbed it, leaning forward and kicking her feet to propel herself away from the ship, the destruction and carnage. They had been told countless times during lifeboat drills that a sinking ship creates tremendous suction and whirlpools that might drown anyone nearby, but now it was real. The water around her boiled with bubbles and debris popped up to the surface as she fought to put distance between herself and the doomed *Heredia*.

She found her voice. "Raymond! Sonny! Lucille!" she screamed again and again, knowing it would be a miracle for her shouts to carry above the cries of the injured and the awful noises of the ship being torn apart by the sea. Her mind was wild with thoughts of losing her children. If only she had held tighter to Lucille. The girl's last plea for her mother haunted Ina's thoughts.

When she stopped for a breath, she felt fish bumping against her legs, sending Ina into a frenzy of kicking to keep them at bay. The darkness of the night and being alone in the water tempted panic. Coupled with the thought of predatory fish, Ina was traumatized. Fortunately she could hear other voices from time to time, men's voices, so she knew others were nearby. She hoped a rescue ship would be arriving quickly—she already felt chilled to the bone.

When morning's grey light crept across the sky, there was no sign left of the *Heredia* nor the U-boat that had sunk it, just debris in the water. After a few minutes, with sunlight now breaking through hazy cloud cover, she thought she could make out the shapes of people in the distance sitting on a raft of flotsam. Her hopes soared. Ina's vision, however, was badly blurred by the oil in her eyes, so she wasn't sure if the shapes really were survivors. Her left eye stung and her eyelid was almost sealed shut. She said a silent prayer, wiped at her eyes with an oily hand, then kicked her legs to get closer to the shapes.

When she was twenty feet away, she could hear the group talking, and she called out, "Sonny! Lucille! Ray!"

"We're sailors!" came the response. "We'll help you."

Arriving at the makeshift raft—nothing more than an oar and two pieces of wood—she asked, "Have you seen my husband and children?"

"No, ma'am," the two sailors responded. One slipped into the water, keeping his naked body out of sight. They all looked around at the horizon, helping Ina scan the bobbing debris for her family, but the heaps of broken wood and scattered pieces of the ship's equipment were thinning out with time and the pull of wind and currents. Nobody wanted to guess if she'd ever see her family again.

While the waves rocked them together and apart, the group shared stories: one sailor had been on watch, the other in the shower when the torpedo hit. Both had been blown free of the ship. Without life preservers, Ina wondered how long they'd last, as they only had bits of wood to hold on to. Ina noticed the naked man's hands turning white as he struggled to continue holding on to the board. He was young and unwilling to bare his body in front of a woman.

"Sailor, get back on your raft," Ina said. "This is no time for modesty."

"No, ma'am, I'm fine, I'm just resting my back," he responded.

Knowing he couldn't hang on to the board indefinitely, Ina didn't resist the current's pull when they began to drift apart. "Well, I suppose I'll keep looking for my children," she said as she floated away. "God bless."

The chill of the night was replaced by the blazing rays of the sun, but Ina decided not to shed her heavy coat, wondering if she could survive another night in water that sucked away her body's warmth. Being adrift in the ocean was terrifying, but even worse were the thoughts about her family and the very real possibility that they had gone down with the ship. *Don't think that way,* she scolded herself; *if I escaped, somehow they did too.* She'd go mad with grief if she thought the worst had happened, and she instinctively knew to put such thoughts out of her mind and focus on saving herself so she could search for them.

Soon Ina found another pair of survivors, one a Filipino sailor who clung to a board, half-conscious, and a ship's officer who'd stayed with him all night, treading water and holding the sailor's head up to keep him alive. "Have you seen my family?" she inquired.

"No, ma'am, I'm sorry," said the officer. "And please, beware of the debris. Some of these boards are sharp. If you bump into them and they cut you, the sharks will come and pick your bones."

She wondered about the men's chances for survival as she paddled on in search of her family. Far in the distance Ina thought she could make out the silhouette of a ship, and she began paddling toward it. After ten minutes, she was out of breath and her arms hung like dead weights over the front of the narrow board she clutched to her chest. The life vest and heavy coat made paddling especially difficult, and she contemplated removing her coat and letting it sink to the depths. But her intuition told her to keep it, no matter how bulky and cumbersome. She did, however, stop her paddling, realizing that she would never make it to the object on the horizon and was expending energy needlessly.

How much longer would it be until help arrived? she wondered. The officer's warning about sharks was causing havoc with her imagination and she shuddered at the thought. Then she saw cork in the water and panicked, thinking her life preserver had ruptured and wouldn't keep her afloat much longer. Despair clung to the edges of every thought, so Ina tried not to think at all. But it was impossible; her mind went straight back to her family, trying to calculate their odds of survival and the chance for rescue. Surely the authorities knew by now that the ship was not only overdue but also sunk; but if that was the case, why weren't there planes overhead or patrol boats in the area? Just thinking about the people "in charge" on land made her furious. Sonny, Lucille, Raymond, and she could have all gotten off at Corpus Christi if the officials had had an ounce of common sense.

Lost in her thoughts, she felt something tug on her tattered nightgown that swayed in the water, trailing behind her. She looked below and saw several pilot fish nibbling her nightgown and swimming between her legs. Then her blurred vision saw much larger shapes pass beneath her. Sharks! She could see about six of the creatures, about four to five feet in length, lazily plying the waters both beneath and around her. Panic and anger at her predicament welled up once again.

"Damn you to hell!" she shrieked, swinging a piece of wood at the fish, slapping the water. She kicked her legs and screamed, frenzied at the helpless feeling of losing her family and fearing a terrible death.

The sharks and pilot fish moved off a bit, but still stayed within sight. *They're like vultures*, she thought, *just waiting for me to weaken further.*

Ina pulled the remains of her nightgown in tight and then pulled down on her heavy coat. Next she brought her legs up so that her knees were near her chest. She didn't want her legs dangling below, and thought the coat offered a measure of protection. The sharks pushed her to the breaking point. *Dear Lord*, she prayed, *I don't want to wait here for the sharks to get me . . . better to just have it over with quick.*

When she looked back down, she could only see a couple of sharks and pilot fish.

A deeply religious woman, Ina put her faith in God, and thought maybe it was God who had prompted her to keep the heavy coat when logic told her to discard it. Now, she renewed her determination to live as long as the Lord wanted her to.

Later, the last of the sharks and pilot fish moved off. But the ordeal left her shaken and feeling utterly depleted of all strength. The emptiness of the ocean settled back around her, sealing out noise and feeling. By mid-afternoon, with the sun's glare adding to the pain of her oil-and-salt-encrusted eyes, she began to doubt anyone was even searching for her. Ina worried that she had drifted far from the accident scene and would never be found. She craved water, her mouth was parched and her lips cracked. Oil-soaked clothing clung to her upper body while her bare legs dangled in the water below. She looked at the empty blue sky and remembered the beautiful sunsets she'd seen while on the ship and how they inspired her to praise the Lord. Now the same sky seemed so blank and unforgiving. Her faith that God was with her was wavering. She tried to summon the energy to pray, to be thankful she was still alive, but was too spent.

Another larger board drifted nearby, perhaps part of a banana crate, and was a welcome find. Ina pushed herself on top of the floating planks, getting most of her body out of the water for the first time in a dozen hours. She struggled with negative thoughts about her family's fate and about sharks in the water below.

Time dragged on, and she cried thinking of a life without Sonny, Lucille, and Ray. She briefly entertained the idea of letting go of the planks and slipping underwater to let the sea take her down. Anything to ease the pain. She doubted she'd last another night at sea, not knowing what had happened to her children and husband. Then a prayer came to mind: "Dear Lord, I will not leave thee or forsake thee. Lord, I put myself in your hands," she murmured. "I lead my family to you; please protect them."

Dusk came, and still no sign of rescue. Not even a search plane could be seen in the dimming sky. Ina second-guessed her decision to leave the sailors on the makeshift raft. The dark void of approaching night, with unseen sharks, terrified her. *With the sailors, I wouldn't have to face this alone*, she thought.

An hour later, in complete darkness, a voice in her head said "Look up in front of you." She saw a light approaching her. Squinting through her damaged eyes, she thought the light was on a mast of a ship. Shouting for help, she paddled on her board in the direction of the boat, now able to make out searchlights in addition to the light on the mast. In minutes, the boat was right on top of her, the noisy engines and energetic voices of crewmen welcome sounds that cut through her exhaustion and despair.

Adrenaline broke Ina's torpor but she was physically unable to help herself get on board the shrimp trawler that was there to rescue her. Hands reached down toward her, but it was all she could do to lift her oil-drenched head.

"It's a Negro," said one of the crewmen. Then they got closer and he said, "Christ almighty, it's a woman!"

A line was thrown down to her, but she was unable to grasp it.

"Are you strong enough to let go of the boards?" asked the fishermen. Ina could only raise her hand toward the boat, looking up at it through one tearing eye.

The crewmen reached down and grasped her arm but it was still slick with heavy oil and she slid back into the water like a seal.

The trawler captain approached to see why the survivor wasn't aboard yet and understood the situation immediately.

"Ma'am," he said, leaning over the side of the boat toward Ina. "Would you agree to us using a rope to help you aboard? The oil is making it difficult, you see."

"Yes, if you would," Ina croaked.

A member of the crew quickly slid a rope under one of her outstretched legs and cinched it down with a knot. "Ready, cap'n," he said.

"Now, ma'am, we will have you out of the water and in some dry clothes forthwith," the captain said, signaling the crew to haul Ina up using a pulley that pivoted over the stern of the trawler. She tried to grasp the rope with one hand while her leg was being pulled above the water, but the angle of the rope pushed her life vest against the lip of the boat, preventing her from being lifted higher.

"Down again, boys," said the captain. He reached out for the rope and moved it away from the boat, then signaled for the crew to try again. As Ina was raised out of the water, the captain grabbed her life preserver and pivoted his catch over the boat, landing her on the deck like a big oily fish.

—⁂—

Ray and Sonny knelt next to her, clutching at her coat and tattered nightgown, helping her to sit up and then showered kisses on her face, which made their own lips black from oil.

Sonny, half crying with joy, choked out the words, "Mom, you made it, you made it."

Ina managed a smile hearing Sonny's voice. Because of the oil, she couldn't see out of her left eye, and her right eye could only make out blurred shadows. She was so exhausted, she bordered on unconsciousness and wasn't sure exactly where she was. All she knew was that she was safe, and she had heard her husband's voice and her son's and assumed Lucille was also with them.

Ray and crewmembers picked her up and gently carried her below and placed her on a bunk, its white sheets slowly turning black as oily water drained from her coat, nightgown, and skin.

Sonny was next to his mother in a flash. Ray was embracing her, and as soon as he released her, Sonny did the same. The boy was at a loss for words, so he said the first thing that came to his mind, crying "Mother, you're beautiful!"

Ina sobbed and hugged her son, saying, "Sonny, what's the matter with you? Look at me."

Then, through blurred vision Ina searched for Lucille. "Where is Lucille? Please tell me she is here!"

Ray and Sonny were silent.

CHAPTER SEVENTEEN

LUCILLE

"I can't swim much longer."

—Lucille

After the ship suddenly lurched, when the family was at the top of the stairs, Lucille found herself trapped by a seething whirlpool on a lower deck. The water around her boiled and swirled, and terrible noises were coming from the structure that had seemed so solid and indestructible just hours before. Though she was a strong, independent girl, being torn away from her family in the darkness shocked her to her core, leaving a frightened, panicked child screaming for her mother. She was flailing around, unsure what to do next when a voice called out to her from above.

"Lucille, I'm coming to help you," said a man. He quickly descended a ladder from a steeply canted upper deck that was pointing toward the sky, then let go and jumped into the water next to her. She recognized him as one of the friendly sailors who had doted on her and Sonny throughout the trip. He spoke with a curious accent that wasn't Spanish and wasn't anything she'd heard in Texas. His name was Roy, she remembered; he was the second mate on the *Heredia*, a tall, tan, and handsome man, Roy Sorli.

"Come with me," he said. "We can't stay in here; we need to get outside the ship."

"But my mother and dad, I need to find them, and Sonny," she pleaded.

"Yes, we will," answered the thirty-four-year-old second mate. "First we need to climb back up there where I was and jump off the other side into the ocean. We need to get away from the ship; it's going to sink. I'm sure your parents are outside in one of the life rafts, and they must be looking for you."

He pulled her from the swirling water and pushed her toward the ladder he had descended. When they reached the top, he boosted Lucille up to the edge of the listing hull, which was vibrating with horrific noises of explosions as bulkheads blew and water rushed into every available space. Just as Sorli climbed to the edge, another sailor's head popped out of a porthole.

"Sorli, is that you?" the man asked as he looked around.

"Robello, you need to get out of there before the ship goes down," Sorli said. "We're about to jump."

"I know, I was trying the door, I thought she was going to roll over," the sailor responded. "I think I can get out this way."

The sailor wiggled one shoulder, then the other, through the tiny porthole, pushing up with his hands until his whole naked body slipped out. Soon he was next to them, his skin glowing in the glare of the searchlight from the U-boat. Sorli took off his jacket and handed it to the sailor, providing the naked man a shred of protection against the sea.

They stepped to the edge of the hull where there was nothing but darkness beyond. Sorli grabbed Lucille's quivering hand. "We jump on three and swim as fast as we can away from the boat," he said.

Lucille looked down at the water, terrified of leaping into the abyss. But she had to put her trust in this man until her parents found her. "I'm ready," she said softly.

"One, two, three!" Sorli shouted, and together they were falling through the humid air, toward an unknown fate.

Lucille hit the water with a smack, and her life vest rose up and covered her face. She frantically pulled it back into place. The first thing she saw was the sagging hulk of the *Heredia*, still illuminated from the U-boat searchlight.

Sorli tugged on her arm. "Keep your head down and swim," said Sorli. "We have to swim fast."

There was no time for the questions that nagged at Lucille: where are the lifeboats, when will I find Mother and Dad, how long will we be in the water?

"Swim, Lucille, don't stop. We need to be far from the ship when it goes down," he said. "You're a brave girl and a good swimmer. Keep swimming."

Just then a louder explosion sent shockwaves through the water, and the stern of the ship completely disappeared beneath the waves. The water swirled around Lucille, tugging at her pajamas. The hissing and spitting of the sinking ship sounded like an angry dragon ready to devour her. She swam as hard as she could, trying to keep up with Sorli and Robello.

There was another man swimming nearby, third mate Thomas Burke, who joined the small band escaping the wreck.

"Keep going," said Sorli.

"No time to stop now," added the other sailor.

"I'm trying," said Lucille.

"Then why do you keep stopping?" Sorli asked.

"Because my britches are falling down," said Lucille, yanking up her waterlogged pajama pants.

Burke snorted. "Okay, can't help that," he said. "I think we're just about out of danger, but we should keep swimming to get clear of the debris and oil."

Lucille had taken swimming lessons in South America and knew how to kick and paddle with her arms, so she kept at it, remembering her mother's glowing approval when she'd advanced a level. That warm, sunny place seemed so foreign and far away now. Lucille felt tears and panic welling up with the memory of her mother smiling when she and Sonny demonstrated the strokes they'd learned. Learning in a Costa Rican lagoon was far different than putting the skills to the test in the open ocean, however. Waves slapped her face, debris from the wreck got in her way, and there was no sandy beach and dry towel waiting for her. She tried to breathe steadily and stay close to Roy Sorli.

Human noises could be heard in the darkness, vague groans and men hollering. But there were no voices Lucille recognized. *My parents must be looking for me*, she thought, *but why can't I hear them calling?*

"Where are the life rafts?" she asked Sorli. "I can't swim much longer."

"We'll take care of you," Sorli said. He grabbed a wooden box that was bobbing nearby. "We might be able to use this." Then he popped the lid open and pulled out a long string of colorful flags. Lucille recognized them as the signal flags that fluttered from the *Heredia*'s yardarms that were snapping in the wind just yesterday when the ship arrived in Corpus Christi. They were a stark contrast to the black water all around, but she couldn't imagine what they'd do with flags. Perhaps wave them at a passing ship?

Sorli grabbed a hatch cover that was floating nearby, and then a piece of wood. Burke helped him lash the flotsam together with the flags. "Okay, Lucille, climb up here," Sorli said, helping her onto the makeshift raft. The two sailors hung on to the edges to stay afloat, sometimes talking softly to each other and looking down into the dark water below.

Lucille looked back at where she thought the ship had been, but it was now dark in all directions.

"Who's that?" called a voice nearby.

"Sorli, Burke, and Robello, and one civilian!" Sorli answered.

A man hanging on to a board appeared from the gloom, another member of the crew. "Any idea how many made it out?" he asked. Nobody answered.

Sorli had been on watch when the first torpedo hit, and he knew the ship's location just a couple of miles from the Ship Shoal Buoy. He worried that the current of the nearby Mississippi River would push the survivors far off course by the time rescue planes were sent out—if and when the New Orleans harbormaster alerted the Navy that the *Heredia* was overdue. Because they were subject to radio silence, the harbormaster might hesitate to send search parties out immediately, giving a ship that was late a buffer of time to reach its destination.

Two torpedoes had ripped through the hull, ensuring that there was no time to send distress signals, and also blowing apart life rafts that would never leave their davits. The survivors would have to rely on the flotsam from the wreck to keep their heads above water until help arrived.

Burke, at twenty-three, was among the youngest of the sailors in the group, a recent Massachusetts Maritime Academy graduate who knew the code of the sea. Sailors always rendered help to others, but war was upending everything he knew. These U-boats were sinking anything they came upon, whether an oil tanker or a merchant ship. After the destruction they had wrought on the East Coast all winter and spring, sailors talked about the Germans' strategy of not only disrupting the supply chain of shipbuilding materials and fuel but reducing the number of sailors who might fight against them. He hoped they had spared the shrimp boats that plied the Gulf, knowing those were the survivors' best opportunity for rescue—if their paths crossed.

Lucille started to cry quietly, the shock and separation from her family starting to set in.

"Now, Lucille, you'll have a lot to tell your mother and dad when they find us," Sorli said to comfort her. "Have you ever swum in the ocean before? Have you ever built a raft like Robinson Crusoe? This is quite an adventure for you."

"I did swim in the ocean, in Costa Rica," she said. "There were big waves at the beach, and Sonny got knocked over by one."

"That's funny," said Sorli. "Now, you're from Texas, have you ever seen snow? I'm from a place with a lot of snow."

"No, but I want to," she said. "Did you build snowmen? I've seen pictures of them."

The chatter helped distract Lucille from her worries, but even she thought it peculiar to be in the ocean in the middle of the night talking about snowmen. She knew Sorli was trying to console her, and she didn't resist.

"Yes, snowmen," Sorli said. "We had so much snow in Norway that I would ski to school. Have you seen skiing?"

Lucille shook her head.

Burke spoke up: "It's like ice skating, except you don't have to be on a pond. Skis are long boards on your feet that let you slide over the snow. I'm from a place that gets a lot of snow too. Boston."

"I would surely like to try that," said Lucille. "Sonny got a scooter for Christmas and he wants to ride it to school when we go back to San

Antonio. Will someone be able to get it out of the ship when we get rescued? And my dad's car, it was on the ship too."

The talk ebbed and flowed, with Sorli doing his best to keep Lucille's spirits up and direct her thoughts away from her family, the plight they were all in, and the cold they all felt right to their bones.

About two hours had gone by since the *Heredia* had been torpedoed, and Lucille shivered as she sat on the hatch cover and boards with her legs dangling in the water. The men were talking among themselves, but she was so tired and cold that she didn't listen. She forced herself to stay awake, afraid of falling off the hatch cover. Amusing herself by splashing a bit of water with her foot, she was fascinated by the phosphorescence that spattered on the surface like a glowing sparkler. Pieces of the makeshift raft knocked together in the trough of each small wave that briefly lifted it, and that too helped her stay awake.

A few minutes later, Lucille laughed and said "Hey, Mr. Roy, quit tickling me."

"Tickling you?" asked the second mate.

"Yes, my feet."

"Maybe you could shift over here a bit and bring your feet up on the raft?" Sorli suggested. "That will make it easier for me to tickle them."

Sorli had seen the large shape of a shark beneath them and knew that was what was brushing up against her feet.

<hr />

Day was breaking, a cloudless sky slowly brightening to reveal a scene of destruction as far as the eye could see: pieces of wreckage, the dead body of a sailor floating face-down in the distance, a dull grey sheen on the water where oil stained the surface. Yet the sky was empty. As the makeshift raft rocked up and over small swells, its occupants scanned the horizon: no sign of ships, rescuers, or Lucille's family. The sailors in the water around Lucille's raft did their best to stay warm and alert, knowing that drifting off to sleep might kill them.

Lucille started to hum.

"What is that tune?" Sorli asked.

"It's 'Nearer My God to Thee,'" she answered. "My mother's favorite. She hums it a lot when she's sewing."

"Praying's not a bad idea," said Burke. "The sun's gonna be brutal soon. Could you pray for some clouds?"

"Sing a little," prompted Sorli. "If you please."

"Well, I don't know all of the words but," then Lucille's voice lilted, just above a whisper, "Nearer, my God, to thee, nearer to thee! Though it be a cross that raiseth me, still all my song shall be, nearer, my God, to thee; nearer, my God, to thee, nearer to thee!"

"That's wonderful," said Sorli.

"Do you miss your family from Norway?" she asked.

"Yes," he said. "I have a daughter there, and I hope she grows up as strong and brave as you are. Now, let's learn something while we're out here."

In order to pass the time, Sorli proceeded to teach Lucille the meaning behind many of the signal flags and how they could be combined to convey a ship's circumstances.

The second mate knew how to make the best of a bad situation. He didn't want to talk in depth about his home and family because many of the memories were painful, having been the youngest of twelve children who learned to work hard at an early age on his family's subsistence farm north of the Arctic Circle. Long sunless winters forced his siblings to make up games to entertain themselves when they had free time. His father had been a harsh taskmaster, and leaving home at sixteen seemed Roy's only option. Yet Roy Sorli was a gentle soul who sought quiet companionship, and he worshiped his fiancée whom he knew would be worried when she didn't hear from him that day. Distracting Lucille was also distracting himself, keeping the sailor from worrying that the future he had planned might not come to pass.

As the day wore on, the sailors took turns holding on to Lucille's little raft, which provided more support than their waterlogged life vests that a few of them had had time to grab before the ship went down. She helped them by pointing out jellyfish that were drifting nearby so they might defend their exposed skin by pushing them away with pieces of wood. And she got a glimpse of a shark below the raft now and then, but never realized that's what had been tickling her feet in the darkness. Sorli had seen the predator and a couple others much earlier, so when Lucille nervously pointed out the shark, he was ready with soothing words. "It's harmless, just a little curious about what we're doing out here."

That was good enough for Lucille. If Mr. Roy wasn't concerned, she wouldn't be either.

"Suppose the captain made it out?" Robello asked no one in particular.

"Don't know, I was on the bridge with him when we were hit," said Sorli. "He had about the same chance as I did."

"The codes? Papers?"

"There was no time to take them from the cabinet and put them in the bag," Sorli said of the procedure of ensuring that the secret naval codes would be destroyed if a ship were abandoned.

"It only took me thirty seconds to put my shoes on, but the deck was awash the minute I stepped outside. I don't suppose we had time to transmit?" asked Burke. Then he answered his own question. "No, never mind. I know the answer. The first torpedo hit amidships. There was no time, the radioman must have been killed instantly. Poor guy."

Silence again descended on the group, who doubtlessly wondered if surviving the attack would turn out to be a blessing or a curse. Like many shipwreck survivors, they might struggle to stay alive only to suffer longer at the merciless whim of the elements. Without food alone, a person may live for days; but without water, that time would be much shorter. The effects of hypothermia, even in the Gulf's mild temperatures, would already be felt as it only takes a few hours for hands, feet, and other extremities to experience numbness and lack of mobility, usually first apparent through slurred speech. It was one thing for a grown man to accept the dangers as part of his job, but watching a helpless child like Lucille suffer galvanized the group, keeping each of them alert to dangers and willing to offer anything to ease her discomfort. As the sun marched toward the western horizon, each of the sailors was summoning his energy for another cold night in the water, trying to assess the odds of lasting without water and with sharks circling beneath.

The slapping of the water against the makeshift raft was like the ticking of a clock, and Lucille was fighting to stay awake. Twilight was coming on and she wanted badly to curl up and sleep on the little raft, but there wasn't quite enough room. Her upper lip was chapped and burned but she tried not to pick at it.

"I heard something," said Lucille.

The sailors perked up, searching the sky.

"An engine? I don't—" Burke began.

"Wait!" said Robello. They were silent again.

Sorli grabbed the loose tail of the flags and slipped a long board under it to raise it high above their heads, propping his elbows on the hatch cover next to Lucille.

"Yes!" said Robello.

Now Lucille could see a stubby aircraft coming nearer, its wings wobbling from side to side, signaling that the group had been seen. The aircraft seemed to take over all of her senses as it passed not far above the tiny raft, shaking her body with reverberations from its engines. The sailors were jubilant, and for a few moments all forgot the discomfort of skin rubbed raw by the salt water, unquenchable thirst, and searing sunburn.

The plane circled back; and when it was almost overhead, a box popped out of the pilot's window, landing in the water not far from the group. One sailor paddled over to retrieve it.

For Lucille, opening the box was as exciting as Christmas morning. Inside were cans of water, candy bars, and skin cream for their sunburned faces. Despite their desperate thirst and a day without food, each waited patiently for a turn to help himself to his share of the contents. More important than the comforting sips of water and soothing skin cream, the box was assurance that help would be coming, that the outside world knew they were here.

The sailors, however, likely tempered their joy with the knowledge that Lucille's family might not have made it off the ship. Each of them had his own remarkable survival story, like Burke's dismay at finding the ship sinking within thirty seconds of the first torpedo or the sailor who squeezed out of a porthole naked because he had been in the shower at the moment of impact. None wanted to speculate on the fate of Lucille's family members, the energetic boy who peppered them with questions, the stern father or the kind mother who was friendly to them all. Keeping a family intact through such a cataclysmic event would be impossible, and seconds spent on board the ship could mean the difference between life and death. There would not be an accurate accounting for all of the forty-eight crew, six Navy Gun crew, and eight civilians for days to come.

The sun continued to set; and once the crew's thirst was quenched, the survivors began to wonder when rescuers would appear. Conversation was muted as all listened intently for another engine sound from plane or ship, keeping watch as before at the crest of every swell. Finally, a wavering light appeared, then an engine could be heard churning in their direction. The drone of the boat's motor was the most welcome sound Lucille had ever heard.

Silhouetted against the sky, the boat was small and low to the water with long poles extending over the ocean on each side. Several crewmen crowded the railing to see the people in the water. One was yelling instructions to the helmsman, telling him to cut the engine as they drew closer. It was a local shrimp boat, the *Shellwater*, with a crew from Morgan City.

Lucille was the first to be lifted from her flotsam perch and onto the deck of the trawler, which was cluttered with pails and piles of fishing net. Sorli was pulled onboard next, and Lucille saw him wince as he took off his life vest for the first time in more than eighteen hours. His exposed skin was badly burned and raw from jellyfish stings.

Two crewmen carried the young girl down the companionway, going first inside the pilothouse and down a small ladder. In a small bunkroom they let her stand on wobbly legs. A crewman asked her name and pointed Lucille to a basin to wash up while he laid some dry clothing on a lower bunk. Lucille's fingers were too raw and stiff to untie the knot her mother had firmly tightened in her life vest, so the fisherman cut it for her. When the sodden weight was lifted from her body, she felt weak and light-headed and began to fall. The two men caught her, placed her on the bunk, then left to get her some food.

Lucille struggled to remove the pajamas she'd worn to bed, her eyes tearing at the memory of her snug stateroom in the *Heredia*, of the anticipation that home was so close at hand before the terrible hours in the water. *Where are Mother, Father, and Sonny?*

"Lucille?" said a voice at the door. Sorli. She finished pulling an over-sized shirt on, feeling its roughness against her raw skin. He poked his head inside, a smile spreading across his red face.

"Good news, Lucille! The captain said your family has been rescued. They're on another shrimp boat. We'll see them when we get to Morgan City tomorrow."

Lucille was overcome with tears. Her emotions were a mix of relief and joy, tempered by the awful realization that they had all been in danger of death.

Sorli stepped forward to hug her, relieved that their ordeal was over, but he tightened up when she put her arms around him because his exposed skin was crisscrossed with raw welts from jellyfish stings.

After a small bowl of broth and some bread, Lucille was happy to stretch out on a bunk and sleep while the boat's engines groaned through the water, rocking her to sleep.

On another shrimper, the radio crackled to life. "Captain, this is the *Shell-water*. Do you have a Raymond Downs on your boat? Tell him I have his daughter."

PART III

PART III

CHAPTER EIGHTEEN

TRIUMPHANT RETURN TO LORIENT

"Those who did not share our hardships will never know the strength of the bonds which tie us together."

—U-boatman Kurt Baberg

While the Downs family was reunited and tried to reconstruct their lives, Commander Erich Würdemann served his country the best he knew how. After leaving the Gulf of Mexico and passing through the Florida Straits, he moved off the American coast on a northeast course, running on the surface with his diesel engines averaging nine knots. The voyage had been interrupted by several crash dives because of enemy aircraft patrols, but the commander wasn't concerned, writing that even though planes were often flying right toward his sub, "we were probably not noticed by any of the aircraft." It's probable he felt like a veteran warrior and considered the opposing pilots rookies who still had a lot to learn about hunting down subs.

The crew of U-506 thought of home with each passing mile, relieved to be away from the terrible heat and humidity of the Gulf and the high-risk hunts they conducted in the shallow waters off the Mississippi River. Some of them marveled that they were not spotted from above by enemy aircraft, and all crew members knew they were fortunate to have slipped in and out of the good hunting grounds without being detected by the U.S. patrol boats that had concentrated in the area. The crew was well aware that if escape was not possible and they found themselves surrounded by the enemy, their orders were to blow up their own sub using demolition charges. Their own fate was secondary: either go down with the U-boat or become a POW if they survived the sinking.

Having been successful in the heart of enemy waters for several weeks, they felt both accomplished and a bit lucky, and now it was likely the crew wanted to head straight to Lorient. They were traveling without torpedoes and expected to be in safe harbor within two weeks.

Würdemann, however, had other ideas. The young commander was free to direct his return journey according to his best judgment without being under the thumb of any on-scene superiors. In any other branch of the military, a twenty-seven-year-old leader would have a more senior officer either working nearby or within direct radio communication. But a U-boat commander was on his own, with no immediate oversight, and could conduct his patrol however he saw fit, so long as it met with Dönitz's Standing Orders.

While northeast of the Bahamas during the night of May 28, Würdemann exercised his authority and made a decision that would put his sub back in combat rather than making a bee-line for Lorient. Lookouts on U-506 had spotted a steamer, and Würdemann ordered a change of course in pursuit.

When the sub had closed the distance from the ship to a mere 2,500 meters, his gunners opened fire with deck guns and Würdemann found himself in "running artillery combat." His War Diary reflects his surprise at the speed with which the ship defended itself: "Freighter turns stern to and returns fire very quickly with stern cannon."

This ship, the *Yorkmoor*, was British, and its crew was more seasoned than those of the American and South American vessels U-506 had previously hunted. These Brits knew exactly what to do when attacked.

The freighter had just left St. Thomas and was steaming to its discharge port in New York. Captain Thomas Matthews was in the chart room when Würdemann's first shell struck, and he immediately turned the ship so that its stern faced where he believed the U-boat attacked from. This maneuver would make his ship a smaller target—presenting his stern rather than the entire hull to the Germans—but still allow him to fire back.

The battle was on. Würdemann and U-506 were taking a bit of a risk by fighting it out on the surface with shells, rather than torpedoes. If just one of the shells from the *Yorkmoor* hit U-506 during its prolonged stay on the surface, chances were the sub would not only lose the battle but eventually sink.

Soon, one of the 105-mm cannon shells from U-506 penetrated the engine room of the ship, and the *Yorkmoor* could only operate at half speed, seriously undermining its evasive maneuvers. Another shell hit beneath the ship's gun platform, blasting the primary gunner from his station. Somehow the injured gunner crawled back and continued firing, directing his aim toward the muzzle flashes in the dark that signaled the location of the Germans.

Würdemann had a fight on his hands, but his vessel was the smaller, less visible target, and his prey was wounded. He watched the steamer make evasive maneuvers, and he countered by changing his own course so that he could position himself off the side of the ship rather than the stern. There had been no loud explosion from the freighter, so the commander had to assume he had not made "perfect hits" that would sink the ship.

Onboard the *Yorkmoor*, Captain Matthews was informed that the engine room was flooding fast. The lights had gone out and the bow was beginning to settle. The Brits were still doggedly manning the deck guns, but after the sub stopped and Würdemann re-positioned it, the gunners on the ship had no muzzle flashes to zero in on. The enemy could be anywhere; its low silhouette blended in perfectly with the ink-black sea. The British gunners could only wait, vulnerable and wounded, until the sub resumed shooting so they would know the direction to return fire.

When Würdemann had U-506 at a right angle to the freighter, he ordered a full artillery barrage fired in rapid succession. He knew beyond a doubt that some of his artillery shells were inflicting damage, writing "a sudden ceasing of the radio messages from the freighter and the slow uncertain, gradually silenced defensive fire are indicative of hits." But the ship didn't sink and he resumed firing. The young commander watched from the conning tower with satisfaction as flames erupted on the bow section of his foe's vessel. A minute later one of the German shells pierced the ship's hull, and a tremendous explosion ripped through the night air when cold seawater flooded onto the red-hot boilers.

The duel was over and Matthews ordered his men to abandon ship. Forty-five sailors had to cram into a lifeboat built for twenty-five because the other lifeboat, which the men cut free of the ship, was riddled with shrapnel.

Würdemann's account says that lifeboats were seen, and "of these one is heavily occupied. Steamer sinks on an even keel. *Yorkmoor* sunk with artillery. Smooth sea, bright moon. New course 90 degrees."

Although the commander made no entry in his War Diary about approaching the lifeboats, survivors later recounted that he brought U-506 alongside and asked the name of the ship, tonnage, cargo, and destination in "German-accented English." After the survivors gave the information, they said the sub motored away, still on the surface.

The forty-five sailors crowded inside the one undamaged lifeboat were left alone, drifting in calm seas over 400 miles from shore with no prospects for help. They were well aware that their radioman had been unable to transmit an SOS. Captain Matthews made two quick decisions that likely saved every man's life. First, he instructed two men to climb onboard the leaking lifeboat and begin making repairs. While those sailors were patching the boat, he and the other men began searching through the floating debris for anything of nourishment. Containers of food and water were found during the search. Fixing the damaged lifeboat, however, did not go as smoothly, but Matthews was convinced that without the second lifeboat, the men crammed into the undamaged one risked being swamped. He stayed at the scene of the disaster for a full day and a half before the battered lifeboat was repaired and able to hold half the crew. The wind was out of the east and Matthews ordered a hoisting of the sails on both lifeboats and began the daunting journey toward the Carolinas.

Six days later, off the coast of South Carolina, the castaways were seen by patrol planes and rescued. Thanks to the cool head of Captain Matthews, all forty-five men survived. Their only injuries were severe sunburn, and rescue crews reported that "no one was hungry or thirsty when picked up."

Würdemann continued his journey to Lorient and two days later, just south of Bermuda, he spotted masts in the distance during daylight. Once again, the young commander couldn't resist trying for one last kill. Perhaps he was thinking of Schacht and their friendly competition. Schacht was a few days ahead of him on the voyage to Lorient, and Würdemann was unsure just how many ships his fellow commander had sunk.

Würdemann instructed the helmsman of U-506 to position the sub well ahead of the ship. Using binoculars, he saw that the vessel was a slow-moving freighter fitted with two large cargo cranes. He also noted that the ship was equipped with a cannon on its stern.

It was another prize ripe for the picking. But the commander, showing his usual mix of cautious determination, decided to bide his time and not take a needless risk. No sense attacking in daylight when time was on his side. He ordered his sub to submerge and wait for nightfall, knowing he'd have a full moon to silhouette his prey.

The ship he had seen was a small (2,292 tons) steamer, the *Fred W. Green*, that was outfitted as a derrick ship with two cranes and 1,000 tons of concrete in its cargo hold to give it stability when lifting heavy objects. The concrete filled much of the hull, essentially making the lower part of the ship impenetrable, as Würdemann would soon find out. Although the ship had been built in 1918 at a Michigan shipyard, ownership had been transferred from a U.S. company to the British War Ministry in 1941 to help in the war effort. She was now on a passage to Africa and had 41 British sailors onboard, including naval gunners.

Using the periscope, U-506 tracked the ship the entire afternoon and finally, under cover of darkness at approximately 8 P.M., the sub burst from the sea and had the *Fred W. Green* in its crosshairs, just 1,500 meters away. The sub opened fire with its 105-mm gun and its very first shell hit the deck, toppling the antennas, thus ensuring that no distress call could be sent. Subsequent shells bounced off the cement-laden hull. But Würdemann had thirty-four shells at his disposal and he later recorded that "after several hits the steamer remained lying stopped." One shell had blown away the ship's entire deck gun platform and another had set the forecastle on fire.

Two lifeboats from the crippled ship were lowered. The last man off the *Fred W. Green* was Captain Sampson, who, after making sure there was no one left onboard, jumped off the bow into the sea. His crew was unable to locate him and he was never seen again. Four other sailors also died during the barrage.

The ship, despite being engulfed in flames, did not sink, and Würdemann ordered U-506 to maneuver much closer to its prey. He was now out of shells, so his gunners opened fire with the machine gun, aiming just below the waterline, hoping to puncture the hull. For the next fifty minutes the Germans fired intermittently, wondering what it would take to sink the ship. Würdemann was ultimately rewarded, writing "Steamer becomes down by the bow and lists to port . . . steamer sinks." The commander then approached the two lifeboats, which had thirty-six sailors crammed in them. He asked the name of the ship, its cargo, size, and destination. After receiving the information, he motored to the east, satisfied that every one of his torpedoes, shells, and even machine gun bullets had been put to good use. All of the survivors from the *Fred W. Green* were found and rescued two days after their ship went down—the last casualty of U-506's spring raid on the U.S.

On June 6, when the men of U-506 were just a few days from Lorient and salivating over the thought of fresh food or imagining the luxury of simply taking a shower, they had yet another delay, this one ordered by Headquarters rather than Würdemann. They were told to rendezvous with another sub, U-155, and transfer their navigational gyro compass globe. U-506 adjusted course slightly to a secret meeting grid, northeast of the Azores, and two days later, after keeping a sharp lookout, sighted the sub and made the transfer.

Würdemann was now close to home but he couldn't let his guard down. British aircraft had been keeping the waters off Lorient hot with their constant surveillance and depth charges. In a radio message to Würdemann, headquarters asked him to go to the aid of Commander Schuch, whose vessel, U-105, had been severely damaged in the Bay of Biscay by an Australian-crewed aircraft coming out of a British base. Würdemann never located the crippled vessel, but later learned it had limped into a port in neutral Spain. Würdemann almost met the same fate on June 11, when he had to crash dive for aircraft, and didn't surface again until almost two hours had passed. Not long after he surfaced, an incoming message told him what he already knew: "Expect increased air danger." In fact, British attacks on subs leaving and returning to Lorient had become so frequent it prompted Dönitz, just a few days later, to issue new instructions to U-boats in the Bay of Biscay. Instead of allowing the vessels to make good time traveling on the surface while having lookouts search the skies for enemy aircraft, the new orders required all U-boats to cross the bay submerged both day and night, with only a brief run atop the ocean under cloak of darkness to recharge depleted batteries. The passage of so many U-boats coming and going out of the Bay of Biscay had become such a rich focal point that the RAF devoted more and more aircraft to the area. And soon the planes would be joined by anti-submarine boats that would make the Bay one of the most dangerous places for a U-boat to pass through.

U-506 managed to dodge enemy aircraft, and after seventy-one days at sea and traveling 11,249 nautical miles, it "made fast Lorient Berth A1" on June 15. The celebration began for the conquering heroes. A band was waiting, and as U-506 fastened her lines to the concrete pen, the musicians struck up a lively tune. Submariner Herbert Werner, author of *Iron Coffin*, described a typical homecoming in Lorient at that time as taking on a dreamlike quality as his U-boat pulled up to the pen. "Our comrades-in-arms stood by in grey-green uniforms, navy blues, and a variety of battle dress. Many girls—nurses from our military hospital—were waiting for us with flowers. How satisfying it was to be expected, how good it was to have survived! The Commandant [of the flotilla] shouted words of welcome, then walked across the gangplank and shook hands with the captain and company. The nurses followed with a smile, a kiss, and a bouquet of flowers for every man. Now we knew we had jumped off the devil's shovel, that life was sweet and rewarding."

The men of U-506 undoubtedly felt the same. Their young commander was wildly acclaimed for leading his men to a stunning success of twelve ships sunk or damaged, and Würdemann became known as the "tanker cracker" for the carnage he inflicted on oil tankers. He had exceeded the veteran Schacht's number of ships hit by two, although both he and Schacht each had nine confirmed ships sunk. Whether or not the two men kept score based on total ships sunk or tonnage destroyed, is not known; but by any measure their patrols were some of the best of the war. Both Würdemann and Schacht were awarded the Iron Cross 1st Class. The medals were important; but the two men would be forever known as commanding the first U-boats to enter the Gulf of Mexico and brave the shallow waters near the mouth of the Mississippi. They had traveled thousands of miles, and would travel thousands more on separate patrols in different parts of the world. Incredibly, their paths would cross again, and both would become involved in another remarkable incident that will be told.

———

Although it's unknown whether Admiral Dönitz conducted a personal de-briefing of Würdemann, this was a practice "the Lion" pursued with returning U-boat commanders whenever possible. Dönitz also made the effort to say a few words of encouragement to the crews. Herbert Werner chronicled a visit in which the Admiral addressed his crew, and he described Dönitz as "lean in appearance, brief in his speech, and stern in his demands," telling the men to follow three overriding duties: pursue, attack, and destroy the enemy. Then Dönitz shook hands with each man, and the crew felt a surge of pride and power, more determined than ever to fulfill their next mission.

———

With U-506 safely at berth, and the ceremonies over, the crew took turns going on a two-week leave. Some of the men remained with the U-boat helping with maintenance, receiving updated training, and assisting drilling new recruits. The other submariners were free of all duties—a chance to try to forget the conditions they had endured inside U-506.

Imagine any group of young men heading out on the town after seventy-one days at sea without alcohol, without so much as a woman's voice to listen to, and without a day off from their daily chores. Now envision that those same young men—some no more than nineteen years old—had been sealed in a sweltering iron tube for most of that time, never knowing if they would step foot on land again. And finally imagine that this tight-knit group knew that in just five weeks they would be sent right back out to sea and an uncertain fate. They would certainly have justification for partying, and that is what they did.

First came the beer and wine, with boisterous singing, followed by a huge dinner. Already on wobbly sea-legs, the bearded crewmembers then staggered to their quarters at a naval complex. Those not totally inebriated had a hot bath or shower and a haircut, and put on their double-breasted blues, the first time all of them had been clean in weeks. Women were their next objective; and with money in their pockets, they set out in small groups to wander through town to find the establishments where the women were waiting.

Some of the French prostitutes had been in the business long before the German occupation, while others joined the trade out of necessity. Author Robert Gildea, in his book *Marianne in Chains*, points out that a million and a half Frenchmen were in German POW camps, "leaving their women alone to fend for themselves." He goes on to say that "the rules that applied at Liberation, when 'horizontal collaboration' was punished by head shaving and possibly prosecution for consorting with the enemy, were not necessarily the same under Occupation, when single women were coming up against Germans in their employment and in social situations." All the French suffered under occupation, and some faced starvation; each citizen did what they felt they had to do to survive.

Once the men had their fill of wine, women, and song in port, those who were on leave often made a quick visit to family in Germany. U-boat men had many perks, such as the opportunity to take an express train from France to their homeland. And once in Germany, the citizens gave U-boat men the highest accolades, treating them as true heroes, gallant and brave. Infantrymen could only stare in jealousy, but yet few would trade places because of the claustrophobia and death rate that came with serving on a sub.

——

While his crew either relaxed or celebrated, Erich Würdemann presented his War Diary to Headquarters. In the "General Remarks" concluding section, the commander had the opportunity to give his opinion rather than merely recording actions he undertook. He was well aware that Dönitz would study what he had to say, and the young commander made the most of his opportunity, explaining why he was so successful. In hindsight, these observations can also be viewed as an outline of what the U.S. needed to do for proper defense from U-boats.

His "General Remarks" read as follows:

"Apparently it [our attacks] came as a surprise to the enemy and hit him unprepared. Only in this way can one explain the lack of:
　　a) Systematic sea patrol.
　　b) Convoy measures (in the relatively small sea area this would be feasible in shallow water with a few escort vessels).
　　c) Instructions (course, zigzag schemes, etc.) to merchant shipping.

The ships proceed independently—sometimes in groups unescorted, mostly unarmed, without camouflage, without zigzagging, steering normal peacetime courses. The fact that this "peacetime operation" continued to run unstopped, even after the almost daily sinking of valuable ships, underlines the vital importance of this traffic route for the enemy.

Undoubtedly boats will find aggravating circumstances in the future and can expect strong air and sea surveillance to be in place off the mouth [of the Mississippi]. Complicating operations and attack was the constant heavy haze associated with an indistinct horizon, mostly smooth sea and strong marine phosphorescence.

The very young, mostly inexperienced crew is well proven. Conveniently the long, quiet time of the outbound transit has an impact on this, training could be encouraged and the crew brought to a certain level of qualification. A decline in performance from the long submerged cruises (about two weeks at a minimum tempera-ture of 35 degrees Celsius in the boat up to 16 hours per day) was not observed."

—⊗—

At the end of the log, Dönitz added his own brief comment, citing the fact that Würdemann made the most of its numerous chances for success: "The Kommandant exploited them well to the last shell and achieved a very beautiful success. Very good shooting performance in torpedo and artillery firing."

While Operation Paukenschlag had proved incredibly successful, and U-boat men could rejoice, there were dark clouds on the horizon for the German war machine. Britain was regularly launching squadrons of bombers into Germany, decimating industrial cities and killing scores of civilians, just as had been done in the Luftwaffe's raids over London. The British were even able to mount their first "Thousand-Bomber Raid" against the German city of Cologne on May 30 and May 31, which seri-ously damaged or destroyed over 5,000 buildings and killed approximately 470 Germans, most of them civilians. On the Eastern Front, Soviet defenders in the Ukraine were still holding out despite massive assaults by the German Eleventh Army, and any idea of a blitzkrieg through Russia had long ago been given up. It was becoming apparent that Germany's fighting forces were stretched thin and their industrial output of military equipment was eroding. The celebration and heady success enjoyed by Erich Würdemann and his crew would not be repeated.

CHAPTER NINETEEN

MORGAN CITY
AND THE HOSPITAL

"Well, I seem to have lost my boat."

—Roy Sorli to his fiancée,
referring to the *Heredia* sinking

S onny, get up." It was Ray shaking Sonny's shoulder. "The boat's at
the dock."

Sonny sat up and rubbed his eyes. Beyond the heavy wooden
pilings visible through the porthole next to his berth were buildings and
people. Deckhands were throwing heavy coils of lines to tie the boat up.

It was the scene Sonny should have experienced 24 hours previously, on the
Heredia. It took him a moment to absorb the reality that the sunburn chafing
on his legs under the bedsheet, the scratches on his arms, and the growling
hunger in his belly meant the shipwreck ordeal wasn't just a nightmare.

"Where's Lucille, Dad?" Sonny asked. He'd heard she had been picked
up by another shrimp boat but was anxious to see his family together

again, to know they'd go back to a normal life after his surreal experience drifting on a raft at sea. It hardly seemed possible now that solid ground was before him and cars were driving past and people around the docks were going about their usual business without so much as a glance at the shrimp trawlers that were docking.

"Now, Sonny," Ray said. "Here are some pants for you. They're not going to fit, but it's better than walking around in your undershorts. Just hike them up and hold on, and we'll see Lucille soon. I have to help your mother now; you go up on deck."

Sonny pulled up the light cotton pants and, despite being tall for his age, was nearly swallowed up by the fabric. A T-shirt on the bed was also for him, so he gingerly slid it on over his sunburned arms and shoulders, remembering briefly how his father had demanded the captain's coat to protect him from the relentless sun. The memory caused a jolt of fear to shake his body, and he put the thought of the barren sea baking in the sunlight out of his mind, moving clumsily toward the companionway leading to the deck.

One of the crewmen, a dark-skinned fellow with a crooked smile, greeted Sonny when he reached the deck. Soon more of the men gathered around and laughed and pointed at Sonny's unusual outfit. One ruffled his hair. Then a shout went up, and the men turned quickly, parting so Ray was able to come up on the deck carrying Ina, who was wrapped in a blanket, her eyes bandaged shut.

"Mama!" Sonny exclaimed. Ina held out a hand to him. Her skin was still greyish and discolored from the oil she had landed in, her hair matted and wild. She looked a little scary, Sonny thought, but his heart nearly burst just to see her in his father's arms. He walked alongside his parents to the gangway, then looked up at the dock and realized it was lined with police cars and ambulances. An orderly waited beside a gurney at the end of the ramp.

The boats had docked right in town, where the Atchafalaya River met Morgan City's Front Street. Sonny felt a little dazed by the jarring change from rocking boat to hard pavement, from the steady hum of the shrimper to the buzz of traffic and voices all around him. A row of buildings across the street from the docks offered shopping and restaurants, while behind him a tug boat growled against a barge as it headed up the brown river under a scallop-shaped bridge. More shrimpers were tying up at the dock, discharging sailors in partial uniforms and covered by blankets. From one boat a man's body was grimly passed to people on the dock.

"Sonny! Mama! Dad!" A high-pitched voice called out to them. Sonny's head whipped around.

"Lucille!" Sonny saw his dad's eyes light up, his mother suddenly looking stronger, a tearful smile spreading across her face. Lucille was a distance away, getting into a car with a tall, dark-haired man who waved enthusiastically.

"Dad, can I go ride with Lucille?" Sonny asked.

Ray lifted Ina onto the waiting gurney. "No, son, just come with me; there are too many people milling around here. We can't lose you now. We'll see Lucille at the hospital, she's got Roy Sorli watching after her," he said.

"Aw, shucks," Sonny said.

"I heard that, young man," Ina admonished. "That language is not acceptable. Now do as your father says."

Sonny flushed, embarrassed that he'd upset his mother, but he'd heard far worse language on the raft just the day before. He thought about his brother Terry, wondering if he'd say "shucks" when he heard about the ship getting torpedoed. He wanted to ask if he could telephone Terry to tell him the story, but his dad was busy helping Ina get into an ambulance. Then Ray took Sonny's hand and led him to another waiting vehicle. Inside were the captain and Mr. Conyea. Ray hesitated outside the car, looking down at the men.

"Good morning, Mister Downs," said the captain very formally. He wore his soiled white coat with borrowed pants and he still had the binoculars around his neck. His face was a fiery red from sunburn, but he looked rested and composed. Mr. Conyea, by contrast, was exhausted and drawn, wearing a T-shirt and ill-fitting pants that Sonny realized must have been donated by the crew like his own garments.

"Captain, Mister Conyea," Ray said with a nod. He motioned for Sonny to ride in the back with the two men while he opened the front door and sat next to the driver.

On the brief ride to the hospital, Sonny gazed out the window at the lush greenery of Morgan City, the graceful, grey Spanish moss hanging from trees, the bright flowers that screamed at his eyes which had been numbed by the days of grey-on-blue he'd experienced at sea. He was excited to see cars and trucks and people again, knowing he never had to get on another ship if he didn't want to.

—◆—

The small hospital was bustling. Sonny was seated in a hallway outside a sterile examination room. Inside, behind the closed door, his mother and Lucille were alone quietly talking as Ina was waiting for a doctor to discuss her recovery.

Sonny didn't understand why he had to wait outside, and he fidgeted in his chair, anxious for the door to open. He spent the time watching nurses move quickly up and down the hallway, dressed in white uniforms from head to toe. Some of the *Heredia* sailors shuffled past in oil-soaked clothing, their arms and faces bright pink with sunburn; one still held a life jacket. Nuns in black habits flew past like blackbirds. One nurse leaned close to Sonny, took his temperature and listened to his heart, scribbling notes on a clipboard.

"Can I see my sister now?" he asked eagerly.

"Young man, you were in a very serious shipwreck," the nurse said as a grin crept across her face. "Are you sure you are well enough to visit?"

"Well, I am hungry," he admitted. "But we didn't know where Lucille was. She wasn't on the raft with Dad and me. And my mom, she was swimming by herself in the ocean. She got all covered with oil. It's in her eyes and her hair."

Sonny heard a familiar voice chirping from the examining room. "That's her, that's Lucille!" he said. The nurse nodded and smiled. Sonny bolted to the doorway and saw Lucille leaning close to their mother, telling her about waving down the shrimp boat with flags on a long piece of wood. Ina's eyes were bandaged but she was smiling, her hand stroking Lucille's hair.

The boy burst into the room and hugged Lucille, both of them crying and laughing at the same time, relieved to be together.

A couple of moments later, Ray stepped into the room, accompanied by a doctor in round spectacles. Ray suggested that the kids go to the cafeteria while he and Ina talked with the doctor.

A small cafeteria in the basement overflowed with hungry sailors, some sitting in the hallway outside. Their eyes brightened when they saw Sonny and Lucille, but the talk was subdued and smiles were rare. To Sonny, the food seemed endless, with glasses of milk, cups of juice, eggs and toast, grits and fruit salad. His stomach grumbled; he wanted to gobble all of it down.

"Not too much coffee now, you two," said a tall man with a mop of curly hair.

"Roy!" Lucille said. "We're so hungry we don't know where to begin. Remember what we talked about while we were floating? How we wanted chocolate cake and ice cream sundaes?"

Sonny recognized the handsome man as the officer, Mr. Sorli, but noticed his clothes were unkempt, his face red with sunburn, and arms laced with grotesque red welts as if he had been whipped. "Glad to see you're doing well," he said to Sonny. "Why don't you start with some toast and maybe juice, but don't eat too much at first," he warned. "You might get sick if you try to eat too much now. Get something and come sit with me."

When they returned to the table with a big plate of toast and jam, the sailor laughed. "That's a small serving of toast? You must be from Texas where everything is big," he joked.

"When we were on the raft, I found a banana in the water," Sonny said, remembering how he'd tried to hold on to the piece of green fruit, then lost it, then found it floating by again. He didn't think he'd ever eat a banana again.

Despite all of the people in the cafeteria, the room was relatively quiet. Some of the *Heredia* crewmembers were still dressed in ragtag uniforms, tattered and dirty. Others wore borrowed clothing like Sonny's, mismatched and too big or too small. Sonny looked around at the men who had been so friendly aboard the ship and knew something had changed with the ship sinking. Something about sitting there eating felt sad and lonely. Suddenly he wanted to be back with his mother and dad.

"Mama's covered in oil," Sonny said to Sorli. "It got in her eyes. Her skin is still blackish. She can't see much."

"But we can still talk to her, she's still Mama," said Lucille. "Let's take her some toast and jam. She'll be hungry too." Lucille wrapped some bread in a napkin.

Seeing the sailors triggered something in Sonny, and he fought to hold back tears. He remembered the shouts for help in the night from both crew and passengers, remembered not knowing if he'd ever see his mother again. His eyes welled up and his lip quivered. "I want to see Mama," he said quietly. Lucille took his hand and they walked down the hall.

When they reached the door of Ina's room, the doctor was gone, but they could hear Ray and Ina talking. Ina was speaking in a soothing voice about things working out, that the Lord had watched over them once, but Ray's voice was stern. "I should never have signed that paper," he said. "All of that work, all of our savings, gone with the ship."

When Sonny and Lucille entered the room, Ray turned to the window with his hands on his hips. The children noticed that one of Ina's eyes was now unbandaged.

"Betty Lucille, come here, I need a look at you," Ina said, turning her head oddly to see with one unbandaged eye. "Sonny, come around this side." The children crowded onto the edges of Ina's hospital bed so their mother could wrap her arms around them as Ray stood by quietly.

"The Good Lord was looking after all of us last night," Ina said.

"How long will we stay here?" Sonny asked.

"We don't know yet. Your dad has some business in New Orleans and I have to wait until the doctor says I can go," Ina said. "Then we'll head back to Gainesville to see Terry, Boy, and your grandparents."

Just then a man interrupted, tapping on the door before he stuck his head in. He wore a crisp tan uniform and carried a clipboard. He wanted to talk to Ray about the ship.

Before he left the room, Ray told Ina he'd try to make a telephone call to Gainesville so their family would know everyone was fine before any news about a shipwreck caused alarm.

Sonny asked his mom what the uniformed man wanted from his father, and Ina explained he was from the Navy, seeking information so other ships would not be torpedoed.

A couple of hours later, Ray returned. The children were curious about everything, but neither Ina nor Ray had the answers they sought. Had Mr. Beach survived the attack? How soon would Ina's eyes be clear? How long would they be at the hospital? How would they get home to Texas? The children didn't know that the same questions gnawed at Ina and Ray. The only question that was easy to answer was when Sonny asked if they would ever see the old family car again, which had been in the cargo hold of the *Heredia*. Ina smiled and asked Sonny to imagine the old Chevrolet with fish swimming around in it. She said they'd never have to change another tire on it again, and that actually seemed funny to Lucille, who was glad to be rid of the old car. It wasn't so funny to Sonny, however, when he made the connection between the sunken ship, the car, and so many other small items they'd left behind when they evacuated.

"My scooter!" Sonny wailed.

"Sonny, we can find you another scooter," Ina said. "What's important is that we're safe and sound."

"Roy and the other sailors said lots of people died. They're dead. The torpedoes killed them," Lucille said.

Ina explained to Sonny and Lucille that yes, some of the sailors they knew had died in the shipwreck, because they didn't make it out of the ship in time or were too badly hurt to survive. It was their first experience with death, and Sonny suddenly understood the quiet cafeteria, the subdued talk in the hospital. He also thought back to his father's frantic, almost hysterical desire to swim back to the sinking ship to find Ina and Lucille. He knew people were dying at that moment.

Ray, who had been silent up to now, took out a bag of clothes and shook out the contents at the foot of the bed. He held up a smock for Lucille and short pants and a shirt for Sonny, not new clothes but clean and in the right size, which was a welcome change for Sonny, who'd been holding up his oversized pants for hours. Ina told them to find a bathtub before they put the clean clothes on, and to be sure to scrub their hair to get all of the salt out of it. Then they could go back to the cafeteria for a little more food.

When the children left the room, Ina took a deep breath. She began to sob. The reality of the situation was sinking in. She felt she'd watched the children age in front of her eyes as they realized people had died, that they'd never see their scooter or old clothes again. It was a loss of innocence and completely out of her control to protect them from it. Crewmen who'd played checkers with them the day before were now dead.

Without saying a word, Ray understood her churning emotions and sat on the bed to embrace her. He told her her parents in Gainesville had received a reassuring telegram, and that United Fruit had been notified and would arrange a meeting.

"What did the Navy man tell you?" she asked. "It was awful, just awful."

"He said we can't share any details of the sinking yet. He just wanted to know what happened before and after the torpedo hit," Ray said. "I was asleep before, so I told him as best I know. If only they had let us off the ship in Corpus the other night."

"I wasn't asleep," Ina said. "Before it hit. I couldn't sleep. I had the most awful feeling, Ray, like I knew something was going to happen."

"We were the lucky ones, Ina," Ray said. "Our whole family made it. All of us. There were 62 people onboard that ship, and so far they've found just 27 alive. A few who were badly injured got picked up by that seaplane and taken to another hospital. Mr. Beach wasn't found. I can't believe he went back to his cabin when they were telling us to evacuate. A few sailors may still be out there, but the Navy doesn't think they'll pick up any more survivors. It's amazing that we survived. Someone was looking out for us."

Ray then announced that his decision to join the military was firm and nothing could change his mind. He explained how he'd seen the dead bodies in a room at the hospital, and the efforts to identify who was who.

A woman knocked on the door.

"Mrs. Guidry, come in," said Ray. "Ina, this is Louise Guidry, who lives nearby and has offered to help."

The woman was a tiny, olive-skinned Cajun with dark hair and bright eyes, who explained that the tiny hospital was so overwhelmed by injured *Heredia* survivors that most of the other patients had been sent home to make room for them. She added that she and others from Morgan City brought the sailors extra clothing from their families and were baking food too.

"We were so surprised to hear there was a family aboard," Louise cooed in her musical drawl. She said she would be happy to take the children during the day so Ina and Ray could rest. Then, noticing Ina's matted hair, the woman said she had something that would get the oil out of her hair. Within an hour, Louise was hovering over Ina with tubs of shampoo, scrubbing and rinsing the sticky oil from her hair as the women chatted about their families, and a lasting friendship was formed. Louise had a granddaughter whose dresses fit Lucille perfectly, and she was able to find Ray, Sonny, and Ina an extra change of clothes for their eventual trip home to Texas.

Ina confided to Louise her worries about Ray's appointment to discuss their lost savings with United Fruit lawyers. Their money had been locked securely in the ship's safe when the *Heredia* sank to the bottom. He'd signed a waiver of liability when they boarded the *Heredia*, acknowledging that the ship's safe passage was not guaranteed and releasing the company from responsibility for loss of life or possessions. But when they boarded the ship under the Costa Rican sun, the possibility of falling prey to a torpedo attack along the way—particularly in American waters—seemed as remote as thoughts of winter, yet the worst had come to pass. The family was now penniless and Ina partially disabled, relying on the kindness of strangers to put together even the most basic necessities such as clothing. While she didn't specify to Louise the amount that was lost, it had been an entire year's pay, which was the family's nest egg and prospect for a future home. They were starting from scratch again.

Four days after the rescue, the Navy ensign who had been in Morgan City to take survivors' statements allowed a newspaper reporter to visit the hospital. As soon as the reporter saw the Downs family, he knew he had struck gold for the front page: Sonny and Lucille were dimpled and smiling, Ray a hulking protector. The story of the family's survival and photos of them smiling from the hospital room raced through papers in the region that were hungry for positive news. When interviewed separately, everyone from the *Heredia* praised Lucille and Sonny for their behavior during the ordeal, and Ray and Ina were quick to publicly credit Roy Sorli with Lucille's safe return.

Underscoring the Downses' incredible night at sea and improbable reunion were the names and addresses of many Louisiana natives from the *Heredia* who never made it home alive, including a "negro mess boy" named Clifton Sayas and chief radio operator Roger Fontana, who had been at sea about six years, according to his wife. Others, like ship's oiler Ramon Barbeito, would go home to New York City without his two friends and fellow *Heredia* sailors who were killed, Luis Gomez and Jose Rege, and with whom he shared an apartment.

In Fort Worth, Texas, Ina's brother J. R. Evans picked up the Sunday paper six days after the torpedoing to find a familiar family smiling back at him. He sent a telegram to the hospital that read: "All of us are thinking of you every minute when ready I will come after you if need be. If we can do anything let us know. Let us hear as soon as possible. Love JR."

Ina's father, John Evans, also saw the picture, and things started to make sense to him. He had been confused by a telegram he received a few days earlier that said the family was simply spending a week in a Morgan City hotel before returning to see Terry. The newspaper photo sent a shockwave through his body, and he immediately resolved to hear Ina's voice to get to the bottom of it. He telephoned the Morgan City hospital, but was only allowed to speak to Ray after the Navy ensign assigned to controlling the release of information had confirmed his identity. Mr. Evans was warned of repercussions if any secret details of the attack were discussed, as the Navy was still trying to squelch rumors and control information about U-boat activity despite civilian involvement.

Ray assured his father-in-law that everyone was fine and Ina's eye treatments were progressing well, as sight was being restored to her right eye. She was still seeing double from her right eye, while her left remained blinded by the oil and of concern to the doctors, who urged rest and provided therapeutic rinses multiple times a day.

When Roy Sorli was allowed to call his fiancée Heddy in a Boston suburb, his delivery of the news was subtle as he hoped to quell her fears about his safety. "Well," he said, "I seem to have lost my boat." She never allowed him to go to sea again.

On Monday, May 25, a photo of the Downses was front and center in the New Orleans *Times-Picayune*, the children smiling on either side of Ina, who had one eye bandaged, and Ray behind them, his arms draped protectively around his family. The perky family photo offset other headlines on the page that blared war news: a successful Russian counter-offensive against the Germans, a possible American warship sunk by an Italian submarine off Brazil, a Japanese plane smashing into an American ship.

Lucille's story about sharks tickling her feet caught the imagination of many copyeditors, who played up the peculiar anecdote as the wire story was used by one newspaper after another. But the story brought sadness to many households whose family members didn't have happy stories to tell, and Ina was eventually the recipient of several letters sent to her in care of the Morgan City hospital by wives and mothers of the dead.

Mr. Beach's wife was one who wrote to Ina and asked about her husband's last days.

"What do I tell her?" Ina asked Ray. "Should I say we told him not to go back to his cabin when the ship was sinking?"

Ray had no response. His mind was on the year's worth of work he had done yet had nothing to show for. The meetings with United Fruit were not promising: it seemed unlikely that the family would receive any compensation for their losses.

Soon another letter arrived at the hospital, addressed to Ina. It was from the mother of one of the sailors, the very young man on the Navy gun crew, Frankie Platts, who didn't seem much older than the children. She said her husband was dead and this boy was all she had left. The son had begged his mother to sign his papers, allowing him to join the Navy before he turned eighteen; and when she finally agreed, this is what happened to him. It was written by her neighbor, as the mother was described as being in a fragile state mentally and emotionally.

Despite her own shock and efforts to regain a little strength each day, Ina found the words to comfort the bereaved women, feeling it was part of giving thanks that her own family had been spared. To Mrs. Beach she wrote, "You were in his thoughts to the very end," a kind way of acknowledging that his return to his cabin was likely retrieving the treasures he'd bought for his family.

To the distraught mother of the Navy crewman Frankie Platts, she summoned a sunny image, writing, "Your son was wonderful to my children. He was a happy young man who played shuffleboard with them on deck when he was off-duty and never missed an opportunity to smile and pass the time. We've been told he did not suffer at the end but was, unfortunately like so many others, standing duty on a part of the ship that took a direct hit. I hope you find some comfort knowing that he brought happiness to others right up to the very end." In truth, Ina did not know how the boy died. She even wondered if he was the young sailor holding on to the plank whose modesty about being naked in front of Ina made him stay in the water. Ina couldn't be sure, because her vision was so blurred by oil at that time.

Three days later Ina received a reply, again written by the neighbor of Frankie Platts's bereaved mother. "Your words brought her [Mrs. Platts] closer to her son Frankie in his last days and hours and somewhat allayed her worst fears for his last moments. This mother and son's whole lives were centered in each other and this loss of one to the other has been a crushing, staggering blow. Your letter, which has given Mrs. Platts such comfort, has been in her hands or close to her person since she received it."

Ina also wrote to Roy Sorli's fiancée to ensure that she knew how much the Downs family appreciated his caring for Lucille through the horrible ordeal. Lucille's stories of his humor and kindness, of allowing her to float atop the wreckage while he was stung by jellyfish and threatened by sharks for many hours, touched them deeply and the two women started a correspondence that lasted for decades.

⁓

The mix of shock and elation receded after two weeks in the hospital. Sonny and Lucille were well fed and entertained by Louise Guidry, allowing Ina to rest and recover. The duo knew the route to Louise's house and covered it eagerly each time they were invited to sample some of her fragrant dinners of étouffée and "snacks" of po'boy sandwiches on crusty bread. She admonished them about getting lost in Morgan City, noting it was bayou country where the legendary Rugaru, a werewolf-like creature, roamed, looking for its next victims. Then she'd laugh and hug them close like they were her own children, sending them back to Ina and Ray with a sack of extra food.

Soon it was time for the family to move forward again. Ray and Ina had to reassemble their life, beginning with a train ride back to San Antonio and then to Gainesville to get Terry. They left the hospital with only the clothes they were wearing and the generous charity of the people from Morgan City. They bade an appreciative good-bye to the hospital staff and Louise, promising to write when they got to Texas. But Ray still had the U-boat on his mind, and Texas wouldn't be their last stop.

CHAPTER TWENTY

THE *LACONIA*:
A SINKING AND
A RESCUE

*"They felt very comfortable on board, though an excited woman
had first asked quite anxiously whether they would now be killed."*
—Erich Würdemann reporting
on survivors of the *Laconia*

Erich Würdemann and U-506 were sent back out to sea on July 28, 1942, just five weeks after their return to Lorient. Harro Schacht on U-507 had been sent out three weeks earlier. Both U-boats were on lengthy patrols of just over 100 days, but the number of ships each sank was less than their prior mission to the Gulf of Mexico. Würdemann conducted his hunting off the coast of Africa near Sierra Leone and Liberia, and sank five ships, while Schacht was sent to the waters of South America where he became the grim reaper of Brazilian souls.

Brazil was considered technically neutral—but the country had allowed the U.S. to base forces on its soil and Brazilian air defenses had attacked German U-boats prior to Schacht's arrival. The Brazilians didn't know that Dönitz and Hitler had planned a wide-scale U-boat assault on the country that summer, another Operation Drumbeat of sorts, but it was scrapped out of concern that they'd provoke all neutral South American countries by doing so. Dönitz, however, convinced Berlin that sending one U-boat, U-507, with explicit instructions to sink only Brazilian ships while carefully avoiding Argentine and Chilean vessels, made strategic sense. Schacht was only too happy to comply, knowing a surprise attack would likely find the ships unescorted and unarmed.

The first ship Schacht sank was the neutral Brazilian steam merchant *Baependy*, which resulted in a horrific 270 deaths of passengers and crew. U-507 continued the carnage over the next three days and sank five more Brazilian ships, extending the loss of life to over 500 casualties. The Brazilian government declared war on Germany almost immediately. One has to wonder in hindsight if the quick sinking of six Brazilian ships, adding 15,000 more tons to Dönitz's tonnage plan, was worth drawing another country into the war against Germany.

While Schacht's one-U-boat lightning strike against Brazil is noteworthy, what happened next—"The *Laconia* Incident," which involved both himself and Würdemann—was truly unusual. In this dire twist of war, three U-boats each ended up with over 200 survivors aboard in an attempt to save lives imperiled by a terrible mistake at sea. It was also an incident that would entwine U-boat captains Würdemann and Schacht posthumously in the postwar trial of Großadmiral Dönitz. [Dönitz became a full Admiral on 14 March 1942 and Großadmiral on 30 January 1943. This was his rank at the time of the Nuremberg trials.]

Part of the story is told through the eyes of a child, similar to Sonny's experience on the *Heredia*.

Five-year-old June Stoneman had been in Singapore with her mother, Ena, and had just been reunited with her Royal Air Force sergeant father,

George, in Durban, South Africa. They were happy to be together, headed home to Plymouth, England after her father's duty in the South Pacific, and the Cunard White Star Line's *Laconia* was a welcome form of transportation, as there were other children to play with and plenty of RAF aboard. While voyaging from South Africa to Great Britain, unescorted by warships, the passengers practiced lifeboat drills daily and carried life preservers with them to dinner. Yet they fell into a predictably complacent rhythm of socializing, paying little attention to the zigzag course the captain steered as the trip went on. The more than 3,000 souls onboard were steaming directly into the crosshairs of a waiting U-boat.

September 11, 1942 began as a routine day for U-156, which was under the command of thirty-two-year-old Werner Hartenstein, patrolling the Atlantic off West Africa. Then smoke from a steamer was sighted in the distance. He estimated it was an old passenger freighter, about 140 meters long and 7,000 GRT. U-156 shadowed its prey until September 12, when it came within firing range as darkness fell.

It took three minutes for two torpedoes to travel from the U-boat into the belly of the steamer, about 2,000 meters away. The ship immediately stopped, its bow settling lower in the water, and life rafts were launched. A radio transmission of "SSS" was heard, giving its name and location, and Hartenstein knew he had hit the *Laconia*.

When the torpedoes hit the ship, June Stoneman had just been put to bed and her parents were dressing for a dance. The lights went out and George grabbed Ena and June by the hands, taking them into the chaos of the ship's passageways. Water was streaming down the hallways, many of which were blocked by debris and passengers attempting to flee. Ena worked hard to keep up with George's long strides to the upper decks where lifeboats were being launched; he carried June through the *Laconia*. Unfortunately, the boat's listing to one side meant that some life boats were uselessly pinned to the side of the ship, making it nearly impossible to free them from the davits that held them above the water. On the other side, the life boats began to hang away from the ship, making it difficult for passengers to climb aboard. One was filled with people, only to tumble against the ship during its launch, dumping its human cargo into the churning ocean.

George deposited June and Ena in one lifeboat and promised to find them after he helped others to safety. As the boat drifted away from the sinking *Laconia* and the water filled with struggling survivors, Ena worried that she'd never see her husband again. But he soon reappeared, having randomly chosen their boat to swim to when it was time to save himself.

As U-156 circled the sinking craft to get a better look, possibly to identify and take the captain prisoner, Italian voices were heard. Hartenstein, the German U-boat commander, was distressed to learn the ship was carrying Italian POW's, allies of the Germans. They were headed for a camp in Great Britain, guarded aboard the *Laconia* by Polish and British troops. Also onboard were dozens of civilian passengers, including women and children like Ena and June Stoneman.

Hartenstein immediately sent the following message to Headquarters: "Sinking by Hartenstein of British *Laconia* in naval square FF 7721 310, unfortunately with 1,500 Italian prisoners. Up to now 90 fished out . . . request orders." Hartenstein, up on the bridge, then watched the *Laconia* disappear below the waves. All was chaos on the surface as passengers swam for rafts, pleading for help and shouting for family members. And it would get worse.

A couple of hours later, in the early morning hours of September 13, Hartenstein's predicament was made clear with another transmission to BdU headquarters: "U-Boat is in debris field full of Italians, cannot help further, have taken 193 on board, this is the extreme limit for prolonged submerging." Headquarters responded with a request for more information, including whether or not the shipwrecked were floating in boats or swimming in the ocean.

In fact, the ocean near U-156 was a scene from hell, with more than 1,000 people floating individually in life jackets and on overloaded rafts and larger lifeboats. Those who weren't able to secure a life vest as they fled the ship were trying to stay afloat on pieces of debris or even by clinging to floating corpses. Many had been injured trying to exit the sinking ship, and some Italian prisoners were bayoneted by guards while trying to escape the *Laconia*, the blood in the water attracting sharks and barracudas that tore at legs dangling below the surface.

Hartenstein's U-boat was overloaded with bodies, having tripled the size of the normal crew contingent in an attempt to save lives and take prisoners (twenty-one of those taken aboard immediately were British). U-156's radio picked up a signal from a ship nearby, so the commander sent the following radio message on open channels, taking the extraordinary step of disclosing his location in order to get help for the shipwreck victims: "If any ship will assist the shipwrecked *Laconia* crew, I will not attack her, providing I am not attacked by ship or air force. I picked up 193 men. German submarine."

Hartenstein requested "diplomatic neutralization" of the area to rescue survivors. It was a completely unforeseen request that threw his superiors into an uproar.

At his Paris headquarters, Dönitz was besieged. Most of his aides saw the situation as a clear-cut act of war and were adamant that Hartenstein should abandon all rescue attempts. The admiral wavered on the matter: he knew that ordering Hartenstein to cast off all of the refugees would demoralize the U-boat crew as well as complicating German-Italian relations, so he weighed his options carefully. He ultimately sided with Hartenstein's decision to aid the survivors, knowing he was risking an attack on U-156 by Allied bombers. The situation would be revisited and scrutinized in Dönitz's post-war trial at Nuremberg, the *Laconia* incident becoming an international benchmark for wartime decision-making about humane treatment of the enemy.

Hitler, then directly overseeing the war front in Stalingrad, Russia, was informed of the situation, and, according to Dönitz's memoirs, the Führer demanded that usual U-boat functions not be compromised by efforts to rescue survivors.

BdU headquarters sent a request to an Italian submarine, as well as orders to U-506 and U-507, commanded by Würdemann and Schacht, to hasten to the scene. None was able to offer immediate assistance, as they were some 700 miles away, about two days away if traveling at top speeds. Until they arrived, Hartenstein's U-156 was in an unusual and precarious position.

The Stonemans found themselves aboard Lifeboat 14, adrift far from the wreckage and the U-boat with no other lifeboats in sight. They suffered searing heat during the day and cold temperatures at night, wearing only what they had on at the moment the first torpedo hit: George was in undershorts but had grabbed a coat; Ena wore a party dress, and June was in pajamas. Supplies aboard the boat had been contaminated, so they went without food or water and were vulnerable to the elements.

Hartenstein's crew worked around the clock in the debris field, at first moving 31 refugees whom he treated out of his U-boat and back to life rafts in order to make room for more that needed treatment. His crew worked diligently through September 13, providing emergency medical care, balancing lifeboat loads and re-provisioning them. Hundreds wearing life preservers mobbed the hull of the U-boat like migrant birds clustered on the only rock protruding from the ocean.

The Italian prisoners told the German sailors that as the *Laconia* sank, British and Polish guards attempted to seal them in water-tight bulkheads belowdecks and kept the Italians from boarding life rafts at gunpoint. About a third of the prisoners overpowered their captors, broke out, and made it off the *Laconia* before the ship settled on the bottom. Yet their ordeal wasn't over.

As dawn broke on September 14, Headquarters repeated that U-boats should only take a limited number of refugees onboard, ensuring that the U-boat would be able to fully function and submerge. After all, the location of the wreck had been widely broadcast on open channels, from both the *Laconia*'s distress signal and Hartenstein's frantic offer of truce to any who helped in the rescue. The worst-case scenario, of course, was that Schacht's or Würdemann's arrival would provide a prime opportunity for an Allied destroyer or bomber to sink more than one U-boat and potentially scuttle scores of Italian soldiers at the same time. Hartenstein and U-156 remained at the scene another day, swarmed by desperate survivors and more nervous by the minute.

Early on September 15, headquarters had news that Vichy French ships were en route, including a cruiser departing from Dakar. Instructions included firing recognition flares and floodlight signals as they approached so U-156 and others would not mistake them for enemy ships.

Soon Würdemann and U-506 met Hartenstein at a secret location away from the wreck site. Survivors were desperate after several days on tiny rations of food and water as not all had been re-provisioned by U-156. Würdemann's U-506 took 132 Italians on board, while Hartenstein's U-156 retained dozens of *Laconia* passengers and crewmembers. U-boat crewmen on U-506 were delighted by British children suddenly playing among them, and they were solicitous to the women aboard, offering cream to soothe sunburn and pot after pot of hot soup to nourish them.

U-156 became a hospital ship of sorts. On its way back to the site of the sinking, it aided a swamped life raft by allowing more exhausted Italians and British refugees aboard. A line secured the foundering life raft to the U-boat so it could be towed back to the massive group of struggling survivors, repaired, and used again. Two more life rafts of survivors were sighted and visited, with U-156 providing them water. They redistributed survivors into the empty life raft, strung them along behind the submarine, and set off again, like a mother duck and her ducklings.

One British woman wrote with astonishment about her U-boat experience after returning home. "The Germans treated us with great kindness and respect the whole time; they were really sorry for our plight," said Nursing Sister Doris Hawkins, who had served in Palestine. "The commandant was particularly charming and helpful; he could scarcely have done more had he been entertaining us in peacetime."

On September 16, Hartenstein returned to the flotilla of drifting life boats again, assisting and feeding survivors out of the crew's provisions, waiting for the French ships to arrive for a complete evacuation.

Then a plane flew overhead. It was a B-24 Liberator, an American heavy bomber.

Hartenstein had previously draped a sheet with a red cross sewn on it across the bow of U-156. He and others on the scene believed it would be obvious they were involved in a humanitarian effort because of the red cross and because the surfaced sub's deck was crowded by survivors with life rafts trailing off the stern. But the commanders at the American base on nearby Ascension Island didn't agree. They ordered the pilot to sink the submarine.

As the plane circled above, a British officer on board U-156 volunteered to signal the aircraft with his identity and information to clarify the situation. The aircraft did not respond; instead, it dropped depth charges, prompting Hartenstein to cut the ropes to the life rafts, eject all shipwreck survivors who were recuperating inside, and abandon his rescue effort in order to save his submarine. The plane returned and dropped more bombs. The periscope was damaged and incoming seawater caused the batteries to emit noxious gases. As U-156 dove, more depth charges exploded around the sub, wrecking more components.

Survivors who were being kept alive by the U-boat were again thrown into peril. Life rafts full of survivors were blown out of the water by the depth charges, and the people were left to their own devices for survival. Hartenstein was forced to abandon the people in the water for several hours, retreating to repair his vessel and ensure it was still fully functional before returning to the survivors.

The incident sparked another sharp debate among those in German naval headquarters, according to Dönitz's memoir. "After this attack on U-156 from the service point of view, it would have been correct for me to abandon all rescue work," he wrote. "There was a very heated discussion at my headquarters during which some of my officers argued, very rightly, that any further attempts at rescue would be wholly unjustifiable. But once I had set my hand to the task I could not bring myself to abandon it and I put an end to the discussion with the words, 'I cannot put those people into the water. I shall carry on.'"

Still, Headquarters was extremely nervous about another attack. "Do not set red cross flags," a message warned. "In no case, at least with the English, has it offered proven protection."

On September 15, Schacht on U-507 was approaching the scene of the *Laconia* sinking, picking up survivors in drifting life boats. Each was documented, and the Italians permitted to relax in the available space inside the U-boat. As they traveled, the Italians told German submariners that they'd been treated badly aboard *Laconia*, including rations of just bread and water. Many of the Italians were emaciated and barely clothed, so the Germans shared what they had aboard to feed and cover them. Soon U-507 trailed a series of jam-packed life rafts from its stern and there were over 150 people aboard the sub.

Schacht continued his rescue into the night and the next day, picking up survivors and treating them, then redistributing bodies more evenly and replenishing their supplies from the U-boat stores. By evening, he had seven life boats in tow and had arrived at the rendezvous point where French boats were to pick up survivors.

When Schacht found Lifeboat 14 drifting alone on the sea, June and Ena Stoneman were among the women and children taken aboard, while George was left in the lifeboat. The women were shown a bunk near the torpedo room, and a sailor who accompanied them handed June a chocolate bar, even holding her on his lap while she ate it and drank a cup of milk, her mother later said.

"In the middle of the night I woke up and saw that June was talking to the German," recalled Ena Stoneman. "He was trying to understand what she was saying. And would you believe, she was trying to tell him she was thirsty and wanted a glass of water. I made him understand. He smiled, went off and came back with the water. Just like any dad getting up in the middle of the night."

"When we awoke in the morning, we got a big breakfast of semolina and some of the sailors took off their heavy socks and gave them to the children. There was quite a festive atmosphere aboard the boat. I think it was because most of the Germans had been away from home for so long and many of them were ordinary family men. They missed their own kids and they were spoiling ours. One sailor—the one whose bunk we used—showed us a picture of his wife and children and looked at it quite longingly."

Schacht gleaned considerable information about the *Laconia* from the ship's navigator, a British seaman named Buckingham. The navigator said the steamer had been used to transport troops to South Africa, then picked up freight and 1,800 Italian prisoners of war, 160 Polish prisoners from Russia who acted as guards, 463 crewmen, 268 military personnel on leave, and 80 women and children, for a total of more than 3,000 souls. The torpedoes had hit the prisoner rooms belowdecks, immediately killing many of the Italians held there.

"The Italians look quite starved," Schacht recorded. "They had recently received only bread and water, according to information from the Englishman, as a punishment because of theft in the mail room and fruit stowage as well as infringement of the prohibition of smoking on the *Laconia*. Clothes were very bad, for the most part prisoner clothing. Many nearly unclothed or naked."

During the rescue, Schacht picked up 16 children, 15 women, and 129 Italian POW's, who all shared German rations in the teeming U-boat. Another 330 *Laconia* survivors in rafts and lifeboats were towed behind U-507.

Würdemann on U-506 reported having 132 aboard, all Italians, and four boats in tow with another 250 survivors in them. Würdemann wrote a long summary of the adventure in his log without a hint of wartime animosity for the British refugees: "The women and children came from Malta and Cairo and were dependents of colonial officials and soldiers," Würdemann noted. "They felt very comfortable on board, though an excited woman had first asked quite anxiously whether they would now be killed. Another woman said at parting she wanted to highlight the helpful attitude of the German U-boats in Churchill circles for which they would have good relations."

German Headquarters continued to worry about the U-boats' preparedness should hostile planes appear again. "Boats must be ready to crash-dive at any time and be fully capable of operating submerged," read another dispatch from BdU. "Deliver the rescued to lifeboats. Keep only Italians on board, go to the meeting place . . . and deliver them to the French. Beware of hostile action by aircraft and submarines."

And they were right in repeating the admonition: a day after Hartenstein's U-156 was depth-charged by the Liberator, another plane from Ascension Island flew over, perhaps in order to locate shipwreck survivors and direct British ships to rescue them. Instead he found Würdemann's U-506 with rafts in tow, assisting hundreds of survivors. Proving that the first attack was not a mistake, this bomber also tried to sink the U-boat, but Würdemann's crew was able to cut the rafts free and dive—with more than 100 refugees aboard—before the plane was close enough to do any damage.

Schacht, anticipating an air attack, took the precaution of reducing the number of survivors on his deck and inside the sub so that he could submerge quickly. Among those he sent back into the lifeboats were the Stonemans. "The lifeboats," wrote Schacht, "were equipped all so well that after removal of the Italian personnel it is highly likely that all would have reached the coast." The commander instructed those in the lifeboats to stay together and remain where they were so the rescue ships could find them.

By midday on September 17, the ordeal was over with the arrival of the French ships *Gloire* and *Anamite*. All shipwrecked survivors onboard the three subs were turned over to the Vichy French.

As a result of the near-sinking of his U-boats during the rescue, Admiral Dönitz issued an order that in the future, U-boats should never assist the shipwrecked, and this became fodder for the Nuremberg trials.

———

Even after the *Laconia* survivors were safely aboard the two French ships, the ordeal wasn't over for the Stonemans. The family was delivered to the Vichy French in Casablanca, where June and Ena were separated from George. In a camp called Sidi El Ayachia, the women lived two months in mud huts on the edge of the desert, suffering daily from the heat, lice infestations, and dysentery. After the Allied invasion of Africa, June and Ena were able to leave aboard a hospital ship and reunite with George at home in time for Christmas 1942.

In an interview decades later, Ena said of the German U-boatmen: "I will never forget them. Even to this day, even though the war went on for three more years when we got home, I still think of those Germans with fondness and gratitude. I look at it this way: without their help out on that ocean, we would have died."

CHAPTER TWENTY-ONE

SPIES, DUTY, AND THE TURNING OF THE BATTLE TIDE

"She'll carry a good load. She isn't much to look at, though, is she? A real ugly duckling."

—President Roosevelt, upon viewing
the blueprints for Liberty ships

W hen Ina's treatment at the Morgan City hospital was complete, she still couldn't see out of her left eye, but the doctors had done all they could. The family returned to San Antonio with only a new set of clothes and train tickets. It was all the family received from Ray's employer, United Fruit Company, after all of their possessions and savings went to the bottom of the Gulf with the *Heredia*. Despite Ray having several meetings with company representatives regarding compensation, they would not budge. He had signed a waiver releasing the company from liability when they boarded the ship, and they held him to it. The Downses had to be content to escape with their lives, and try to rebuild the savings and possessions that were lost.

Ray's resolve to join the service and do his part fighting the foes of the United States was strong before he left Costa Rica, but it was galvanized by the torpedoing of the *Heredia*. Once his family was safely back on land, he immediately sought to enlist in the Marines. Despite his youthful vigor and excellent physical condition, his age was a factor: at thirty-seven, he was near the upper age limit of candidates any branch would take.

Indeed, the Marine Corps turned him down. But the Navy's Coast Guard needed many hands on deck after the tremendous shipping losses of early 1942 and fears that U-boats could be transferring spies and saboteurs to the U.S. The few ships they had couldn't cover a thousand miles of coastline, so shore patrols were instituted, adding thousands of civilians with dogs and on horseback, ensuring nearly constant surveillance.

In June, the Navy put out the word that owners of small working boats and pleasure craft were needed to assist with the Coast Guard's near shore patrols. While 1,200 boat owners had already enlisted, another 1,000 were requested for this temporary reserve force, and the Navy planned to equip each with "radio, armament and anti-submarine devices." (On Cuba, author Ernest Hemingway had a similar idea. He had his private yacht outfitted with 50-mm guns and sought to hunt down U-boats the way he had once hunted big game in Africa—but he only spotted one that summer, and it was too far away to fire on.)

Ray was accepted by the Coast Guard in September 1942, just months before policies changed to using Selective Service only and establishing thirty-eight as the upper age limit for servicemen without specialized skills. Some of the limits were established because the War Manpower Commission was concerned that skilled workers would be drained from essential war industries. Ray's mechanical skills could have earned him a bigger paycheck in the private sector, but he was fixated on settling his score with the U-boats that had nearly killed his family.

Many citizens like Ray volunteered for the military after the American losses at Pearl Harbor and stories of Nazi atrocities began circulating. The country had been on the doorstep of war since Germany's invasion of France in 1940, but in the aftermath of Pearl Harbor, the armed services swelled from just over 450,000 servicemen in 1941 to 3.9 million by the end of 1942. That number would leap again, to over 9.1 million by 1943, and to over 12 million by 1945. The Coast Guard's strength rose from 19,235 members in 1941 to 171,192 in 1945.

According to Rutgers University's Eagleton Institute, "appropriations for the Army grew from about $500 million in 1939 to over $8 billion in 1940 and $26 billion in 1941. The Naval Expansion Act signed in June 1940 authorized the construction of new battleships, aircraft carriers, destroyers, and aircraft. After the Japanese attack, the President announced goals to produce 60,000 airplanes in 1942 and 125,000 more in 1943 and 120,000 tanks over the 1942–43 period."

Dim-outs and curfew requirements in most coastal cities put Americans' ignorance of the U-boat threat to rest, but the severity of the offshore war was still obscured by the media's conflicting reports. The same day in July 1942 when 24 sailors shipwrecked by U-boat action washed ashore in British Guyana after seven days adrift and another 27 survivors of two ships simultaneously torpedoed swam to Key West, a dispatch in the *New York Times* declared that the tide of the war was turning against U-boats. The article cited improved coastal patrols, convoys, and submarine-hunting technology. At that time more than a half-dozen U-boats roamed the Gulf of Mexico, still picking off unescorted ships.

Not all newspapers supported the government's actions. An opinion piece published in the New Orleans *Times-Picayune* picked apart a White House statement that building more ships was the answer to the "shipping problem," noting that the statement's euphemisms avoided mentioning the loss of precious lives. The author, Walter Lippmann, argued that the problem was getting worse, pleading that young officers should be put in charge of ensuring protection for merchant ships, using any craft available, as had proven effective in World War I. "While we wait for the delivery of enough orthodox combat ships to master the submarines, it would be reassuring if something of the same sort were at least being attempted," he wrote.

In mid-1942, Admiral Dönitz redirected U-boats from America's East Coast to redouble efforts hunting convoys between North America and Great Britain with great success, leading many in Britain to wonder about the possibility of starvation due to food shortages. Production allowed the Germans to keep an average of over 100 U-boats active every day while American shipbuilders could not keep up with the number of freighters, tankers, and passenger ships needed to replace those sunk during what the Germans called "The Second Happy Time" due to so many successful torpedoings.

By late 1942, however, the Allies were slowly gaining the upper hand, in both sending more ships to sea and the fight against U-boats. The mass production of American Liberty ships certainly helped: at the height of the war they were ready to sail approximately 42 days from the moment a keel was laid. "I think this ship will do us very well," said President Franklin Delano Roosevelt when viewing the blueprints for the ships. "She'll carry a good load. She isn't much to look at, though, is she? A real ugly duckling." With that, the nickname "ugly duckling" stuck to the quickly assembled ships.

The advances in seaborne war technology were impressive on both sides, particularly the Allies', but the full effects would still take months to be felt. The World War I-era sonar used by ships to detect submarines, called ASDIC, had been vastly improved, but it was closely matched by the Germans' Metox, a receiver on submarines capable of detecting airplane radar, often giving the submarine time to dive before the aircraft was sighted. German crews were at first elated when radar was installed on a handful of U-boats in the second half of 1942, but their excitement was tempered when they realized its limitations. The radar was fixed and forward-looking, so crews were forced to navigate in a circle to determine what was showing up on their radar as well as securing an estimate of the object's speed and direction of travel. Near the end of the war, the Germans also developed a "snorkel" device that allowed the use of the submarines' diesel engines while submerged. The snorkel protruded out of the water like a periscope to allow fresh air to enter the vessel to offset the noxious fumes of the diesel. Unfortunately for the Germans, the device was still in its rudimentary stages and came too late in the war to make a significant difference.

None of these German technologies matched the power of just a few employed widely by the Allies, including HF/DF (called "huff-duff") that tracked U-boats by their radio transmissions. Germans were unaware of this technology, so they didn't change their liberal use of radio transmissions to avoid detection. Two additional Allied inventions also helped greatly: one was a device that found submerged subs by magnetic fields, and the other was an acoustic torpedo that followed the sound of propellers to their targets. Equally important was that the American-made Consolidated B-24 Liberator heavy bomber had a range of nearly 800 miles that closed gaps in previously unreachable portions of the ocean, allowing U-boats little of the protection they had once enjoyed and forcing them to submerge more frequently and for longer periods. On ships, a new bow-mounted anti-submarine mortar quickly proved to be more deadly than depth charges as they detonated upon contact with a submarine's hull. Also, British agents working in the country's top secret Room 40 in Bletchley Park had cracked the Enigma code and were thereafter able to quickly adjust to new code combinations, allowing the Allies an advantage in reading encrypted German orders to U-boats and other forces.

The combination of these advances was evidenced by the number of U-boats sunk, which climbed from 86 lost in 1942 to 243 lost in 1943. In May 1943 alone, Allies using new technology and refined convoy tactics sank 41 U-boats. Once lost, the skilled U-boat commanders and experienced crews were harder and harder to replace. The psychological edge the Allies claimed is more challenging to quantify than hard numbers. U-boat commanders repeatedly heard their peers radioing emergencies due to attacks; they began to have difficulty meeting with milk cows for refueling because they had to take evasive action more frequently; and fewer of their comrades in arms returned to the U-boat bunkers to celebrate victorious missions. The once-dominant U-boat crewmen no longer had the upper hand at sea.

Ray reported for duty at the plush former Ponce de Leon hotel in St. Augustine, Florida, which was converted for Coast Guard training. While his resolve to serve was just as strong as any soldier's, he was fortunate to get turned down by the Marines and therefore able to fulfill his service close to his family. His rank was Fireman First Class, with duties including operation and maintenance of boat engines, which earned his growing family a meager $213 per month including dependent and housing allowances. Other less-skilled Coast Guard enlistees were paid as little as $78 a month.

Built by industrial magnate Henry Flagler in the 1880s, the grand Ponce de Leon hotel towered over a rustic Spanish coastal fort and wasn't far from a miles-long stretch of white-sand beach. Presidents and celebrities had once been guests; but in 1942, instead of a bell captain in the portico offering to open doors for well-dressed couples, guards demanded identification from any non-uniformed visitor. The concierge desk was taken over by the Officer of the Day; the plush rugs, oil paintings, and lavish furnishings had been removed and steel furnishings installed to enable essential military functions like processing recruits, medical checkups, and issuing uniforms. More than 2,000 Coast Guardsmen entered the service through this facility, the windows of its fancy salons blocked to enable showing training films and the guest suites now bunking several seamen each. Here Ray learned to identify stealthy U-boats by their phosphorescent wake and the particulars of boat-engine repair. More importantly, he was able to channel his anger over the sinking of the *Heredia* into productive work.

While he trained in Florida, Ina and the children prepared for another new home. They had been staying with her uncle and aunt, Victor and Beulah Hill, in San Antonio. As arrangements were made for another Chevy that would take them across the Gulf States, they packed up the kitchen utensils, towels, and other necessities provided by generous friends and family. They had little to start with but looked upon the move as another adventure, even as the reality of their situation continued to sink in, such as when Terry asked his mother where his paint set was.

"I'm sorry, son, it was on the ship with everything else," she answered.

Their rented home was among modest bungalows on Oneida Street, a neighborhood between the Matanzas and San Sebastian rivers, just a few blocks from the Ponce de Leon where Ray trained. It was just across a bridge from the lighthouse, his eventual permanent duty station, where he was assigned to a PT (Patrol Torpedo Boat) patrol.

The three-bedroom home had the right amount of space for the family, and Ina immediately sought approval from the landlord to dig up a patch of grass and plant a victory garden. Terry found a job as a soda jerk and Lucille, now twelve, began babysitting. Everyone pitched in to ease the family's financial burden, which was their way of sharing their father's sense of duty. Sonny was taught to run laundry through the wringer on the home's old washing machine, and to wipe down the clotheslines before hanging the family's shirts and pants out to dry. He also hoed the weeds in the garden and helped Ina sterilize canning jars when it was time to put up the vegetables they'd grown.

When school started, Sonny was a little shy. Old enough to understand that he was the odd man out, he squirmed when the teacher introduced him to his new third-grade classmates, explaining he was from Texas.

"You're from Texas? Are you a cowboy?" one boy sneered. The label stuck, branding him as "cowboy" around school and making Sonny feel stigmatized. He began to crave the time he had with Terry and his Dad on weekends, which usually revolved around playing sports. It would turn out to be an investment in time that paid dividends later in life.

The monthly pay of an enlisted man didn't go far with three growing children to feed, particularly as Ina was unable to work full-time as a seamstress until her eyes had completely healed. Yet she took on the challenge of scrimping and saving while rebuilding their nest egg, and that became her work. She figured out the government's newly instituted ration system that allowed each household limited quantities of goods—from car tires to sugar and shoes—and sought to rebuild their stock of basic necessities that had been lost in the ship's sinking.

"You're spending too much money on food," the children heard Ray say one night.

"Well, we can't just do without it," Ina responded, never one to back down.

After duty hours Ray returned home to echo Ina's emphasis on education and the children complied, bending closer to their books and composition pages when he appeared. Ray also spent more time reading the Bible and began teaching Sunday school at their church, changes the children surmised were related to the *Heredia* sinking. Ina had been the family's pillar of religious faith in the past, but now Ray invoked God's name just as often. Some of his new-found religious fervor might have been out of appreciation for his family's survival and some might have been Ray's grasping for a higher meaning in his life, a reason he and his family had been spared. But his children knew, too, that his sleep was racked with nightmares after the *Heredia* incident and Ray might have been seeking peace from a higher source for that affliction as well.

The *Heredia* and its aftermath slowly faded from family conversation, perhaps to avoid inflaming Ray's terrible nightmares or because the family had a new sense of purpose: fighting the enemy by participating in the war effort on the home front. But the wrenching experience would always be part of their history and sense of strength and resilience.

⁂

When Ray first arrived for duty in St. Augustine, the residents were still talking about the sinking of the *Gulfamerica* tanker close to shore in April (sunk by U-123). The ship, on its maiden voyage, was loaded with 90,000 gallons of fuel oil, which exploded into flames visible for miles along the coast and burned for days. Reports say the U-boat was brazenly on the surface between the flames and the shoreline—even firing its deck guns to administer the coup de grace to the flaming vessel—providing onlookers a menacing profile of the sub as sailors tried to jump through the flames to safety. Floridians didn't need a newspaper to tell them the war was hitting very close to home after that incident. The *Gulfamerica* sinking, however, was the last near-shore torpedoing off Florida's east coast. Ray felt a sense of pride that his service and those of many others who patrolled the beaches and coastal waters had made a difference.

With military bases and uniformed men all around, Terry jumped at the chance to do his part in the war effort and he volunteered to man a shore patrol position with some of his buddies from the high school football team. That involved staying overnight in a raised lookout hut at the beach and recording any unusual activity in a log book. The huts were checked regularly by a Coast Guard patrolman on horseback.

Sonny and Lucille wanted to go with Terry, but he explained that they couldn't. "This is serious business," Terry said. "We are trained to watch for certain unusual things. We're not out there playing ball."

Like Terry, all Americans were asked to be alert for unusual activity in their midst. This heightened state of alert caused rumors to persist that Germans were given aid by recent immigrants or sympathizers, whether radioing the location of vulnerable ships, warning them of air defenses, or providing fuel for long-range U-boat missions. Most rumors were untrue; but on June 13, 1942, a U-boat dropped four saboteurs off on Long Island, New York, with explosives, maps, and orders to damage key assets such as transportation hubs and hydroelectric plants. A young Coast Guardsman on patrol stumbled upon the men in the early morning hours and became suspicious enough to alert other men in his barracks. One of the spies had attempted to bribe him while the others were burying the explosives on the beach. The Germans confused the Coastie long enough to make their escape, later blending in with commuters on a train into New York City.

The U-boat that delivered them was also detained but not by any shore patrol: it had entered water too shallow and was stuck, but it ultimately managed to slip away when the tide turned.

Four days later another team of four saboteurs was dropped by a U-boat on Ponte Vedra Beach, between Jacksonville and St. Augustine, Florida. They, too, were armed with cash, explosives, and information about sensitive American targets in order to wage a prolonged campaign of destruction. They buried their explosives, split up, and took trains to Cincinnati and Chicago.

The saboteurs had been selected due to their knowledge of the U.S., as all had lived in America for some period of time (one had served in the U.S. Army, and another was a naturalized citizen). They were trained in German manufacturing plants to know the most vulnerable places to strike. And most alarming, the long-range plan was to drop many more teams of saboteurs along America's coastline in succeeding weeks until there was a significant network wreaking havoc on the country's infrastructure and undermining its ability to supply war materials.

The commitment and fortitude of the spies, however, was weak. The oldest of the saboteurs, George John Dasch, had a change of heart when he arrived in New York. He told a co-conspirator, Ernest Burger, that he was going to inform the F.B.I. about the espionage plans and Burger agreed to help dismantle the plot. Dasch contacted the F.B.I., then traveled to Washington and confessed to the whole scheme. At first the F.B.I. thought he might be mentally unstable and making up the story. Then Dasch dumped $84,000 in cash on one agent's desk, and the Feds knew he was for real.

The F.B.I. had been hunting for the German spy teams following the Coast Guard's earlier discovery of the buried explosives, along with German uniforms, on the beach in Long Island, but Dasch gave the F.B.I. everything they needed to find all of his accomplices, using the code name Pastorius, so the episode became known as Operation Pastorius. Dasch even turned over a handkerchief with invisible writing that revealed contact information for Nazi sympathizers in the U.S.

All of the spies were rounded up quickly without having done any damage. In fact, one spy had spent two days playing cards, another frittered time away in movie theatres, and a third spent some of the espionage money on a new car.

A military commission found all the captured spies guilty and sentenced all to death except Dasch and Burger, who were spared because they had revealed the scheme. Both served time in prison until 1948, when they were repatriated to Germany under certain restrictions. The remaining six men were executed in Washington, D.C.

The public never heard a word about the incident until November 1945, when the Attorney General revealed details of the attempted espionage and the information was published in *The New York Times*.

The execution of Operation Pastorius conspirators was not the end of Germany's attempts to infiltrate America: two more spies were dropped on the shore in Maine in late November 1944. One was Erich Gimpel, a German who had cut his teeth by tracking shipping in South America for the Germans before he was deported by the Peruvian government. He was paired with William Colepaugh, a native-born American whose mother was German and who signed on as a kitchen crewman aboard a ship in order to defect to Germany when the war began.

Together Gimpel and Colepaugh crossed the Atlantic on U-1230, which after two months at sea spent several more days submerged in the Gulf of Maine to observe shipping and tides. They were rowed ashore at remote Hancock Point, near Bar Harbor, Maine, in dress clothes and topcoats under cover of darkness, carrying $60,000 in cash and diamonds. Their mission was named *Unternehmen Elster* or Operation Magpie. It called for the spies to gather information on American technology and manufacturing and relay it to Germany via a radio they were supposed to build.

A local woman saw the two unusually well-dressed men walking along the road at night during an already-snowy Maine winter and it piqued her interest, so she allegedly alerted a local sheriff the next day. But Colepaugh and Gimpel had, by then, taken a cab to Bangor, where they arranged transportation through Boston to New York. When a ship was torpedoed near Bar Harbor on December 3 (the *Cornwallis*, a Canadian steamer) suspicions were confirmed that spies had been dropped off by a U-boat lurking among Maine's many small islands and inlets.

Colepaugh and Gimpel didn't do much damage as spies: they stayed together about three weeks, trying to gather the necessary components for the radio and finding a place to live in New York. But Colepaugh freely spent the espionage money on wine, women, and song, eventually telling a friend that he was a spy. He was turned in to the F.B.I., which quickly hunted down Gimpel as well.

Convicted for spying, both men were sentenced to death by hanging, but they avoided the death sentence through a series of lucky breaks. First, President Franklin D. Roosevelt died, which suspended all death sentences for several weeks. Then President Harry Truman commuted their sentences after the war was over. Colepaugh was released from jail in 1962 and went on to lead Boy Scout troops in Pennsylvania later in life. Gimpel served a ten-year sentence before being deported to Germany. He lived out his life in South America.

U-boats were clearly more effective at hunting ships than at delivering spies, but Ray Downs, on his beach patrols at St. Augustine, was keeping an eye out for any suspicious activity. He had not given up his desire to seek revenge against the Germans, and whether that was fulfilled by capturing a potential spy or spotting a U-boat for a plane to depth-charge didn't really matter.

CHAPTER TWENTY-TWO

PASSAGES SO FAR FROM HOME

"All are living under constant tension, produced by living in a steel tube."

—U-boat ace Erich Topp

After Commander Harro Schacht assisted in the *Laconia* rescue, the remaining portion of his patrol was one of aggravation and anxiety, without the satisfaction of sinking any enemy ships before returning to Lorient 30 days later. Compared to his successful hunting off Brazil, this period of no kills must have chafed at the daring officer's sense of duty. Adding to his frustration was that some of his crew members had become sick shortly after taking on the shipwrecked survivors from the *Laconia*, perhaps contracting a contagious illness from them. In his War Diary, the commander said, "Have had for some time constant feverish illnesses with diarrhea, headaches and general exhaustion onboard. Started after survivors were onboard."

There are few places, if any, worse than the confines of a U-boat to have an illness rampaging through the crew. Making matters more difficult, one of the sick men, crewman Obersteuermann, was deteriorating fast, and Schacht had to briefly take on a doctor as well as fuel and provisions from a milk cow U-boat.

As far as the hunting of enemy ships went, that too was frustrating. An example occurred on October 5 when U-507 came upon a promising target, and Schacht was able to maneuver into a perfect position for a submerged attack. As he had the men prepare to launch the torpedo, however, the tube door became stuck. This time the problem became a lucky break because as the steamer came closer, the commander realized it was a neutral Swedish "red cross steamer." The malfunctioning tube, however, continued to cause him problems, leaking whenever the sub was on the surface.

On October 7, the seriously ill crewman took a turn for the worse: "turns blue, out of breath. Cardiazol and Lobelin injected," wrote Schacht. Then two hours later: "Obersteuermann deceased. After two hours of artificial respiration . . . revival attempts stopped because beginning of rigor mortis. . . ." Twenty-four hours later, under cover of darkness, "The body of Obersteuermann laid to rest in the sea."

To top off the bitter days after the *Laconia*, Schacht was admonished in an incoming message to stop writing "novels" in his War Diary situation reports. And upon his return to Lorient, BdU Headquarters wrote that Schacht would have had better success had he gone to the operations area of "U-130," where there was strong traffic for targets and that, by so doing, Schacht's patrol "would have been shorter." Headquarters closed their comments by again noting that the commander's colorful entries were not needed when they wrote "Be more succinct in the Kriegstagebuch."

After the *Laconia* debacle and subsequent maintenance and re-provisioning in Lorient, Schacht made another patrol. Once again he and U-507 headed across the Atlantic in a southwest direction to the waters off Brazil, where he had done so much damage in his earlier voyage. He left Lorient on November 28, 1942, and made his first kill approximately one month later, when he sank the British ship *Oakbank* two hundred miles northeast of Brazil. Of the complement of sixty-four onboard, twenty-four crewmembers were lost, and the master and apprentice were taken prisoner by Schacht. The others who survived the attack found salvation in various ways: thirty were rescued at sea by another British ship, one was rescued by an Argentine ship, and two others survived a 200-mile ordeal in a raft before finally landing on the coast near Para, Brazil, a full nineteen days after the *Oakbank* sank!

Seven days later, Schacht was hunting closer to the Brazilian coast. Opportunity to find ships would be greater there, but so would the risk. Aircraft from U.S. Naval bases in Brazil frequently patrolled the area, searching for U-boats and protecting passing convoys. Whenever U-507 was on the surface, spotters on the bridge would have to be extremely vigilant scanning the skies. Should an enemy plane be spotted, every second counted in the crash dive. Damage from a bomb might be slight, but that could still doom a U-boat: if the hydroplanes did not respond, a U-boat could continue its dive far beyond the vessel's limit, causing it to be crushed by the water's pressure. Even if a damaged U-boat was not crushed, if it was unable to surface the fate of the crew would still be death, only a prolonged and tortured one as their air supply slowly gave out. The best chance for part of the crew to survive a damaging attack would be if the U-boat was hit on the surface. Men up on the bridge might be thrown into the sea, and even those inside the conning tower could have time to sprint up the ladder to the bridge and escape; but those in the belly of the boat almost always were drowned as water poured inside.

While still off Brazil on January 3, 1943, U-507 intercepted another target, also a British steamer, *Baron Dechmont*, which was sunk by multiple torpedoes. Seven were killed out of a crew of 44, and Captain Donald Mac-Callum from Glasgow was taken prisoner. (Taking the captains of ships prisoner prevented them from skippering another vessel, and the Germans hoped it would slow down Allied shipping, by removing the most experienced hands.) Schacht continued his hunting, and five days later sank another British steamer, the *Yorkmoor*, in the same area. Again, Schacht took the ship's master prisoner.

With the rate of successful attacks it looked like Schacht would duplicate his earlier patrols off Brazil and in the Gulf of Mexico. Admiral

Dönitz was pleased with the situation reports Schacht filed to Headquarters, and satisfied that the coast of South America was worth sending a few subs to. Along with being fruitful in terms of ships sunk, the area was a bit safer for his U-boats than the coast of North America. But not safe enough.

A squadron of PBY Catalina aircraft had arrived at Panarmarin Field in Natal, Brazil and were becoming quite familiar with the coast and adept at spotting U-boats. Just three days after Schacht sank the *Baron Dechmont*, another U-boat, U-164, was sunk by American aircraft 80 miles northeast of Fortaleza, Brazil.

Gone were the days when Schacht could hunt with impunity. He'd had aircraft spot him several times while in the Gulf of Mexico, but the pilots still had a lot to learn about finding and surprising subs. Those encounters in the Gulf were little more than harassments.

On the morning of January 13, a U.S. pilot by the name of Lieutenant Ludwig was preparing his PBY at Natal for a routine patrol when he was told that a sub had been sighted following a convoy. The sub was U-507.

That day, Schacht sent a message to Headquarters telling them that he had spotted a convoy, and his superiors replied that he should attack and not report back until the operation was over.

Headquarters waited for Schacht to report the outcome of the attack, and when none came, they requested him to give a report. There was no response. Over the next four days, Headquarters kept asking for U-507's position and situation, and still no reply. They feared the worst, and they were right.

Lieutenant Ludwig had launched and quickly located U-507 on the surface. The men on the U-boat spotted the plane as it came at them in a steep dive, flying at almost 200 knots. Schacht of course sounded the alarm, and he and the men on the bridge piled down the ladder into the sub and sealed the hatch. But it was too late. Ludwig was directly over the sub, perhaps as close as fifty feet, when the pilot released four depth charges. He later reported that he saw "Niagara Falls turned upside down" as great plumes of water went shooting into the sky. The PBY circled the scene, knowing they had hit the sub, but did not see any survivors.

Daring and genial Harro Schacht had fought his last battle. All hands were lost, as well as the captured ships' captains who were onboard U-507. Schacht met his death over 5,000 miles away from his homeland, after surviving a total of 227 days at sea on four different war patrols.

When Schacht and U-507 were lost, Erich Würdemann was on his fourth patrol, which began on December 14, 1942. It is unknown when the young commander learned that Schacht was dead, but the news must have been a bitter blow to Würdemann, as he and Schacht had been through so much together, often operating their U-boats just a few miles from each other. Like Würdemann, Schacht was the only other commander who had experienced the initial daring missions to the Gulf of Mexico and the improbable rescue of the *Laconia* survivors. The loss of Schacht and U-507 also drove home the fact that German submarines were being lost at an alarming pace. In 1943 a U-boatman's average estimated life span was a mere six months, and Admiral Dönitz was forced to conclude that "the losses have therefore reached an unbearable height." But there was little he could do until German technology countered the advances in Allied sub hunting. And the death of seasoned men like Schacht, who were totally committed to maximizing their kills, meant that their replacements were less expert and resolute.

Würdemann's fourth patrol reflected the increased dangers to U-boats as a result of Allied aircrafts' improved sub-hunting abilities, including new equipment that could detect a submerged sub's magnetic field from aloft. In fact, U-506 had encountered extreme danger the moment they left Lorient as they traveled through the Bay of Biscay. The commander's War Diary has one entry after another reporting: "Dived due to enemy aircraft," even during the nighttime hours. Consequently, the beginning of the patrol was taking much longer than past missions, and there were more challenges to come. The voyage would demand that the young commander put extra emphasis on keeping the morale of his crew at a high level in the face of an enemy that now had the advantage in their deadly game of cat-and-mouse.

Würdemann set a course for the waters off South Africa, but he kept hundreds of miles out to sea as he made his way south, not daring to be near the coast where enemy aircraft could spend longer periods in the air searching for him. That part of the voyage took a full seven weeks, and upon reaching a point off Cape Town, U-506 was refueled by a milk cow. Würdemann then conducted a methodical six-week search for ships, changing course often, and moving slightly westward. But even as far as South Africa, British aircraft were keeping things hot for him. The commander made one attempt to attack a convoy, but found himself surrounded by escort ships that had heavy air support. The sub was detected and the crew of U-506 had to endure an agonizing hour of being depth-charged.

It wasn't until the night of March 7, not far off Knysna, South Africa, that Würdemann found a target that was unescorted. It was an average size British merchant ship named *Sabor*, carrying salt and sixty-three bags of mail, with a crew of fifty-eight sailors. When U-506 was in range, multiple torpedoes were fired and all missed because "enemy speed overestimated." Würdemann had his combat helmsman maneuver the sub ahead, and two more eels were launched. The crew of the U-boat anxiously counted down the seconds, waiting for the sound of an explosion. None was forthcoming from the first torpedo, which hit the *Sabor* directly in the bow but did not detonate. But the second torpedo exploded forty-five seconds after it was launched, traveling 1,000 meters before it hit the ship's engine room. The freighter came to a halt, and Würdemann watched most of the crew (seven were killed in the blast) abandon ship in three lifeboats. Because the ship did not sink, the commander decided it was safe enough for U-506 to stay on the surface and blast the *Sabor* with artillery. But, like so much of the patrol, issues with the cannon arose and it became inoperable after just three shots.

Further complications ensued when Würdemann ordered the U-boat to submerge in preparation for launching the "coup de grace" torpedo. As the sub started to descend, it collided with an unknown object, rocking the vessel with three "severe concussions." Luckily the sub could still surface and when it did, the commander found that the air search periscope was bent, an antenna was missing, and the "port motor was frozen." Remarkably, twenty minutes later the Germans were able to fire the long-awaited coup de grace torpedo and the *Sabor* broke apart and sank.

While the sub was damaged, the problems were not critical, nor did they affect the ability of Würdemann to locate another ship two days later with a name similar to one just sunk, this one called the *Tabor*. It was a Swedish merchant ship, also filled with salt, located farther out to sea than his last victim. U-506 sent two eels into the ship, and Würdemann recorded watching the surviving crewmembers leave the vessel in three lifeboats. Then the coup de grace torpedo was launched, hitting under the ship's bridge but showed "not the slightest effect" on getting the *Tabor* to actually sink. Artillery was fired, which set the ship ablaze and eventually sent her to the bottom of the sea. Würdemann had the sub approach the lifeboats and demanded information about the ship. In this exchange the commander was either told the wrong name of the ship or he recorded it incorrectly, because his log showed it to be the *Pearlmoor*, rather than the correct name, *Tabor*. Most, but not all, of the survivors eventually made it to shore, although they suffered greatly from exposure caused by several days adrift in lifeboats in stormy weather.

When no other ships presented themselves as easy targets, Würdemann ordered repairs made to the sub, sending crewmembers into the ocean in breathing apparatus to fix the port shaft and propeller. Just after the work was completed, it was time to begin the return transit, again being refueled by a milk cow off South Africa.

As the commander approached Lorient—dodging enemy aircraft frequently—he must have felt glum. He had sunk only two ships during a grueling 143 days at sea. Compared to the 71 days U-506 spent on the Gulf of Mexico patrol where they sank the *Heredia* and either damaged or sank ten other vessels, this patrol to South Africa was a failure. The total distance covered was an incredible 19,624 nautical miles with little to show for man-hours and fuel spent. Würdemann attempted to put the patrol in the best light possible, writing how his men displayed an excellent attitude on the "extraordinarily long—and yet not very successful—war patrol. They [the crew] provided their service freshly, cheerfully, and skillfully from the first day to the last day."

Once in Lorient it would have been impossible for the crew of U-506 not to notice the difference in both their greeting and shore accommodations after this trip compared to prior returns. Instead of lavish celebrations, the welcome-home meal was muted and meager. A crewmember who served with Würdemann on the South African patrol later said that because of British aircraft bombing Lorient, they had to reside in a bomb shelter that was appalling. "The whole ship's company lived in one medium-sized room," he reported. "The light continually went out. Water, of which there was plenty, was quite undrinkable." Another crewman who later became a British POW told an interrogator that morale plummeted at Lorient: "Whereas formerly new drafts showed enthusiasm and keenness to join their U-boats, they now invented every possible excuse and trivial sickness to avoid it."

Although Würdemann had his own room with a bunk, wash basin, and chair, his mind was likely on his hometown, Hamburg, because he would have heard the distressing news that it had been repeatedly bombed by British aircraft. One attack in March killed 27 civilians and injured 95 when 417 planes rained bombs on the industrial port city. And still to come was the horrific bombing on July 27 and 28, 1943, where 42,600 Hamburg civilians were killed in a firestorm caused by air raids.

The anxiety and grief that the young commander must have felt was shared by Admiral Dönitz himself. On May 19, 1943, his son Peter was killed in the North Atlantic while serving aboard U-954 when it was sunk with all hands lost. (A year later, Dönitz's other son, Klaus, was killed when he was on a German torpedo boat [S-141] during a raid.) Adding to his stress was the loss of experienced men like Schacht, and the knowledge that Allied radar had become more effective and virtually impossible for U-boat radio operators to detect.

Erich Würdemann was well aware that the U-boats were falling behind the Allies in technological advances, and he must have wondered how long he and the crew of U-506 could continue before they met the terrible fate of so many U-boatmen before them.

After two months on land, Würdemann and a crew of 54 men were sent out on yet another patrol. A crewman later commented that as he prepared to board, the U-boat was covered in flowers, and to him "it looked like a grave." Included in that crew was a surgeon, which prompted one crewman of the sub to complain it was bad luck to have a doctor onboard. Also onboard was a German war correspondent who hoped to produce a propaganda video and brought with him "two heavy bags containing a cine-camera, 14,000 feet of film, and his own electric accumulator." This crew, many of them reluctant and inexperienced 19- and 20-year-olds, was a far cry from the enthusiastic men that had sailed with Würdemann in the past. Even the commander himself was observed to be "a bundle of nerves," and "looked to be 40 years old." It's little wonder he was anxious: during his last patrol and while in Lorient he either heard about or saw for himself the last messages from several U-boats that had been sent to the bottom of the sea. Many transmitted final messages saying "Attacked, bombs, sinking," and one hauntingly added a final word at the end of the communication: "imprisonment."

On July 12, six days after U-506 left Lorient, an American Liberator aircraft was patrolling the Atlantic approximately 200 miles west of Vigo, Spain. At the controls was Lieutenant Ernest Salm of the First Antisubmarine Squadron of the 480th Group. He had launched his aircraft from its base in French Morocco and this was his first mission as aircraft commander. The day was misty with poor visibility, but the Liberator was equipped with the latest radar. At mid-afternoon, Salm had the plane cruising well above the clouds at 5,600 feet, traveling at 176 miles per hour, when its radar sensed an object on the ocean's surface several miles away. The pilot turned the plane toward the object and started his descent, increasing his speed to 250 miles an hour as he readied his crew for an attack on what they suspected was a U-boat.

U-506 was cruising on the surface, recharging her desperately depleted batteries. On the bridge were the first lieutenant, another watch officer, and six crewmen, all wearing life jackets and all with their eyes to the sky. Erich Würdemann was below them in the conning tower.

The men on the bridge were hyper-alert. They could only see 1,000 yards through the mist and felt more vulnerable than ever. In good weather they would use their binoculars and be able to spot an aircraft far enough away that it looked like a tiny black fly in the sky, leaving them just enough time to crash dive. Not this time.

Suddenly, all heads turned toward a roaring sound above them, and the cry "Alarm!" went up in unison. But it was too late, the Liberator rocketed out of the clouds and came plunging directly at them, its machine gun emitting flames as it raked the sub's deck. The plane did not level off until it was a mere 35 feet above the ocean's surface, and within a second was almost directly over the sub. Seven depth charges came tumbling out of the aircraft. Most of the bombs exploded within just feet of the sub, and one exploded directly on the forward deck. Parts of the diesel engine broke through the pressurized hull and tremendous geysers of water shot up into the air, temporarily obscuring the sub from eyes that looked down from the Liberator.

When the bombs exploded most of the men on the sub's deck were hurled into the sea, while crewmen below were thrown off their feet, crashing into equipment. Thousands of gallons of ocean water entered the sub through cracks in the hull, and additional water poured down the hatch from the bridge. Erich Würdemann was stunned. He started to call for a crash dive, but stopped himself when the reality hit him that the sub was mortally wounded.

The commander then looked for a life jacket but, finding none, scrambled up the ladder to the bridge. Plumes of oil were spreading out from the sub in all directions, and he could hear shouts from those in the ocean and others coming up the ladder behind him. He saw the stern of U-506 disappear under the sea while the bow rose steeply into the air.

There was nothing more he could do, and Würdemann jumped into the ocean, just as the bow slid beneath the surface, taking those still inside with her.

Approximately 15 men were in the water, many wounded from either machine-gun bullets or from the exploding bombs. All were covered in oil and in shock, just like the *Heredia* survivors had been 14 months earlier. Two crewmen located the commander, who may have been injured and struggled to tread water without the aid of a life jacket. They held his head above the waves. Then Erich Würdemann clearly said "Let me go," and he pushed away from the two crewmen holding him up, and slowly drifted away. He was never seen again.

Lieutenant Salm regained some altitude and banked the Liberator so that it returned to the spot where he had bombed the sub. Giant blue oil bubbles rose from the sea where the U-boat had been.

Salm saw survivors floating in the oily and debris-filled sea, some wearing yellow life jackets and some without. Salm had his men drop a life raft and he also laid down a ring of smoke bombs to mark the location.

Only six of the survivors bobbing on the surface had the strength to make it to the life raft; the others drowned, slipping under the ocean, joining Erich Würdemann and those trapped on U-506 in their watery grave.

CHAPTER TWENTY-THREE

SONNY

"It's true. It's all true."

—Sonny

The months that the Downs family spent in St. Augustine were ones the children would remember fondly, especially because they were able to spend more time with their father than they had in the past. Ray's daily appearance in his crisp Coast Guard uniform made the entire family proud. But the man's strict composure crumbled when he began feeling poorly. Several doctors appointments confirmed he'd need immediate surgery to remove a kidney.

The children were alarmed to see their big, strong Dad in a hospital bed after his surgery. He looked ashen and weak. Ina was admonishing him about his recovery.

"Ray, you need to take the medicine the doctor gave you," she insisted.

"I won't," he said.

She threw up her hands. "Ray, they said you may lose the other kidney too. You have to take the medicine to prevent that."

He spent weeks in the hospital recovering, particularly after reopening his sutures when he kicked at an orderly who insisted, like Ina, that he swallow medicine that was brought to him. It was clear that Ray didn't like lying on his back, feeling helpless and being told what to do.

But soon he was home, listening to the radio in the evening again, talking to Sonny about baseball scores and Ted Williams's batting average against the Yankees. The youngster had a head for facts and numbers, his parents noted, as he kept a notebook full of team statistics and pored over the nightly newspaper in search of more sports news.

"Dad, can we listen to the fight?" Sonny asked one evening.

"Of course, if your homework is done," said Ray. "I think it's Marty Servo and Sugar Ray Robinson."

Sonny started out lying on the floor in front of the radio, but as announcer Don Dunphy wound up, breathlessly following the action, blow-by-blow, he got up and threw jabs and hooks at an imaginary opponent, bouncing around on his feet.

"Sonny, don't get so worked up, it's nearly your bed time," said Ina. But Ray's enjoyment of Sonny's performance won him a pass, and he continued to bob and weave.

As much as Sonny was everyone's favorite playmate at home, he knew his parents' expectations for him were high. Ina let him figure out the cost of their allotment of gasoline and how much was available to spend at the grocery store, while Ray helped develop his baseball and basketball technique, which showed real promise. The boy was also doing well with his school studies.

That's why Sonny was shocked to receive an "F" at school one day.

He gasped at the red failing grade on his composition. His careful pencil lettering seemed to blur and his stomach knotted as he scanned the essay: it was certainly his, but could Mrs. Hall have made a mistake?

"Mister Downs," she said, standing over his desk. Every other child in the classroom held their breath to hear what Sonny had done. "Remember, I assigned this as a nonfiction essay. That means a true story. That's why you received a failing grade. You must pay closer attention to your assignments."

"But Mrs. Hall," Sonny stammered. "It's true, it's all true."

His teacher, in her dark blue dress and hair tucked into a net behind her ears, pursed her lips and shook her head in disapproval. "Now, Mr. Downs, you'd better not say another word. I asked you to write a true story about the war, and you wrote how your family was torpedoed by a German submarine. Your imagination has gotten the best of you."

⸺

It was several years before Sonny ever wrote about or talked about his ordeal in the Gulf of Mexico.

EPILOGUE

SURVIVORS OF U-506

The six U-boatmen who were able to climb into the life raft dropped from the Liberator began paddling toward Spain. For two days and two nights they paddled, often seeing aircraft but none close enough to signal. They lived on chocolate and water found in the life raft. On July 14 they spotted an American aircraft and were able to fire a signal flare which the pilots saw and reported the position to the destroyer *Hurricane*, which was 60 miles away. On July 15, Allied Headquarters in Gibraltar received the following message from the destroyer: "*Hurricane* has picked up survivors of U-boat sunk by Aircraft 4220 N—1451 W. Congratulations."

Two days later the German prisoners found themselves in Great Britain where they were interrogated about every aspect of the patrols of U-506. The sub commanded by Erich Würdemann had sunk 15 ships and been at sea for a total of 344 days before it met its demise.

THE WAR GRINDS TO A CLOSE

There were still many loose ends to the war in 1945 despite clear indications that the Germans had lost. Refusing to give up without a fight, Dönitz sent six type IXC U-boats equipped with snorkels across the Atlantic toward the U.S. in March 1945 in a wolfpack formation. Thanks to their superior code-breaking technology, the Allies were prepared for the group's approach and had destroyers and carrier escorts ready to receive them. Four of the six U-boats were sunk, while only one of the destroyer escort ships was successfully torpedoed.

Within months, a series of unforeseen events unfolded as German leadership crumbled in the face of defeat. In his memoirs, Dönitz describes an atmosphere of distrust and unpredictability, including getting a telegram (presumably from Hitler) that said Heinrich Himmler, the high-ranking Nazi party official and leader of the SS, had offered to surrender to Sweden, so Dönitz should be prepared to take "instant and ruthless action against traitors." Himmler had expected Hitler's nod as successor, but his unauthorized communication with the Allies eliminated that possible transfer of power. Hitler had expelled successors-in-waiting Hermann Göring and Himmler from the Nazi Party for disloyalty after Göring requested to be put in charge while Hitler was in the Führerbunker in Berlin during the final days of the war. On April 30, 1945, Hitler committed suicide, which put a surprising chain of succession in motion: he had named Dönitz his successor and Joseph Goebbels as Head of Government and Chancellor. But on May 1, Goebbels also committed suicide with his wife after killing all of their children, leaving Dönitz alone to orchestrate Germany's surrender to the Allies.

"[T]hat I myself might be entrusted with the task had never entered my head," Dönitz wrote in his memoirs, noting that he had not spoken to Hitler face-to-face in more than nine months. "Having spent the whole of my life as a serving officer in the Navy, that any such idea should have occurred to me seemed quite improbable . . . I could not understand what could have led to my appointment."

Soon after Dönitz took leadership as President and Head of State at Flensburg, Himmler came to him, accompanied by a contingent of SS guards, seeking a leadership role in the new post-Hitler government. According to Dönitz's memoir, he received the man warily—with a revolver under some papers on his desk, ready to be used if necessary. Dönitz showed him Hitler's final wishes, which banished Himmler from any leadership position, and Dönitz rejected Himmler's request to have a role in the succession.

His greatest fear, Dönitz wrote, was that surrender would be followed by chaos and further bloodshed both by uprisings against German forces that continued to occupy portions of the Netherlands and Norway and by liberating forces entering Germany. He broadcast a radio message to German citizens on May 1, promising to hold on to the Eastern Front as long as possible before surrender, although he knew General Eisenhower would demand that German troops surrender to the Russians, eliminating most barriers to Russian occupation of Germany. He said Eisenhower did not understand the determination of the Soviets to conquer Eastern Europe and sent the chief of the Operations Staff of the High Command, Generaloberst Alfred Jodl, to negotiate, but Eisenhower would not back down. On May 7, just a week after Hitler's suicide, Dönitz approved Jodl to sign a surrender at Reims, France.

Dönitz sent the following radiogram to those still serving in the Kriegsmarine: "My U-boat men, six years of war lie behind you. You have fought like lions. An overwhelming material superiority has driven us into a tight corner from which it is no longer possible to continue the war. Unbeaten and unblemished, you lay down your arms after a heroic fight without parallel. We proudly remember our fallen comrades who gave their lives for Führer and Fatherland. Comrades, preserve that spirit in which you have fought so long and so gallantly for the sake of the future of the Fatherland. Long live Germany. Your Grand Admiral."

Reflecting on the capitulation, U-953 commander Herbert Werner wrote in his memoirs, "The murdering had finally come to an end. Henceforth we would be able to live without fear that we had to die tomorrow. An unknown tranquility took possession of me as I realized fully that I had survived. My death in an iron coffin was finally suspended."

That sense of relief was well-founded, as the war at sea had been relentlessly brutal. More than 2,600 Allied merchant ships were sunk, along with 175 naval vessels and 784 of the fleet of 1,162 U-boats.

While Dönitz negotiated the terms of surrender, he kept the German army on the battlefield and as many ships moving as possible to enable the evacuation of hundreds of thousands of soldiers and civilians from northeast

Germany and the Berlin area so they would not be harmed by Soviet troops described by historians as "frenzied" and "vindictive." The Red Army was not just intent on conquering Berlin but also taking revenge for the brutal way Germans had waged war on them starting in 1941, including the nearly 900-day siege of Leningrad during which people starved and human flesh was reportedly sold for food. The result was that much of Germany and countries to the east suffered severely as the Red Army rampaged through, executing prisoners and civilians at will, raping and pillaging. "The fact that the women of Germany were largely innocents, swept up in the horror rather than being responsible for it, meant nothing to an army that had lost 13.5 million casualties at the Germans' hands," according to the British news site *The Daily Mail*. The Soviets, including Marshal of the Soviet Union Josef Stalin, were never held accountable for war crimes as the remaining German leaders were.

German war crimes were addressed in the International Military Tribunal in Nuremberg, Germany, a process that ran from November 1945 to October 1946. The course of action had been vetted and approved by Allied leaders, with panels of prosecutors and judges representing each of the major Allied nations. The location was a courthouse in the town that was symbolically acknowledged as the birthplace of Nazism—but with these trials the town would forever be associated with the end of functional Nazism.

During the trial all were required to watch a film of Allies liberating concentration camps, and psychologists were employed to record the defendants' reactions as well as to interview them afterward. The footage included prisoners being burned to death in a barn, corpses piled high and being thrown into pits, a doctor describing medical experiments on female prisoners, and more. Some of the defendants buried their faces in their hands or looked away. Afterward, Dönitz was recorded as speaking emotionally, asking how he could have known about the atrocities. "I never had a thing to do with the Party," he claimed.

Admiral Dönitz and other German leaders were generally charged with planning to wage a war of aggression, crimes against peace, war crimes, and crimes against humanity. Crimes against peace included planning to annex other countries, such as the secret agreement Hitler struck with Stalin in 1939 that divided up Poland and the Baltic countries.

Dönitz's specific charges included planning the war; upholding Hitler's secret Commando Order that required killing potential POW's even if they were surrendering; use of slave labor in shipyards; sinking merchant ships without warning; and requiring that his underlings not render aid to those shipwrecked. He sat in the prisoner dock alongside military colleagues accused of the worst imaginable crimes, including some who created concentration camps and enabled the extermination of tens of thousands of noncombatants, such as Hermann Göring, Alfred Jodl, and Ernst Kaltenbrunner, who were all sentenced to death.

According to one source, Dönitz's defense had significant assistance from his former—and forever loyal—Kriegsmarine, who smuggled helpful documents and technical information to his counsel.

When he was asked about firing on sailors fleeing sinking ships, Dönitz denied that it was his policy or that any member of the Kriegsmarine had done so, with the exception of "the Eck affair" that concerned the machine-gunning of survivors from the wrecked *Peleus*, the Greek ship torpedoed by U-852. The commander and two members of the crew who took part were executed, two others served sentences up to life in prison.

"Firing upon these men [from *Peleus*]," Dönitz testified at his trial, "is a matter concerned with the ethics of war and should be rejected under any and all circumstances." Dönitz said that he reprimanded the captain at the time, and added: "In the German Navy and U-boat force this principle [not firing on survivors], according to my firm conviction, has never been violated, with the one exception of the Eck affair. No order on this subject has ever been issued, in any form whatsoever."

When pressed, he acknowledged in his testimony that Hitler wanted Allied sailors killed so they couldn't return to work on another ship. "I think in the summer of 1943 I received a letter from the Foreign Office in which I was informed that about 87 percent of the crews of merchant ships which had been sunk were returning home. I was told that was a disadvantage and was asked whether it was not possible to do something about it," he said. "I wrote that I had already been forced to prohibit rescue because it endangered the submarines, but that other measures were out of the question for me."

An acknowledgement from American Fleet Admiral Chester Nimitz that he had also ordered attacks on merchant ships without warning and other proof that neither the Americans nor British rendered aid to those shipwrecked by submarine attack were introduced as evidence during his trial, helping Dönitz to avoid a sentence on those actions despite being found guilty. The tribunal decided that Dönitz's orders were ambiguous regarding giving aid to shipwreck survivors as well as potentially ordering such survivors shot.

He was found guilty and sentenced primarily on the charge of using slave labor, even though he maintained his innocence, saying he was not in charge of procuring shipyard workers. He spent ten years in Spandau prison, and later wrote two books of memoirs.

The final tally of the war showed that approximately 40,000 men served in German U-boats but only a quarter of them survived to return home after the war. Thanks to the Allies' superior air power and sub-detection technology, the Atlantic Ocean is littered with sunken U-boats, most that will forever be tombs for their crews.

THE DOWNS FAMILY

After Ray's two-year stint in the Coast Guard at St. Augustine, the Downs family was again on the road, searching for the right combination of employment and luck that would allow them to rise above their meager circumstances. From St. Augustine, they packed up and went west again through the Gulf states in a cautiously optimistic return to Texas. Ray had a job with the railroad, back to doing what he knew best, and they would be closer to family.

Their new home, however, turned out to be a tourist court near the railroad yard in bustling Abilene, hardly a step up from St. Augustine. The two-bedroom efficiency was a tight squeeze for everyone, and the children—now ages sixteen, fourteen, and ten—tried to put a good face on starting at yet another new school. Terry immediately fell in step with other football players as his physique was filling out, but Sonny remained scrawny and somewhat shy. Lucille took after her father in her athletic talents, still playing ball with the boys at age fourteen. She inherited Ina's strong will, which allowed her to withstand the "girls can't" attitude of teen boys.

One of the bright spots for Sonny was being near enough to the railroad to see his father come in on a locomotive at the end of the day. The boy would climb the ladder to the platform of a nearby billboard that advertised Butterquick Biscuits and wave to Ray as he approached. Once, Ray even scooped Sonny up into the moving locomotive for a brief ride.

When they arrived in Abilene, the nearby Camp Barkeley Army base was in the process of decommissioning but still held 800 German POW's. It's possible that some of them lived more comfortably than the Downses, as the Geneva Convention required 140 square feet of space per enlisted man. Many prisoners still lived a quasi-military existence, marching in formation to the mess hall and to classes. They were also paid for work, such as agricultural jobs, when it was available. Most camps were equipped with a library, and prisoners took mandatory classes. Some even participated in activities like singing groups. It was reported that many German POW's were shocked when shown films of Allied troops liberating Nazi concentration camps. Reacting with anger and disgust at the scenes of depravity, many burned their uniforms. In the next few years they were repatriated to their home country and Camp Barkeley eventually became Dyess Air Force Base.

After just a few months in Abilene, the Downs family was on the move again, this time "home" to San Antonio. Ray went back to work for the Post Office and Ina, with her sight restored, returned to sewing and baking for some of the clients she'd had nearly four years earlier. They lived just a few blocks from the home they had left in 1941—which seemed a lifetime ago.

In San Antonio, Ray made a basketball hoop and backboard and nailed it on the garage so Terry and Sonny could play ball, which they did—for hours. Terry's sport of choice was football, but Sonny still wanted to do it all, with baseball continuing to edge out other sports for the moment.

Ever busy as a soda jerk and trimming neighbors' lawns, Terry saved his earnings in hopes of going back to St. Augustine to work for a summer on his friend's family's shrimp boat. But family finances remained tight, and when it was time to use the money he had saved on a train ticket to

Florida, Ina had to admit it had been spent on other necessities, dashing Terry's dream.

Sonny took on a newspaper route, riding his bike before school in the morning to toss newspapers on the doorsteps of about fifty customers. He knew the story of Terry's savings being depleted so decided to keep his cash in a sock rather than giving it to his mother to hold. He had to move it frequently to avoid impromptu "loans" to his siblings. Later he sold papers on the busy corner of Commerce Street and New Braunfels Avenue, near the entrance to Fort Sam Houston. After a tipsy but grateful soldier gave him a $100 tip for returning his lost wallet, Sonny opened his first savings account.

In high school, Terry's size and athletic prowess caught the attention of San Antonio's Brackenridge High School football coach Red Forehand. The teen had proportions that resembled his father's: he was over six feet tall, broad-shouldered and strong. His father's "get it done" attitude shone through as well, and as a result Terry was scouted by college teams—an educational milestone his parents never envisioned. He went to Baylor University on a full athletic scholarship and studied dentistry. He married twice, had two sons, ran his dentistry practice in San Antonio for fifty years, heading the Texas Dental Association before "retiring" to a position with Aftco which he holds as of this writing.

In high school Sonny's interest in sports began to narrow. When he shot up several inches to over six feet tall during the year between junior high and high school, his desire to play baseball was challenged by his coach, Day Brandt, who took notice of his ability to hit a basket from any point on the court. Brandt counseled Sonny to focus solely on basketball, and Sonny agreed.

At one point Terry was home from college and challenged Sonny to a game of basketball. The older brother spent the scrimmage blocking Sonny's right hand, making Sonny frustrated. Ray saw the lopsided game and started to rebuke Terry for picking on his "little" brother. But the result was that Sonny began shooting with his left as well as his right hand. Both Ray and Terry took note of Sonny's new-found talent, and wondered just how far it might take him.

When Lucille graduated from high school she received a heartfelt letter from Roy Sorli and his wife, Heddy, congratulating her and reminding her that she had been a brave young lady. "The best of luck and may God's blessing be with you as it was that night," he wrote. In fact, Ina stayed in touch with the Sorlis for many years following the *Heredia* torpedoing.

Lucille did not attend college but became an executive secretary, working for the Federal Reserve Bank in San Antonio for most of her career. She married twice and had four children, with whom she was always active, including playing tennis and swimming. She's remembered for her beauty, larger-than-life personality, and strong will that anchored her children's lives, yet she also struggled with crippling depression. Sadly, she died during surgery at the age of sixty-seven.

Roy Sorli, the Norwegian second mate of the *Heredia*, returned to the arms of his sweetheart, Heddy, in Lynnfield, a coastal town north of Boston. She didn't want him to go to sea again and he eventually complied, spending the rest of his life working as a union carpenter and raising two children (he had two daughters in Norway by a previous marriage). His carpentry work is still visible on a church steeple facing Boston Common, and he and Heddy were active in the Lynnfield Historical Society. He had a small fishing boat and later a cabin cruiser, which his family enjoyed, but they stayed close to shore. As Flotilla Commander of the local Coast Guard Auxiliary, he taught seamanship courses.

Roy Sorli's children say he rarely spoke of his childhood, which compelled him to go to sea, or the *Heredia* sinking that sent him home for good. They do remember the Merchant Marine Meritorious Service Medal he received in 1946 for saving Lucille that hung in the family's home, but their dad was reluctant to talk about the ordeal. When Roy died of lung cancer in 1976, Heddy had a Viking longboat carved on their shared headstone.

Both Ray and Ina Downs lived long lives after their harrowing experience, but they eventually lived apart. While they had been rich in love for their children, the financial stress of providing for the family became challenging to endure and resulted in strong disagreements. The couple was divorced in the late 1950s while continuing to live and work in San Antonio, Ina as a seamstress and Ray for the state employment commission.

Sonny's survival at sea was just one chapter in a rewarding life. After graduating from high school he went to the University of Texas at Austin on a basketball scholarship, racking up high points as a rare ambidextrous player. He holds both the career scoring average (22.3 points per game) and single-season scoring average (26 points per game) records at UT-Austin today—nearly sixty years later—despite being followed by national star Kevin Durant decades later. He was named All-Southwest Conference in 1956 and 1957, then was drafted by the St. Louis Hawks of the new National Basketball Association in 1957. However, the NBA was in its infancy then—none of the multi-million-dollar contracts that are common today—so Sonny sought a more stable future, having experienced many financial ups and downs through his childhood. He entered the Army and never played a professional game. While at Fort Eustis, Virginia, he began selling insurance policies to his fellow soldiers and former basketball teammates, eventually becoming a top producer (including being named Manager of the Year for the Mutual Life Insurance Company of New York for expanding the company's business by over 150 percent in Wichita, Kansas in the early 1980s). Yet Texans will forever claim him as their own: when asked to vote for the "All Time Texas Basketball Team" in 2011, more than 12,000 people weighed in and Ray "Sonny" Downs received the most individual votes. He married Betty Gayle Lowther of San Antonio (a neighbor of teacher Mrs. Hall) and has three sons. Today Sonny lives in Massachusetts and is still a top salesman in the financial industry.

Nobody remembers, or perhaps they just forgot to ask, what the Downses thought in 1992 when an oil slick appeared in the Gulf of Mexico. Many potential sources were investigated, with the eventual determination that it was the remaining fuel oil seeping out of a weathered wreck called the *Heredia*, which sits mostly intact 80 feet under water, a silent legacy of a terrible war and a family's resilience.

Acknowledgments

Alison O'Leary and I would like to thank a core group of people by starting at the very beginning.

The idea for this book came about in a surprising way. I was giving a presentation about leadership to employees at a financial company when I had the good fortune to meet attorney Jim Hoodlet. Jim and I found we had a mutual interest in both history and fishing, and he invited me out on his boat to fish for striped bass the next weekend. During a slow part of our excursion, as we drifted over the Billingsgate shoals off Cape Cod, Jim brought up the name of a friend of his, Ray "Sonny" Downs Jr., who was a top salesman and financial advisor. Jim explained to me how Ray had survived a U-boat attack in the Gulf of Mexico when he was just 8 years old.

Maybe it was because Jim and I were on a boat at sea, or maybe it was my fascination of how people survive the most challenging of ordeals, but Jim had hooked me the same way he later did with a couple big fish. Now he just had to reel me in.

Later that week I received an e-mail from Jim, and attached to it was a summary of the *Heredia* sinking, a 1942 newspaper article about the Downs family, and a photo of the vessel. I shared the information with Alison, and she said something to the effect of "What are you waiting for? This is right up your alley. Let's meet this Ray Downs." I wasn't quite as sure. I'd done several works of non-fiction and knew how daunting the research could be, but I had to admit Ray's story was intriguing.

Alison and I did a little bit of digging around on U-boat sites to see which German commander had sunk Ray's ship. Part of the reason we started investigating was how surprised we were that a ship was sunk in the Gulf of Mexico by a U-boat. As we did a bit of cursory research, we were further surprised to learn that the *Heredia* was far from the only ship sunk in the Gulf, and realized this was a part of World War II history that most Americans know little about. Alison and I also marveled that there was a survivor of a U-boat attack living just a half hour away from us in Massachusetts. How could we not want to meet him?

Jim must be a mind reader, because before I even had the chance to e-mail him about meeting Ray, he beat me to it, suggesting that Alison and I join Jim and his wife Penny for dinner with Ray. Three weeks later we were all in a restaurant enjoying a great meal. Ray had yet to even talk about his experience on the *Heredia*, but I had already made up my mind that this was a story I wanted to dive into, simply because I knew Ray was someone we could work with. He was so personable, so articulate, and so full of good humor, I knew he would make a good partner. It wasn't until after we had finished the meal and were having coffee that Ray gave us an overview of what had happened to his family in May 1942.

Jim sat back and smiled as Ray walked us through the events. Being a fisherman, Jim would likely call this part of the evening "setting the hook." All along, Jim had known Ray's story needed to be chronicled, and now he had his writers. So to Jim, a big thank-you for recognizing a great piece of history and introducing us to Ray. And to Ray, our initial impression of you was exactly what we got—someone who helped us in every way and made the project fun.

Besides Jim and Ray, there was someone else who was indispensable to Alison and me: Jerry Mason, who created the website uboatarchive.net.

Jerry is not just a wealth of information; he is flat-out brilliant, and more importantly kind and patient. He answered my every question, no matter how dumb, no matter how complex, and went out of his way to help make this a better book. Jerry, retired from the Navy in 2005 as a captain, after a distinguished career that included his start as a Naval Aviator and later graduating from both the Naval War College and Air Force Air War College. And now, after building www.uboatarchive.net, he is using his passion for history to help people like Alison and me. A perfect example is how Alison and I were able to get Erich Würdemann's War Diary (Kriegstagebucher, "KTB") from the National Archives, but it was in German! It was Jerry and his team (listed on his website under the section "U-boat KTBs") that translated the War Diary and helped us understand some of the terminology. So, to Jerry, a heartfelt thank-you.

Many other people went out of their way to offer us a helping hand and/or help make this book a reality, and some are listed here: publisher Claiborne Hancock, agent William Clark, copyeditor/proofreader Phil Gaskill, researcher Tony Cooper, publicist Megan Beattie, librarian Cecily Christensen, and historian Eric Wiberg.

Other key contributors are discussed in the Sources section that follows.

Sources

Ray "Sonny" Downs spent many hours discussing his experience with us, and shared a summary of his ordeal that he had written years earlier. His brother Terry did the same, relaying the details that his parents and Lucille disclosed to him about their survival at sea. We also had a written interview Ina had conducted with a friend. In the middle of the project, when we thought we had all the information we could gather from the Downses, Lucille's daughter surprised us by producing a lengthy audio tape that her grandmother, Ina, had recorded chronicling every aspect of the *Heredia* voyage and subsequent sinking including the personal struggles of both Lucille and herself when they were adrift in the ocean. Each member of the Downs family also talked with newspaper reporters, and the articles that resulted rounded out their experiences. Using all of this firsthand material allowed us to create the dialogue of the Downs family based off their own recollections.

For Schacht and Würdemann, their War Diaries were essential. In the case of the sinking of U-506 and the death of Erich Würdemann, we were fortunate that six crewmembers survived and chronicled what happened when they were interrogated by the British, and a lengthy report was subsequently produced. (The report is housed in The National Archives of the U.K. Our thanks to Tony Cooper for securing a copy for us.) These survivors/POW's also discussed Würdemann's personality and style of leadership. The report by the pilot that bombed U-506 (Lieutenant Salm) was also of great help.

A declassified document from the U.S. Navy, Office of Naval Intelligence, about the *Heredia* was invaluable for giving us a perspective of the sinking by survivors other than the Downses. The document is titled Summary of Statements by Survivors, SS "Heredia."

Credits for the photos used in this book include the Steamship Historical Society of America, uboatarchive.net, Roy Sorli Jr., and the Downs family.

One of our favorite websites, in addition to Jerry Mason's, is uboat.net, run by Gudmundur Helgason. It has precise maps of U-boat patrols with sites of where ships were sunk, details of allied ships hit, U-boat commander profiles, and much more. Gudmundur's and Jerry's websites will keep you up at night once you start digging.

Of the many books we read, *Iron Coffins* was our favorite. Author Herbert A. Werner gives his personal account of his service on U-boats and makes you feel you are by his side. He was a damn good writer as well.

Our bibliography gives the complete list of our source material, and we wish to thank every author and historian listed for their work. Any errors in this book are ours, and ours alone.

Authors' Notes

ALISON O'LEARY

It was an honor and a privilege to be trusted with this wonderful story by Ray Downs and to work with veteran author Michael Tougias in shaping it. As soon as Ray ("Sonny") started telling us this story in his silky soft South Texas accent, I was entranced. I could still see the young boy in him as he recalled sitting on the life raft with his father, distracted from his fear and hunger by playing the seagull game. Emotions still welled up when he spoke about seeing his mother hauled aboard the shrimp boat, covered in sticky oil. Without his clear recollections of these events, as well as the emotions he felt at the time, there would be no book.

The era we write about is in the distant past, but the family's struggle to stay together and seek the best opportunities for financial advancement are achingly familiar to anyone who has lost a job, relocated for advancement, or tried to stretch meager dollars to cover all the needs of growing children. To this end, we sought to portray Ray and Ina Downs, the parents, as honestly as possible, using their own words from family documents and their children's memories. Along with frequent conversations with Terry and Sonny Downs, we were fortunate to have access to personal letters describing many of the decisions and events as well as audiotapes of Ina telling her own version of the torpedoing. For the latter, we are indebted to Lucille's daughter Valerie Cusino.

Ina and Ray were simple people with high school educations. They had never traveled far prior to these events but took chances in pursuing the most basic dream: relief from scrimping and saving, living week to week, and hoping to provide their children with a few pleasures like a scooter or a radio for entertainment. In the end, they were never materially wealthy but left indelible impressions of determination, perseverance, and resilience on their children.

The objective in writing this book, it seems, changed somewhat during the process. As we got to know the characters and their circumstances, it was impossible to pen a romantic good-versus-evil story. As a result, *So Close to Home* encapsulates a microcosm of the human condition: hard work isn't always rewarded, the fruits of one's labors can be snatched away, and retribution isn't always possible, even for the clearest transgression.

Our research about the German Kriegsmarine was fascinating. We immersed ourselves in every book we could find about U-boats, Operation Drumbeat, and German war strategy. Despite being history buffs, at many points in the process we expressed astonishment at our own lack of knowledge about World War II. Friends we spoke to were similarly unaware of the loss of ships and lives along the East and Gulf coasts during 1942, which strengthened our resolve to bring this story to a wide audience. (We also learned that the highest-ever death toll for a single ship sinking was when a Russian submarine torpedoed the *Wilhelm Gustloff*, a transport ship packed with approximately 8,000 German military men and civilians. This occurred in the icy North Sea in January 1945, during the downfall of the Third Reich, when Germans were fleeing from Soviet troops.)

At one point, many months into the writing process and feeling very familiar with the protagonists and facts, I had to double-check a simple item: how many days U-506 had been at sea when the tanker *Halo* was sunk off Louisiana. I counted the days three times and was astonished again: it was the 44th day of a three-month stint at sea. The text describes the humid, stinking, crowded conditions of a U-boat in the steamy Gulf Coast climate, but I sat back and thought about it again: they were only about halfway through their mission. I wondered at how people could withstand that discomfort for such a prolonged period: because the alternative of serving in land battles was worse? Because there was some shared sense of purpose amid those dank, stinking conditions?

In contrast I re-read the account of the *Halo* sinking: it was done by stealth, of course, with 39 crewmen unaware at one moment that anything was out of the ordinary, and the next moment they were fighting for their lives. The German sub sailed away while the *Halo* was still burning, and dozens perished either in the flames or over the next few days of exposure to the elements, a desperately painful end—close to a safe port. Can one both admire and despise the actions of the sub crew, or mourn for the dead and their fractured families while at the same time acknowledging that the sinking of ships is a common and accepted part of being at war?

So Close to Home is just a small slice of history, a moment in time, a glimpse into the struggles that both sides faced. Let's not forget or gloss over the sacrifices made.

MICHAEL TOUGIAS

A surprising result of researching and writing this book was the respect I gained for U-boat commanders and the men who served with them. Prior to this project, I thought of them all as fanatical Nazis, when in fact most weren't even members of the Nazi party, but rather were young men fighting for their country. Had they been born in the U.K. or the U.S., they would have served in the Allied cause, and served with distinction.

Writing about Erich Würdemann setting out on his final patrol was difficult. I wanted to shout at him and say "don't go, you know it's a lost cause." I'm sure he knew his days were numbered, yet he went anyway. Was it loyalty to his country, his crew, or to Dönitz? Or did he believe Germany still had a chance to turn things around? We will never know. Nor will we ever fully comprehend why, after U-506 was torn apart by bombs dropped by the Liberator, he decided to detach from the two men who were holding him up in the water. Those two survivors later said Erich Würdemann did not want to decrease their own chances of survival by keeping him afloat. That was part of the commander's decision, but perhaps he simply had enough of this war-torn world and the thought of becoming a POW was more than the proud man could bear.

Reading Schacht's and Würdemann's War Diaries gave me a glimpse into their decision-making, their leadership, their focus on destroying the enemy, and at times even their compassion. I hope this book paints a balanced picture of them. The real crime is that their lives were wasted because of the actions of one monster, Hitler.

———

I can't blame Sonny's teacher for not believing his story: it really is more remarkable than the best fiction the imagination can conjure up. The fact that all four family members survived is a testament to their inner fortitude and timely bits of luck. Sonny was fortunate that when the ship lurched and he was torn from his father's hands, the boy emerged not far from the ladder that led to the gun deck. And what are the odds his father would kick out a window, climb to the very deck where Sonny was, and pull the raft from its mounts when the captain and George Conyea had failed in their attempts? I wondered: Could Sonny have survived if his father had not found him at that very moment? Would Captain Colburn and George Conyea have protected the boy the way his father did?

Lucille's big break came in the form of Roy Sorli, helping the girl through that terrible night and throughout the next day. But it was Lucille herself who found the strength to swim from the sinking ship and to keep calm through the entire ordeal.

Ina's survival story is unique because she made the decision to forgo the help of the sailors she found floating on some wreckage. Normally your odds of survival are better with a group, but because of the naked sailor, she decided to go it alone. And she was later rewarded with her own bit of good luck when the shrimp boat located her as twilight was fading to black. I don't think she could have survived another night.

As I was writing the book, I kept thinking, what an unusual family the Downses were. Each one showed a sense of resilience that was off the charts, both during their ordeal at sea and in the months that followed. It was an honor to write their story.

Bibliography

INTERVIEW AND LETTERS

Several interviews with Ray "Sonny" Downs. Ray also wrote a description of the attack and his survival ordeal

Interviews with Terry Downs

Several letters written by Ina Downs. Ina later dictated a description of her survival story to a friend, Joan Swanson.

Ina's audio recording of her voyage on the *Heredia* and her survival at sea ordeal, which included a discussion of Lucille's experience as told to her

Letters to Ina from parents of sailor killed on *Heredia*

Letters from Roy Sorli to Lucille and Ina

Some of our best information came from the Germans on U-506 (see U.S. and U.K. National Archive Section)

BOOKS

Clay Blair, *Hitler's U-boat War*, NY, NY, Random House, 1996

Lother-Gunther Buchheim, *U-Boat War*, NY, Bonanza Books, 1986

Rainer Busch, *German U-Boat Commanders of World War II: A Biographical Dictionary*, Annapolis, MD, Naval Institute Press, 1999

C.J. Christ, *WWII in the Gulf of Mexico*, Houma, LA, CJ Christ Publishing, 2005

Peter Cremer, *U-boat Commander*, Annapolis, MD, Naval Institute Press, 1984

Peter Darman, *Warships and Submarines of World War II*, London, Grange Books, 2004

Karl Doenitz, *Memoirs: Ten Years and Twenty Days*, NY, NY, World Publishing Company, (English Translation) 1959

James P. Duffy, *The Sinking of the Laconia and the U-Boat War*, Santa Barbara, CA, Praeger, 2009

James Dunnigan and Albert Nofi, *Dirty Little Secrets of World War II*, NY, NY, William Morrow, 1996

George Feldman, *World War II Almanac*, Detroit MI, Gale Group, 2000

Wolfgang Frank, *The Sea Wolves*, NY, NY, Ballantine, 1955

Michael Gannon, *Operation Drumbeat*, NY, NY, Harper and Row, 1990

Robert Gildea, *Marianne in Chains*, NY, NY, Metropolitan Books, 2002

Winston Groom, *1942*, NY, NY, Atlantic Monthly Press, 2005

Max Hastings, *Inferno*, NY, NY, Knopf, 2011

Homer Hickman, *Torpedo Junction*, Annapolis, Maryland, U.S. Naval Institute, 1989,

Richard Hough, *The Greatest Crusade: Roosevelt, Churchill and the Naval Wars*, NY, NY, William Morrow Company,1986

Edwin Hoyt, *U-Boats Offshore*, NY, NY, Stein and Day, 1978

Wilfred Chuck Huettel, *War in the Gulf of Mexico*, Santa Rosa Beach, FL, Hogtown Press, 1989

Robert Jackson, *Kriegsmarine: The Illustrated History of the German Navy in World War II*, Minneapolis, MN, Zenith Press, 2001

Hans Adolf Jacobsen and J. Rohwer, *Decisive Battles of WWII*, NY, NY, G Putnam and Sons, 1960

Warren Kimball, *Churchill & Roosevelt, the Complete Correspondence (Book I, Alliance Emerging)*, Princeton, NJ, Princeton University Press, 1984

Ernest McKay, *Undersea Terror*, NY, NY, Julian Messner Publishing, 1982

Arch Mercey and Lee Grove, *Sea, Surf and Hell*, NY, NY, Prentiss Hall, 1945

Nathan Miller, *War at Sea*, NY, NY, Scribner, 1995

Arthur Moore, *A Careless Word . . . A Needless Sinking*, Kings Point, NY, American Merchant Marine Museum Press, 1983

Samuel Eliot Morison, *History of United States Naval Operations in WWII: The Atlantic Won*, Chicago, IL, University of Illinois Press, 1956

Axel Niestle, *German U-boat Losses During World War II*, Annapolis MD, Naval Institute Press, 1998

Ed Offley, *The Burning Shore*, NY, NY, Basic Books, 2014

Peter Padfield, *Dönitz: The Last Fuhrer*, NY, NY, Harper & Row, 1984

Léonce Peillard and Oliver Coburn, *U-boats to the Rescue: The Laconia Incident*, London, J. Cape, 1963

Gunther Prien, *U-boat Commander*, NY, NY, Award Books, 1976

J. Rohwer and G. Hummelchen, *Chronology of the War at Sea*, NY, NY, Arco Publishing, 1974

Jurgen Rohwer, *Axis Submarine Successes, 1939–1945*, Elstree, UK, Greenhill Books, 1998

H. Trevor-Roper, *The Last Days of Hitler*, NY, NY, MacMillan, 1974

Theodore P. Savas, *Silent Hunters: German U-boat Commanders of WWII*, Boston, MA, Da Capo Press, 1997

Theodore Savas, *Hunt & Kill: U-505 and the Battle of the Atlantic*, El Dorado Hills, CA, Savas Beatie LLC, 2012

Anthony Shaw and Peter Darman, *World War II Day by Day*, London, Brown Reference Books, 1999

Jak Mallmann Showell, *U-boat Commanders and Crews*, Wiltshire, UK, Crowood Press, 1999

U-Boat Commander's Handbook written by the German Navy translated by the U.S. Navy and later published by Thomas Publications of Gettysburg PA

Jordan Vause, *Wolf: Uboat Commanders of World War II*, Annapolis, MD, Naval Institute Press, 1997

Herbert A. Werner, *Iron Coffins*, NY, NY, Holt, Rinehart and Winston, 1969

David Westwood, *The U-Boat War*, London, UK, Conway Maritime Press, 2005

Melanie Wiggins, *Torpedoes in the Gulf*, College Station, TX, Texas A&M University Press, 1995

Melanie Wiggins, *U-Boat Adventures*, Annapolis MD, Naval Institute Press, 1999

Gordon Williamson, *Grey Wolf*, Oxford, UK, Osprey Publishing, 2001

Malcolm Willoughby, *The U.S. Coast Guard in World War II*, Naval Institute Press, Annapolis, MD, 1957

DOCUMENTS

Harro Schacht U-507 War Diary "U-boat Kriegstagebücher (KTB) For patrols 2, 3, 4, 5 (National Archives and Uboatarchive.net)

Erich Würdemann U-506 War Diary "U-boat Kriegstagebücher (KTB)" For patrols 1, 2, 3, 4, 5 (National Archives and Uboatarchive.net)

Werner Hartenstein U-156 War Diary "U-boat Kriegstagebücher (KTB)" For 4th patrol (National Archives and Uboatarchive.net)

An enclosure to U-506 War Diary, 3rd patrol, labeled "Report on the reception and care of *Laconia* shipwrecked" (National Archives and Uboatarchive.net)

Dönitz War Diary: "War Diary and War Standing Orders of Commander in Chief, Submarines" (Des Führers/Befehlshaber der Unterseeboote (F.d.U./B.d.U.) Naval History and Heritage Command, Washington DC, and uboatarchive.net

U-506 Interrogation of Survivors, C.B.04051 (75). Naval War Division (of U.K), London, August 1943. U.K. National Archives

Confidential summary of Anti-submarine action by Aircraft (ASW-6) report completed after 2LT Salm's flight. (uboatarchives.net)

"Summary of statements by survivors, SS *Heredia*, American passenger and cargo ship, 4732 GT, United Fruit Company, New Orleans, LA." U.S. Navy, National Archives

NEWSPAPERS

"Allston Mate of Torpedoed Ship Tells of 16-hour Struggle in Gulf," *Boston Daily Globe*, May 26, 1942

"M. C. General Hospital Closes with Many Laurels To Its Credit After 15 Years of Service to This Area," *Morgan City Daily Review*, November 25, 1955

"First Hospital in Patterson," *Morgan City Daily Review*, Sept. 1, 1978

"Oceaneering divers to plug sunken submarine's oil leak," *Morgan City Daily Review*, August 14, 1992

"Young Navy Blimp Crews Itch to get U-boat on Daily Tours," *New York Times*, February 12, 1942

"City Still Glows in Haze of Light After New Dimout," *New York Times*, May 19, 1942

"Roosevelt Weighs Pipeline to Ease Gasoline Shortage," *New York Times*, May 19, 1942

"Rationing of Spending By Public Urged to Bar Inflationary Buying," *New York Times*, May 19, 1942

"Battle is Fiercer: Nazi Chutists and Tanks Fail to Halt Red Army Before Kharkov," *New York Times*, May 19, 1942

"Convoy is Largest: First Armored Forces of Our Army Land in British Isles," *New York Times*, May 19, 1942

"War on Submarine Gains, Says Vinson; House Chairman Voices His Confidence of Ending Threat to Shipping," *New York Times*, June 8, 1942

"Navy Seeks 1,000 Boats for U-boat Patrol; Relaxes Requirements, Offers Commissions," *New York Times*, June 28, 1942

"U.S. Ship Among Three Lost," *New York Times*, July 8, 1942

"U-boats Attacked 111 Ships and Sank 92 Along Gulf-Sea Frontier During the War," *New York Times*, June 4, 1945

"87 Land in Brazil from 3 Lost Ships," *New York Times*, August 15, 1942

"Sinkings by U-boats Cut Sharply Under Navy's Coastal Convoying," *New York Times*, August 15, 1942

"Nazi Saboteurs Planned to Blow TVA and Hell Gate, Clark Reveals," *New York Times*, November 8, 1945

"Dutch Ship Sunk, Gun Crew Among 14 Losing Lives," New Orleans *Times-Picayune*, May 13, 1942

"Battle for Oil Speeds War to Supreme Crisis," New Orleans *Times-Picayune*, May 14, 1942

"Catalina Flying Boat Praised on Submarine Guard," New Orleans *Times-Picayune*, May 14, 1942

"Higgins Reveals Plans to Speed Output of Ships," New Orleans *Times-Picayune*, May 14, 1942

"Submarine Bill is Signed by President," New Orleans *Times-Picayune*, May 14, 1942

"Fourth Gulf Ship Hit by Torpedoes Towed Into Port," New Orleans *Times-Picayune*, May 15, 1942

"Neutral Mexican Ship Sunk as Axis Torpedo Crashes Into Lighted Flag on Side," New Orleans *Times-Picayune*, May 15, 1942

"Declaring War on U.S. Hitler's Biggest Blunder, Louis Lochner Discloses," New Orleans *Times-Picayune*, May 16, 1942

"Vast Funds in Gold, Silver and Securities Assembled at Corregidor, Brought Safely to America," New Orleans *Times-Picayune*, May 16, 1942

"Reds Near Kharkov, Allies Bomb Japs," New Orleans *Times-Picayune*, May 17, 1942

"Both Sub, Shark Hit Him, Relates Survivor of Ship," New Orleans *Times-Picayune*, May 18, 1942

"Greatest Boom to Follow War, Banker Believes," New Orleans *Times-Picayune*, May 19, 1942

"American Troop Convoy Reaches Port in Ireland," New Orleans *Times-Picayune*, May 19, 1942

"Doolittle, Record Maker During Peace, Leads U.S. Tokyo Raid," New Orleans *Times-Picayune*, May 20, 1942

"Through Rose-Colored Glasses," New Orleans *Times-Picayune*, May 20, 1942

"America Solving Problem of Sub, Says President," New Orleans *Times-Picayune*, May 22, 1942

"Injured Seaman Saved by U-boat as Vessel Sinks," New Orleans *Times-Picayune*, May 24, 1942

"21 Lost as One Craft Escapes; 36 Die on Other," New Orleans *Times-Picayune*, May 24, 1942

"U-boats Sink Vessel, 57 Lose Lives," New Orleans *Times-Picayune*, May 24, 1942

"Slick: Oil Seeping from Ship Sunk in WWII," New Orleans *Times-Picayune*, August 14, 1992

"Story of WWII Spies Lives on in Maine," *Bangor Daily News*, July 15, 2003

"Stalin's Army of Rapists: The brutal war crime that Russia and Germany tried to ignore," (UK) *Daily Mail*, October 24, 2008

MISC.

"War Diary: The Submarine Situation," Eastern Sea Frontier, April 1942

"Torpedoed Once—Bobs Up in USCG," Coast Guard newsletter article about Ray Downs, 1943

Timothy Warnock, "The Battle Against the U-boat in the American Theater," pamphlet, Air Force Historical Research Agency, 1994

"Thunder in the Gulf," *Louisiana Life* magazine, Summer 2000

WEBSITES

www.Uboat.net

www.Brownmarine.com

www.Uboatarchive.net

www.Uboataces.com

http://ahoy.tk-jk.net/macslog/IndextotheSubmarineArticl.html

http://historisches-marinearchiv.de/projekte/crewlisten/ww2

www.raf.mod.uk/history/bombercommandtenthousandbomberraids3031may.cfm

http://www.usmm.org/wsa/shiploss.html; http://www.usmm.org/battleatlantic.html

http://www.americainwwii.com/articles/sharks-in-american-waters/

http://www.learnnc.org/lp/editions/nchist-worldwar/5908

http://www.wreckhunter.net/u-boats.htm

http://www.pbchistoryonline.org/page/the-enemy-presence-german-u-boats

http://www.history.navy.mil/library/guides/germanuboat-warlogs.htm

https://www.youtube.com/watch?v=mrawPHAWznU

http://salutetofreedom.org/nc.html

http://www.history.com/interactives/inside-wwii-interactive

http://articles.baltimoresun.com/1992-11-02/news/1992307117_1_sinking-ships-u-boat-war

http://www.ubootarchiv.de/ubootwiki/index.php/U_506

baseballinwartime.com

history.com

http://www.history.army.mil/documents/mobpam.htm

http://uboatsbermuda.blogspot.com/2014/01/all-143-u-boat-patrols-off-bermuda-1942.
html

http://www.history.navy.mil/research/library/online-reading-room/title-list-
alphabetically/g/german-espionage-and-sabotage/eastern-sea-frontier-war-diary.html

http://www.nationalww2museum.org/learn/education/for-students/ww2-history/
ww2-by-the-numbers/us-military.html

http://www.uscg.mil/history/articles/northatlanticcampaign.pdf

http://www2.census.gov/prod2/statcomp/documents/1946-04.pdf

http://theoceancountylibrary.org/beacon/1942-01-01%20front%20page.pdf

https://www.navycs.com/charts/1941-military-pay-chart.html

http://www.cv6.org/company/muster/organization.htm#Grades

http://www.nps.gov/casa/planyourvisit/upload/World%20War%202.pdf

http://www.drbronsontours.com/bronsonponcedeleonhotelcoastguard.html

http://www.museumoffloridahistory.com/exhibits/permanent/wwii/sites.
cfm?PR_ID=75

https://en.wikipedia.org/wiki/Operation_Torch

https://www.uscg.mil/history/docs/USCGRating_Warrant_Marks.pdf

http://www.ibiblio.org/hyperwar/USN/ref/Ranks&Rates/index.html

staugustinelighthouse.org

theshipslist.com

unitedfruit.org

flpublicarchaeology.org

About Author
Michael J. Tougias

Michael Tougias is an award-winning author and co-author of twenty-five books covering a wide variety of subjects. He speaks to groups and businesses across the country on leadership and resilience, and he also has a presentation based on *So Close To Home*. You can learn more about him at www.michaeltougias.com (interested organizations can contact him at michaeltougias@yahoo.com). The author also has an archive of maritime rescue articles and personal stories on his blog, michaeltougias.wordpress.com, and he has an author page on Facebook at Michael J. Tougias.

Through research into dozens of survival stories, Tougias has prepared an inspirational lecture for businesses and organizations titled "Survival Lessons: Peak Performance and Decision-making Under Pressure." Tougias describes this presentation as "an uplifting way to learn some practical strategies and mind-sets for achieving difficult goals from those who have survived against all odds."

Tougias also offers a presentation on leadership and resilience based on his co-written international bestseller *The Finest Hours*. The lecture is titled "Leadership Lessons from The Finest Hours" and it includes amazing visuals from the rescue. He has given the presentation across the country for all types of organizations, including General Dynamics, John Hancock, International Administrative Association, the Massachusetts School Library Association, New York University's Surgeons' Round Table, Lincoln Financial Services, Goodwin Procter LLP, the United States Coast Guard, and many more. For more details, see www.michaeltougias.com.

SUMMARY OF
MICHAEL J. TOUGIAS'S
LATEST BOOKS

The Finest Hours
The True Story of the U.S. Coast Guard's Most Daring Sea Rescue
(Coauthored with Casey Sherman)

On February 18, 1952, an astonishing maritime event began when a ferocious nor'easter split in half a five-hundred-foot-long oil tanker, the *Pendleton*, approximately one mile off the coast of Cape Cod, Massachusetts. Incredibly, just twenty miles away, a second oil tanker, the *Fort Mercer*, also split in half. On both fractured tankers, men were trapped on the severed bows and sterns, and all four sections were sinking in sixty-foot seas. Thus began a life-and-death drama of survival, heroism, and tragedy. Of the eighty-four seamen aboard the tankers, seventy would be rescued and fourteen would lose their lives.

An interview with Michael Tougias and photos of the disaster unfolding can be found on YouTube "Finest Hours—Adam Knee (producer)"

"A blockbuster account of tragedy at sea . . . gives a you-are-there feel."—*The Providence Journal*

"A gripping read!"—James Bradley, author of *Flags of Our Fathers*

Overboard!
A True Blue-water Odyssey of Disaster and Survival

The latest nerve-racking maritime disaster tale from the masterful author of *Fatal Forecast* and *The Finest Hours*. Michael Tougias has left countless readers breathless with his suspense-packed, nail-biting disaster-at-sea narratives. And now one of the survivors of a perilous tale has sought Tougias out to tell his terrifying story, for the first time described in *Overboard!*

In early May of 2005, Captain Tom Tighe and first mate Loch Reidy of the sailboat *Almeisan* welcomed three new crew members for a five-day voyage from Connecticut to Bermuda. While Tighe and Reidy had made the journey countless times, the rest of the crew wanted to learn about offshore sailing—and looking for adventure. Four days into their voyage, they got one—but nothing that they had expected or had any training to handle. A massive storm struck, sweeping Tighe and Reidy from the boat. The remaining crew members somehow managed to stay aboard the vessel as it was torn apart by wind and water. *Overboard!* follows the simultaneous desperate struggles of boat passengers and the captain and first mate fighting for their lives in the sea. (An interview with the author and survivors, along with actual footage from the storm can be found on YouTube "Michael Tougias—Overboard Part I, II, III.")

> "A heart-pounding account of the storm that tore apart a forty-five-foot sailboat. Author Michael Tougias is the master of the weather-related disaster book."—*The Boston Globe*

> "*Overboard* is a beautiful story deserving of a good cry."
> —*Gatehouse News Service*

> "Tougias has a knack for weaving thoroughly absorbing stories—adventure fans need this one!"—*Booklist*

Fatal Forecast
An Incredible True Tale of Disaster and Survival at Sea

On a cold November day in 1980, two fishing vessels, the *Fair Wind* and the *Sea Fever*, set out from Cape Cod to catch offshore lobsters at Georges Bank. The National Weather Service had forecast typical fall weather in the area for the next three days—even though the organization knew that its only weather buoy at Georges Bank was malfunctioning. Soon after the boats reached the fishing ground, they were hit with hurricane-force winds and massive, sixty-foot waves that battered the boats for hours. The captains and crews struggled heroically to keep their vessels afloat in the unrelenting storm. One monstrous wave of ninety to one hundred feet soon capsized the *Fair Wind*, trapping the crew inside. Meanwhile, on the *Sea Fever*, Captain Peter Brown (whose father owned the *Andrea Gail* of *The Perfect Storm* fame) did his best to ride out the storm, but a giant wave blew out one side of the pilothouse, sending a crewmember into the churning ocean.

Meticulously researched and vividly told, *Fatal Forecast* is first and foremost a tale of miraculous survival. Most amazing is the story of Ernie Hazard, who had managed to crawl inside a tiny inflatable life raft—only to be repeatedly thrown into the ocean as he fought to endure more than fifty hours adrift in the storm-tossed seas. By turns tragic, thrilling, and inspiring, Ernie's story deserves a place among the greatest survival tales ever told.

As gripping and harrowing as *The Perfect Storm*—but with a miracle ending—*Fatal Forecast* is an unforgettable true story about the collision of two spectacular forces: the brutality of nature and the human will to survive.

> "Tougias skillfully submerges us in this storm and spins a marvelous and terrifying yarn. He makes us fight alongside Ernie Hazard and cheer as he is saved . . . a breathtaking book."—*Los Angeles Times*

> "Ernie Hazard's experiences, as related by Tougias, deserve a place as a classic of sea survival history."—*The Boston Globe*

> "Tougias spins a dramatic saga. . . . (He) has written eighteen books and this is among his most gripping."—*National Geographic Adventure Magazine*

Ten Hours Until Dawn
The True Story of Heroism and Tragedy Aboard the *Can Do*

During the height of the Blizzard of 1978 the pilot boat *Can Do*, with five men onboard, set out from Gloucester to assist a lost Coast Guard boat and an oil tanker that was in a Mayday situation. *Ten Hours Until Dawn* tells the story of what happened on that awful night when the seas were producing monstrous waves of 40 feet and the wind was screaming at 100 miles per hour.

This is one of the few ocean tragedies where we know exactly what happened due to the existence of audio recordings which were taped the night of the storm and feature both the voices of men of the Coast Guard and the *Can Do*. The tapes span a ten hour period during the men's fight for survival.

"The best story of peril at sea since Sebastian Junger's *Perfect Storm*. Superb!"—*Booklist*

"What a story! Tougias's research and writing make the reader feel as if they are onboard the *Can Do* during the Blizzard of '78."
—Governor Michael Dukakis

"An incredible tale of heroism and sacrifice."
—Nathaniel Philbrick, National Book Award Winner

Selected as an American Library Association "Top Book of 2005"

A Storm Too Soon
The True Story of Disaster, Survival, and an Incredible Rescue

Seventy-foot waves batter a tattered life raft 250 miles out to sea in one of the world's most dangerous places, the Gulf Stream. Hanging on to the raft are three men, a Canadian, a Brit, and their captain, J. P. DeLutz, a dual citizen of America and France. The waves repeatedly toss the men out of their tiny vessel, and J.P., with 9 broken ribs, is hypothermic and on the verge of death. The captain, however, is a tough-minded character, having survived a sadistic, physically abusive father during his boyhood, and now he's got to rely on those same inner resources to outlast the storm.

"By depicting the event from the perspective of both the rescued and the rescuers and focusing only on key moments and details, Tougias creates a suspenseful, tautly rendered story that leaves readers breathless but well-satisfied. Heart-pounding action for the avid armchair adventurer."—*Kirkus Review*

"The riveting, meticulously researched *A Storm Too Soon* tells the true-life tale of an incredible rescue."—*New York Post*

"Tougias deftly switches from heart-pounding details of the rescue to the personal stories of the boat's crew and those of the rescue team. The result is a well-researched and suspenseful read."—*Publishers Weekly*

"Few American authors—if any—can better evoke the realities that underlie a term such as 'desperate rescue attempt.'"
—*Fall River Herald*

"Already a maven of maritime books with *Overboard!* and *Fatal Forecast*, Tougias cinches that title here. Working in the present tense, Tougias lets the story tell itself, and what a story! Anyone reading *A Storm Too Soon* will laud Tougias's success."—*The Providence Journal*

Rescue of the Bounty
Disaster and Survival in Superstorm Sandy

The harrowing story of the sinking and rescue of *Bounty*—the tall ship used in the 1962 classic *Mutiny on the Bounty*—which sailed into the path of Hurricane Sandy with sixteen aboard.

On Thursday, November 24, 2012, Captain Robin Walbridge made the fateful decision to sail *Bounty* from New London, Connecticut, to St. Petersburg, Florida. Walbridge was well aware that a hurricane was forecasted to travel north from the Caribbean toward the Eastern seaboard. Yet the captain was determined to sail. As he explained to his crew of fifteen: a ship was always safer at sea than at port. He intended to sail "around the hurricane" and told the crew that anyone who did not want to come on the voyage could leave the ship—there would be no hard feelings. As fate would have it, no one took the captain up on his offer.

Four days into the voyage, superstorm Sandy made an almost direct hit on *Bounty*. The vessel's failing pumps could not keep up with the incoming water. The ship began to lose power as it was beaten and rocked by hurricane winds that spanned over a thousand miles wide. A few hours later, in the dark of night, the ship suddenly overturned 90 miles off the North Carolina coast in the "Graveyard of the Atlantic," sending the crew tumbling into an ocean filled with crushing thirty-foot waves. The Coast Guard then launched one of the most complex and massive rescues in its history, flying two Jayhawk helicopter crews into the hurricane and lowering rescue swimmers into the raging seas again and again, despite the danger to their own lives.

In the uproar heard across American media in the days following, a single question persisted: Why did the captain decide to sail? Through hundreds of hours of interviews with the crew members, their families, and the Coast Guard, Michael Tougias and Douglas Campbell create an in-depth portrait of the enigmatic Captain Walbridge, his motivations, and what truly occurred aboard *Bounty* during those terrifying days at sea.

Dripping with suspense and vivid high-stakes drama, *Rescue of the Bounty* is an unforgettable tale about the brutality of nature and the human will to survive.

"Coauthors Tougias and Campbell superbly re-create the disastrous voyage, providing just the right amount of detail to bring every character involved in this dramatic tale to life. A thrilling and perfectly paced book."—*Booklist*

"Tougias is the master of this genre . . . an artfully crafted recounting of a needless tragedy."—*Windcheck magazine*

"A terrifying, true disaster—the authors explore [the crew] in profiles so detailed that when Sandy hits, you feel their pain quite literally as they are tossed about . . . as waves the size of city buildings batter the ship."—*Philadelphia Inquirer*

SOME OF TOUGIAS'S
OTHER BOOKS INCLUDE:

The Cringe Chronicles: Mortifying Misadventures With My Dad
(coauthor Kristin Tougias)

Until I Have No Country: A Novel of King Philip's Indian War

King Philip's War: The History and Legacy of America's Forgotten Conflict
(coauthor Eric Schultz)

Derek's Gift: A True Story of Love, Courage and Lessons Learned

There's a Porcupine in My Outhouse: Misadventures of a Mountain Man Wannabe
(Winner of the Best Nature Book of the Year Award
by the Independent Publishers Association)

The Sinking
of the *Heredia*
May 19, 1942

Mississippi R.

Morgan City

New Orleans

Corpus Christi

see inset

× sinking

U-506 patrol

GULF
of
MEXICO

Heredia voyage

N

YUCATAN PENINSULA

31901059292146